Music and Society

World music,
politics and
social change

D1569079

Music and Society

Series editor Peter Martin

This series covers all kinds of music – ethnic, 'classical' and popular, ancient and modern – in relation to the human needs served. Each lively study gives a new approach to the understanding of music and the society which creates it. These titles will be essential reading for listeners, concert-goers, record buyers and performers who enjoy any kind of music.

Edited by
Simon Frith

World music, politics and social change

Papers from the International Association
for the Study of Popular Music

Manchester University Press
Manchester and New York
Distributed exclusively in the USA and Canada by St. Martin's Press

Copyright © International Association for the Study
of Popular Music 1989

Published by Manchester University Press
Oxford Road, Manchester M13 9PL, UK
and Room 400, 175 Fifth Avenue,
New York, NY 10010, USA

*Distributed exclusively in the USA and Canada
by* St. Martin's Press, Inc.,
175 Fifth Avenue, New York, NY 10010, USA

Reprinted in paperback 1991

British Library cataloguing in publication data

World music, politics and social change. Papers from
the International Association for the Study of Popular
Music.–(Music and Society).
1. Popular music. Sociological perspectives
I. Frith, Simon   II. International Association for
the Study of Popular Music III. Series
306'.484

Library of Congress cataloging in publication data

World music, politics, and social change : papers from the
International Association for the Study of Popular Music / [edited
by] Simon Frith.
    p.   cm. –(Music and Society)
ISBN 0–7190–287   .
1. Music and Society. 2. Popular music – History and criticism.
I. Frith, Simon   II. Series.
ML3795.W58   1989
780'.42 – dc19   89-2775

ISBN 0 7190 2879 5 *paperback*

Typeset by Megaron, Cardiff, Wales
Printed in Great Britain by
Billings Ltd, Worcester

Contents

General editors' preface

We live, we are often told, in a museum culture, clinging on to artefacts of the past because we cannot invent appropriate ones ourselves. Yet even if this is true, it is also true that more people than ever before are interested in and enjoy some form of music: people who attend concerts of some or other kind and people who play music themselves, as well as the countless millions who buy records and tapes (themselves the products of a major industry) or simply experience the pervasive effects of music on radio and television and in films. Though heterogeneous, this public is enormous, including both those who are professionally involved in the production of masterworks and those who just 'know what they like' when they chance to hear it. For despite another of the claims often made about contemporary societies – that their rationalistic and utilitarian values have all but erased the spiritual, the emotional, in a word the distinctively human qualities of life – it is evident that the clamour for music not only survives but indeed is intensified, in such societies.

In short, music matters. For some it is the paramount expression of human creativity, for others the symbolic affirmation of the Western cultural tradition. Others again hear in their music an explicit denial of the values of such a tradition: for them music may mean the sound of protest, rebellion or even revolution. What is common to each of these, and other, orientations is an undeniable, if usually unstated, belief in both the power and the importance of music in society. In this context, the usefulness of the books in this series – to students, teachers and the general public – should spring from the fact that they aim to enhance enjoyment by way of understanding. Specialist knowledge will not be assumed, the

axiomatic - self evident

volumes being written in a lively style, primarily for non-specialist, albeit thoughtful, enthusiastic, and diligent readers.

We take it as axiomatic that, since music is made by human beings, it cannot but be a manifestation of human experience – of the problems and despair, the triumphs and joys which are an integral part of living together in particular social contexts. Some of the books have a musical, others a sociological, bias, but in all the musical and sociological aspects are inseparable. We are concerned simultaneously with the external manifestations of music as revealed, historically and anthropologically, in ritual and in religious, civic, military, and festive activities, in work and in play; and also with the social, psychological and philosophical undercurrents inherent in music's being made by human creatures. Although matters have been complicated, over the last century, by the fact that industrial capitalism in the West has to a degree fragmented the cultural homogeneity of earlier societies, this interdependence of music and society has not been radically changed. It is true that in our 'pluralistic' society we may detect at least three overlapping musical discourses: a folk or ethnic tradition, a classical or art tradition, and a commercial or commodity tradition. Even so, Music & Society starts from a recognition of the fact that these 'discourses', however distinct, cannot be independent, since they are coexistent manifestations of the world we live in.

The point is emphasised in each of the papers which Simon Frith has brought together in this volume. Individually, they remind us of the complexity of musical culture in every society, especially in an age when indigenous traditions in all parts of the world, are being forced into a dynamic accommodation with Western pop. Taken together, the papers constitute a powerful challenge to certain well-established assumptions. Even the notion of an indigenous tradition becomes questionable, as Professor Frith points out, once it is realised that 'there is no such thing as a culturally "pure" sound'. Everywhere, at an accelerating pace, conventions are challenged, new styles emerge, and innovations appear, spurred on by urbanisation, migration, international mass communications, and the availability of radios and recorders which allow more and more people, for the first time in history, to create their own musical environments. This may mean cheerfully absorbing the new sounds, or adapting them to one's own ends, or defensively trying to drown them out; whatever the response, the significant point is that ordinary individuals to an unprecedented extent, have the ability to decide for themselves.

For Professor Frith, the implication is that the kaleidoscopic nature of modern musical culture need not be interpreted in terms of progressive decline and the corruption of traditional forms. On the contrary, the papers collected here suggest that the process of cultural cross-fertilisation is more likely to result in the enrichment rather than the decay of musical life. Much more evidence could be assembled in support of this thesis: the blossoming of jazz in particular, and the whole Afro-American movement in general, are only the most spectacular examples in the twentieth century. It is not surprising, then, that for Professor Frith, popular music remains 'a progressive, empowering, democratic force'.

What is surprising – some would say disgraceful – is the extent to which all forms of popular music have been ignored by the academic establishment. The comprehensive catalogue of doctoral dissertations and theses on music which were submitted to North American universities between 1961 and 1983 runs to 255 densely-packed pages, yet the section devoted to 'Jazz and Popular Music' takes up just *one and a quarter* pages. The historical period covered by the catalogue, moreover, is precisely that in which Afro-American style became the most penetrating influence on global music-making, and in which the American music industry came close to world domination. Whatever the main preoccupations of academic musicologists have been, these have not included a concern to understand the musical cultures of their own societies. It is a sorry state of affairs, and one which the members of the International Association for the Study of Popular Music are concerned to put right. The appearance of the present volume is thus doubly welcome: firstly because of the insight which it provides into neglected areas of modern musical culture, but equally because in beginning their work the researchers have shown an awareness of the vital idea that most academic musicologists seem to have forgotten – the fundamentally social nature of musical experience.

Even the solitary composer, who may think that his personal motivation is to transcend the society he finds himself in, owes his 'loneness' to the world that made him. Beethoven himself – who in his middle years believed that his music should and could change the world, and in later years knew that his transcendent music had changed the self, ours as well as his own – could not but be dependent on his music's being *heard*; and this inevitably involved other people – as performers and listeners, but also as patrons, sponsors, agents, managers, instrument makers and the whole host of unseen but vital others without whom musical performances would be no more than unfulfilled dreams.

Music does not create or realise itself, but is always the result of people doing things together in particular places and times. To understand music is to understand the men and women who make it, and vice versa. The approach promulgated in Music & Society is, we believe, basic. It needs no further explanation or apology, except in so far as its self-evident truths have sometimes, and rather oddly, been forgotten.

Wilfrid Mellers
Pete Martin

Contributors

Alenka Barber-Kersovan was born in Velika Kikinda, Yugoslavia and now works at the Institut für musikalische Bildung in Hamburg. She is secretary of the German branch of the IASPM.

Bernard J. Broere is a musicologist who did extensive field work in Colombia and taught Latin American music at the University of Amsterdam. He is currently living in Geneva.

Judith R. Cohen received her PhD from the Université de Montréal, with a dissertation on Judeo-Spanish songs in Canada. Based in Toronto and Montréal, she performs and teaches medieval and world musics. Currently, she is on the faculty of the Royal Conservatory and coaches the Balkan vocal ensemble at the University of Toronto.

John Collins is a sociology graduate of the University of Ghana and has been working on the African music scene as musician and writer since 1969. He is currently working with the Ghana Arts Council and is running a recording studio and African sound archives at Bokoor House near Accra, Ghana.

P. L. van Elderen is Lecturer in Cultural Studies in the Department of Sociology, Tilburg University, the Netherlands. He has written several articles on youth-culture phenomena: rock music and football hooliganism, and is presently writing a book about the sociology of Thorstein Veblen.

Franco Fabbri is editor of the series 'Popular M/R' and member of
the editorial board of 'Musicà/Realtà'; he is also director of the
Computer Division at G. Ricordi & C. publishers, Milan.

Martin Hatch is Associate Professor of Music and Asian Studies at
Cornell University. He is the editor of *Asian Music* and directs
the Cornell Gamelan Ensemble.

Geir Johnson is a musician and journalist based in Norway.

Peter Manuel has researched extensively on contemporary and
traditional musics in India, Cuba and elsewhere. He currently
teaches at Columbia University in New York.

Mottie Regev has recently completed a PhD in sociology: 'The
Coming of Rock, The Contest over the Meaning and Content of
Popular Music in Israel', at Tel-Aviv University. He teaches
there at the Departments of Sociology, of Musicology and of
Film and TV. He is interested in the production of hierarchies of
'quality' between cultural products, and in the production of
belief in them.

Paul Richards teaches anthropology at University College, London.

Stan Rijven is a Dutch pop critic, DJ and scholar in sociology. He
writes for a leading daily newspaper and publishes regularly in
several Dutch and foreign magazines. He pioneered European
interest in world music, founded the magazine *Afrika* and hosts a
weekly show on world music on Dutch radio. As a founder music
of PAN, Stichting Pop Archives Netherlands, Rijven is
currently setting up a centre for the active archiving of Dutch
pop culture.

Will Straw is Assistant Professor of Film Studies at Carleton
University in Ottawa, Canada. He is a member of the Executive
Committee of the Canadian branch of the IASPM.

Anna Szemere is a research fellow of the Institute of Musicology,
Budapest. She is currently working in California.

Simon Frith is director of the John Logie Baird Centre at the Universities of Glasgow and Strathclyde and a columnist for the New York *Village Voice*.

Simon Frith

Introduction

The International Association for the Study of Popular Music (IASPM) was founded in 1981 on the initiative of Philip Tagg, a rock musician and classically trained musicologist based in Gothenburg; Gerhard Kempers, a music educator and broadcaster based in Amsterdam, and David Horn, a music librarian and American music scholar based in Exeter. Tagg, Horn and Kempers had quite different pop tastes and experiences, but shared a mission: to get popular music on to the curriculum of academic music studies.

For Tagg and Kempers, who'd both been working with school music teachers and pupils, the pressing problem was pedagogic – there was an increasingly troublesome gap between the interests and ambitions of the children and the expertise and ideology of their tutors. In Holland the foolishness of a situation in which young people's demand to learn rock techniques was unmet because rock musicians were 'unqualified' to teach them was becoming obvious to both musicians' and teachers' organisations (see P. L. van Elderen's essay below). In social-democratic Sweden there was an additional anxiety that schools were failing to address an important part of young people's lives – the question was how to train pupils in *critical* pop consumption.

From a British (and American) perspective the problem was seen slightly differently. The phenomenal growth of the rock industry following the Beatles' world-wide success and the new scholarly interest in youth subcultures had led to serious studies of popular music (not least in the new rock press), but research tended to be sociological; the academics examined the production and consumption of sounds, the journalists argued about ideology.

With few exceptions (most prominently Wilfrid Mellers in Britain and Charles Hamm in the USA), musicologists continued to treat popular music with disdain. In Britain too, then, as David Horn argued, formal music education neglected most pupils' interests, while popular music scholarship itself was in danger of being confined to people (like myself) with no proper musical knowledge at all.

These concerns were publicly expressed at a conference on popular music in Amsterdam in 1981, and it was immediately apparent that they were widely held – hence IASPM, which now has branches in Canada, Britain and Ireland, the USA, the Nordic countries, Benelux, Italy, France, West Germany, Australia and Japan, and individual members in Cuba and the Philippines, the Soviet Union, East Germany and Hungary, Ghana, Israel and Uruguay. There have been three international IASPM conferences since 1981 – in Reggio Emilia in 1983, in Montreal in 1985 and in Accra in 1987, and I think it is now clear what 'popular music study' is as a discipline, and what distinguishes our approach from that of other scholars.

First, in terms of academic convention, popular music scholarship has, in fact, to be a multi-discipline. This was reflected in IASPM's initial membership profile – the Amsterdam conference brought together sociologists, musicologists and anthropologists, historians and political economists, cultural and literary theorists. None of us could make proper sense of pop without drawing on each other's expertise.

Second, popular music has to be studied as an international phenomenon. The point here is not just that popular music exists in all countries (and all countries have popular music scholars) nor even that the terms of their research cross national boundaries. What matters, rather, is that all countries' popular musics are shaped these days by international influences and institutions, by multinational capital and technology, by global pop norms and values. Even the most nationalistic sounds – carefully cultivated 'folk' songs, angry local dialect punk, preserved (for the tourist) traditional dance – are determined by a critique of international entertainment. No country in the world is unaffected by the way in which the twentieth-century mass media (the electronic means of musical production, reproduction and transmission) have created a universal pop aesthetic. One of IASPM's most fruitful activities has simply been to compare notes on this, and if the 'Americanisation' (or 'Anglo-Americanisation') of their music is a matter of equal concern to scholars from Canada and Cuba, from Norway and the Philippines, from Hungary and Scotland, it is also clear to IASPM members now that musical impact and influence aren't just an effect of economic power. Popular music in the USA, the sounds that now echo round the world, were shaped by the powerless, by black musicians and poor white communities, by migrant tunes and rhythms coming in from Latin America and the Caribbean, by old forms being played back by new audiences. If nothing else, popular music study rests on the assumption that there is no such thing as a culturally 'pure' sound.

It follows from this, thirdly, that to study popular music is to study musical change, to study struggle and competition between different producers, tastes and money-makers – IASPM has had to take account of the politics of pop. This is, again, reflected in our membership profile, which is not confined to the academic world but also includes musicians and journalists, music policy-makers and entrepreneurs, radio and TV employees. For such musical activists, tastes matter: studying pop means making a practical intervention, encouraging some ways of doing things, discouraging others, addressing questions of community and opportunity, art and market. IASPM is not in itself a political organisation, it has no 'line' on any pop practice, but there is agreement that each member should have her or his own line, that their tastes are as important to music scholars as to anyone else – which makes IASPM gatherings fraught as well as instructive events.

In making this selection of papers from IASPM's first three conferences I have tried to reflect the above concerns as well as make available stimulating and fascinating work. The authors here do, on the whole, ignore disciplinary boundaries, address popular music's international formation, and engage with the political issues of pop power and taste. Each essay save the last is focused on a different country; each is a case study in musical continuity and change; each deals with the relationship between musical form and cultural identity.

Part 1 contains two papers which show in historical detail that the effect of Anglo-American commercial music on supposedly 'under-developed' countries need not be the destruction of indigenous sounds, but can mean their enrichment. Imported pop is a resource, a supply of new sounds and instruments and ideas which local musicians can use in their own ways to make sense of their own circumstances. Both John Collins and Paul Richards' examination of West African music history and Martin Hatch's survey of recent Indonesian pop demonstrate that musical change has to be related to the economic and cultural relations in which *musicians* are embedded – they are the mediators between pop's institutional forces and cultural effects.

The two papers in Part 2 look more closely at how musical 'traditions' (and traditional musicians) adapt to changing contexts – to the rise of the mass sound media, to the experience of migration. The authors here use the concept of 'acculturation' – their interest is what happens to a community's music when it is absorbed into a new system of communciation – but as both studies show, the problem is to define 'traditional' or community music in the first place. Judith Cohen, for example, points out that for a migrant group like Canada's Spanish Jews, song and dance has always meant acculturation, using a 'host' country's local musical forms for one's own expressive ends. Alenka Barber-Kersovan argues that for young Slovenians in the 1970s, acculturation (in this case the use of Western rock) was a more effective way of establishing a local musical identity than the preservation of the region's folk sounds.

Not surprisingly, perhaps, the commonest question at IASPM conferences concerns speaker's definitions of 'popular music', and as the papers in Part 3 suggest, the immediate task is to examine the way labels work in pop practice – to trace the use of genre rules in music marketing, taste formation, and musicians' creative short-hand. Unlike IASPM's experts, 'unschooled' players and listeners continually make musical distinctions without stopping to think about them! This is to raise at the individual, subjective level the questions of taste and value previously treated in terms of culture and community. Franco Fabbri (writing about Italy), Bernard J. Broere (writing about Colombia) and Motti Regev (writing about Israel) are each concerned with the complexity of the labelling process, the range of non-musical factors (performing conventions, packaging styles, lyrical modes, etc.) that feed into it. But they also make clear that in linking different types of music, people identify with them, hear songs and sounds and styles as embodying certain values and attitudes. How such identification works, how it changes, is, for me, the most fascinating (and difficult) question for popular music research.

The papers in Part 4 tackle one aspect of this, the politics of music. Each paper here is concerned with the ideology of rock in particular, but in contrasting settings – Communist Cuba and Hungary, Welfare State Norway and the Netherlands, the global TV setting of Live Aid. The point all six authors make is that judgements of rock's 'value' inevitably confuse political, moral and aesthetic criteria (though it is good to learn that the Cuban authorities are – correctly! – so confident of the aesthetic power of their music and musicians that they've made little attempt to keep US rock off the air-waves).

When I was putting this anthology together, I deliberately excluded papers on British or North American popular music – I've learnt most at IASPM meetings from students of other countries' sounds, and I decided that readers of this book would too. But in editing these pages I came to realise that Anglo-American pop is always present here anyway – it is the way of music-making to which all other musical changes in the last thirty years must be referred. And what has become equally clear to me (which, I now realise, is why I so enjoyed these papers when I first heard them) is that whatever rock's role as the 'sound of corporate America' (promoter Bill Graham's words), its part in world-wide popular culture is still essentially as an extra – which is what gave Live Aid, which is discussed here, its poignancy.

The essays here celebrate, then, the richness of local music scenes, and document the remarkable skill, vigour and imagination with which local musicians and fans and entrepreneurs take over 'hegemonic' pop forms for themselves. Popular music, even in the era of Sony-CBS, MTV-Europe and Michael Jackson as global Pepsi salesman, is still a progressive, empowering, democratic force, and my only regret in compiling this book is that I couldn't include a tape or disc to illustrate it – every writer makes me want to *hear* the music being discussed. Perhaps it is not a coincidence that IASPM has grown as an academic organisation just as 'world music', the sounds of countries other than North America and Western Europe, has begun to be recorded, packaged and sold as a successful new pop genre. This is not to imply that IASPM is by its nature facilely optimistic (as scholars of musical traditions tend to be facilely pessimistic) but, rather, that as the music of the multimedia, multinational centre of the entertainment industry becomes ever more uniform (Whitney Houston and Phil Collins providing a world-wide commercial soundtrack), so the diverse sounds from the margins become ever more important as evidence that music-making remains a human activity. If nothing else, we can learn from other people's popular music *and* dance to it!

facilely

hegemonic

Part 1

Creating a mix

Editor's note

One of the pleasures of pop music is that we feel its effects before understanding its causes. We like (or dislike) a song immediately – move to a rhythm, respond to a melody or voice – without needing to know how or why or where it was made. In commercial terms, this is the reason why all sorts of sound can sell, why every global genre gets its moment of chart glory; in academic terms, it means that the trickiest task of musical analysis is to explain the relationship of cause and effect. How free can our response to music really be? How are the conditions of production coded into sounds?

These general questions lurk behind the more specific theme of this section: why and how does popular music change? There are two familiar positions on this in musicology. The first suggests that popular music 'evolves', simple (or 'primitive') forms becoming complex, 'spontaneous' expression becoming art, 'traditional' music becoming modern. The second rests on a model of corruption, 'pure' sounds becoming subject to commercial manipulation, collective expression becoming a commodity, 'traditional' music becoming pop.

The trouble with both these positions is that they muddle up musical and social judgements. They rest, that is, on dubious assumptions about the relationship of musical cause and effect. As all the papers in this book suggest, definitions of music as 'traditional' or 'modern', 'folk' or 'pop', can't be derived from formal qualities alone; they depend on judgements too of music's use. And as the two papers in this section make clear, this means that the logic of musical change can't be derived from a study of songs or performances in isolation. If all contemporary popular music is, in one way or another, a mix of sounds from different societies, genres

and eras, then the question is, why this mix at this moment? What
are the musical choices available in fact? To which musicians, which
entrepreneurs, which audiences?

John Collins and Paul Richards address these questions with
respect to the history of popular music in West Africa, and they
write from a materialist perspective. For them, to place musical
forms in their socio-historical context is to place them in a mode of
economic production, in a particular class structure. Musical
change is an effect of social change, and what historians have to
understand, therefore, is the *function* of music in a society. In
the West African case, a long historical view reveals music's place in
a merchant economy. Even before colonialism West African
musicians had an essentially ideological role: their music was
used to confirm status and prestige, to give scattered trading
peoples a sense of the social order, to carry messages and confirm
beliefs. Colonialism didn't change the purpose of West African
music, then, but, rather, introduced new ideological elements to it –
among other things, the colonialists introduced the concept of
'traditional' music to legitimate their own claims to progress and
modernity. Methodologically, then, the most important aspect of
Collins and Richards' paper is the way it combines straight musical
data (discographical work) with ideological data, evidence of the
discourses that surround musical forms and events. In order to
understand patterns of musical continuity, influence and invention,
they argue, we have to understand what different sounds mean to
people.

This argument is made too in Martin Hatch's paper on the
popular music scene in Indonesia. He writes as a musicologist,
trying to classify current Indonesian pop genres with reference to
traditional forms such as gamelan but drawing our attention to
the irrelevance of the traditional/modern distinction for today's
audiences and musicians. Hatch himself concludes that pop genres
can't be defined simply in terms of their musical characteristics;
musical meaning is dependent too on context and use. And he
develops two of Collins and Richards' other points: first, he shows
that for musicians in Indonesia, as in West Africa, Western pop is a
resource not a threat, a store of musical ideas and techniques that
can be used for local ends; second, he emphasises the positive aspect
of technological change – the now flourishing Indonesian pop scene
followed the spread of the cassette tape player.

The theme of this section, in short, is that the development of a
music market does not necessarily mean the swamping of a local
culture by multinational commodities. Technological and commercial forces may also support the changes in music-making
practice that enable popular forms to continue as a vital part of a
dynamic social structure (rather than as an anachronistic residue of
the past).

1 *John Collins and Paul Richards*

Popular music in West Africa

Introduction

The West African musical styles considered in this paper have been
the subject of relatively little scholarly attention. An earlier
generation of European ethnomusicologists interested in African
music tended to dismiss these musics as 'commercial' phenomena of
little substance or to deprecate them as byproducts of 'culture
contact'. African researchers have been preoccupied with more
urgent projects in connection with major cultural traditions
threatened by colonialism. 'Counter-colonial' scholarship has had
little time to spare for music which emerged under colonialism.
This neglect is to be regretted. The subject is worth more than trite
generalisations about cultural 'syncretism' and stylistic 'diffusion'.
African art is too often viewed ahistorically and the analysis of West
African music suffers, in particular, from the fact that without their
history the sounds are robbed of much of their significance and
meaning. Accordingly, we attempt to discuss the social context in
which a number of 'popular' styles emerged – we focus in particular
on *highlife* and *juju* – and then raise questions of how social
meanings are constructed in these musical idioms.[1]

Our argument is that these idioms are best understood as a
cultural phenomenon particularly closely associated with the
elaboration of merchant interests. This is a position opposite to that
adopted in the versions of 'modernisation' theory underlying
'syncretist' explanations of the relationship between music and
social change, in which the emphasis is placed upon the enormous
impact of colonialism in dynamising a somnolent pre-colonial social
formation. This latter viewpoint itself is derivative of the rhetoric
surrounding the changing ownership of trading networks. Colonialism strengthened its control over these networks by defaming

African propensities for trade,[2] circumscribing Nationalist and Pan-Africanist movements and allowing politics to operate only at the level of the most local 'ethnic' units, while recruiting funds and legitimacy for its own infrastructural ventures (e.g. railways) by emphasising the extent to which the unorganised and isolated character of rural production acted as a constraint on commerce.

A broader perspective on the evidence suggests that merchant capital had become a powerful transforming influence in most parts of West Africa long before the advent of colonialism, and that in all probability, this influence predates the period of direct contact with Europe via the coast. It should be remembered European perceptions of West Africa have been unduly affected by the fact that the site of initial contact, along the coast, was for long West Africa's 'backyard'. Early West African societies looked north and east to the Mediterranean and to Arabia, and desert-edge kingdoms most remote from direct European access, e.g. Mali, were among early non-European centres of capital accumulation of world importance.

It is argued in this paper, then, that many characteristics of cultural change are best understood in terms of the dynamics of merchant capital, as the main economic force shaping recent history in West Africa, and yet to be entirely eclipsed by other forms of capital accumulation and systems of economic organisation. The depth to the history of trade and merchant capitalism in West Africa revealed by modern scholarship provides grounds for suspecting the validity of the 'dualist' and 'syncretist' approaches hitherto emphasised in writing concerning culture change in the region. If, as we shall argue, it is the long-established characteristic of a trade-dominated social formation constantly to absorb 'new' and 'alien' cultural influences, much as a new fashion in commodities stimulates trade, then the 'modernisation' and 'westernisation' rejected in the name of musical 'authenticity' or which 'syncretism' is supposed to graft on to the 'traditional', are terms empty of meaning. Although 'syncretism' and 'authenticity' equally lose their analytical value as critical concepts this is not to deny their ideological potency, or to underestimate their value as political positions (see below).

The nature of merchant capitalism in West Africa

Merchants organise the purchase, sale, transportation, storage and insurance of commodities, but do not often, or necessarily, aim to organise or directly control the production process. This is left to peasant farmers and craftsmen who still own the means of production, working partly for their own subsistence and partly for sale, and heavily reliant upon 'non-wage' labour sources (i.e. 'family' labour and its extensions, e.g. reciprocal labour co-operatives).

There are distinct advantages to merchant capital in not risking attempts to control the production process directly. Where the production of commodities remains in the hands of peasants and part-time craftsmen (with 'subsistence' holdings) a continuous and flexible adjustment of balance between production for market and production for subsistence is possible in response to changing market conditions, with a minimum of social and political dislocation. Merchants, in preferring not to seek to organise production directly (were this possible) are, in effect, exercising a choice to conserve this flexibility. British attempts, in the Okitipupa region of western Nigeria during the depression years of the 1930s, to dissolve a permanent specialist palm-harvesting 'proletariat' of migrant workers in order to hand back exploitation to palm-grove landlords otherwise little disposed to undertake the hard and dangerous work of climbing their own trees, suggest that colonial officials similarly perceived a threat to political 'stability', with consequences for the expected revival of trade in subsequent years, when an African rural labour force became too far divorced from its subsistence base.[3]

Merchants typically gain access to commodities by the following 'indirect' means:

(1) managing 'demand' – this involves attempts to manipulate notions of 'innovation' and 'fashion'. Gifts and social occasions are important as means of 'opening' trade. The Royal African Company's agent, Richard Smith, trading in the Sherbro in the eighteenth century, describes how the ruler of the Bulom seized Company property to compensate for not having been invited (unlike other local chiefs) to the wake of the Company's deceased agent, Clark.[4] Business and politics were as important as the social focus to such occasions, to which music was an essential accompaniment.

(2) indebtedness – merchants frequently act as bankers to rulers and peasants, financing political campaigns (even wars), supplying arms, and advancing loans to ameliorate the effects of poor harvests. At present, for example, it is estimated that up to half of all peasant producers in Sierra Leone borrow money or arrange credit in kind to cover rice shortages in the hungry season. Typically, this credit is

described as being provided by 'family' and 'friends' – such 'friends' frequently prove to be village produce traders. For short-term loans it is most usual to mortgage future harvests. Longer-term loans are often advanced against 'pledged' land.[5]

(3) ideological manipulation – in the market place the isolated peasant or craft worker learns the social value of that portion of family labour directed to non-subsistence ends. But through the merchants' manipulations the values of commodities shift in unpredictable ways. Commodities become, in Marx's phrase, 'social hieroglyphics', 'abounding in metaphysical subtleties and theological niceties'. Through marketing, commodities assume an aura of meaning as 'possessions' which transcends their practical utility, conveying messages about the power and prestige of their owners. Markets are, in consequence, places of mystical danger which require the attention of ritual experts. Witchcraft accusations and violence often go hand in hand with trade difficulties. Musicians are among the consultants retained to help manage this disorder.

Merchants, as entrepreneurs in the narrow sense, tend first to reinvest their profits in their trade networks rather than in the productive process. Any commercial network is complex, combining technology and social know-how. Pathways, roads, ferry points and bridges have to be built and maintained. Detailed, up-to-date, commercial intelligence is required, as are the social skills to recruit teams of carriers or reliable vehicle crews. In the West African trade European maritime skills were matched by African traders' skills in social 'navigation' overland, through densely populated districts of great political complexity. 'Hospitality' was, and is, a fine art in Africa, perfected in the context of intense mercantile activity; 'landlords' and 'brokers' are two of the most widely understood roles in the West African public life.[6]

Frank argues that an important characteristic of mercantile networks is their hierarchical character, which in turn, helps ensure monopoly profits.[7] It is clear that he has in mind a tree-like graph allowing the merchant alternative sources of supply but permitting no alternative sales to the producer. There is much argument about whether such spatial structures operate at a world scale, facilitating, in Frank's view, the development of the metropolis at the expense of the periphery through the extraction of monopoly profits. At the local scale such studies as are available for West Africa suggest that merchant profit margins are not invariably excessive.[8] Nevertheless it can be argued that something like Frank's model provides a blueprint – an ideal type – upon which many merchants have endeavoured to build.

A key aspect of network construction, then, is the attempt made to secure its distinctiveness. This may involve legal charters or attempts to eliminate competing routeways, or physically to isolate competing market places.[9] Appropriate spatial differentiation may also involve cultural separation, via language, dress, music, religious sectarianism and the manipulation of 'ethnicity'. These elements will be used by merchant groups as identifiers to maintain discipline and loyalty to 'house' and 'line', to attract clients, structure transactions and facilitate expansion. The elaboration of trading networks through such cultural resources has been described by Cohen for the Hausa trading out of Ibadan, by Curtin for the Jakhanké in the Senegambian hinterland, and by Northrup for the pre-colonial Aro in eastern Nigeria.[10] The Aro, priests as well as traders, expanded their network by investing profits in 'bride price', marrying women from the communties in which they traded, but refusing to allow Aro women to be married to non-Aro men. Thus their social networks expanded relative to those of local peasant communities.[11]

In recent times such processes may have changed in their surface characteristics while retaining their structural logic. Colonial governments built railways and associated feeder roads in competition with trader-chiefs organising local labour into the construction of many thousands of miles of 'private' roads, the foundation for subsequent fortunes made in vehicle ownership.[12] The major colonial trading companies, and more recently their multinational successors, have tended to elaborate networks with similar structural characteristics to the 'ethnically' differentiated networks of local trading groups. Gyllström's study of tea multinationals in Kenya isolates structural characteristics and principles of network growth equally applicable to commodity-exporting companies operating in West Africa.[13] In effect, he demonstrates that over time an increasing proportion of the London commodity market price is devoted to the maintenance and expansion of the company network at the expense of the earnings of the peasant producer. To this extent the commodity exporting firm becomes an end in itself.

It should be noted, however, that although a differentiated 'tree' network linking two ecologically or economically distinct regions is advantageous from the point of view of monopoly profits it is not an easy structure to sustain. The drive to maintain 'monopoly' control over a network but to improve 'connectivity' are in contradiction. New linkages improve transportation but increase the likelihood of effective competition. Sometimes a network then proves especially vulnerable to rapid take-over by a rival group. It is possible to interpret the period of colonial conquest in West Africa (1885–1900), and 'ethnic' violence in northern Nigeria (1966) in these terms as 'coups' visited upon trading networks. The relatively short duration of the struggles involved reflects the fact that it is the ownership of the network rather than its structure which has been called into question.

Colonialism in West Africa is to some extent a puzzling phenomenon because of the rapidity of its advance, the flimsiness of its apparatus of administrative control during its heyday, and the equal rapidity and relative 'peacefulness' of colonial withdrawal. The puzzle arises in part because there has been a tendency for commentators to overstress the social and economic changes wrought by the growth of British, French and Portuguese political influence. West African colonialism was at all stages firmly grounded in mercantilism. Even when its theorists, such as Lugard, affected to despise 'commerce', their ideological commitments – witness the pseudo-mediaevalism of northern Nigerian Indirect Rule – served to protect mercantile opportunities against the inroads of industrial and finance capital. A well-known instance is Governor Clifford of Nigeria restricting Lever Brothers to commodity trade at a time, in the 1920s, when they wished to acquire land for plantations.[14]

In an important sense, therefore, colonial regimes were acting in a way that was more consonant with pre-colonial mercantilist interests than if they had embarked on schemes to transform the productive base of the economy along Rhodesian and South African lines. Thus despite the fact that colonialism favoured overseas trading interests, this was tolerable, politically, in the short term because dominant sections of the conquered communities of West Africa saw this as a temporary phenomenon – as a change of ownership which might just as rapidly be reversed. Colonialism in West Africa was notable, therefore, more for its congruence with the past than for the new social and economic forces which it unleashed, and it served to help prolong the political dominance of merchant capital into the twentieth century.

Instruments and merchants

In the music with which we are concerned 'innovation' and changing fashion are virtues, and nowhere is this more strongly to be seen than in the case of the instruments involved. Part of the appeal of *highlife* has always been the glamour of the exotic instruments – to begin with guitar and trumpets, later clarinet, saxophone, piano, electronic organ, and even violin.[15] Musicians attain prominence by claiming to be *first* with a new instrument or style of playing. It is often said, for example, that veteran Yoruba musician I. K. Dairo transformed *juju* music from a street-corner idiom into a sophisticated modern style because he was the first to introduce the electric guitar.[16] A *juju* band of the 1980s is likely to have instruments, including synthesisers and amplification, worth many thousands of Naira.[17] A recently re-equipped band will take space in the press to announce the launch of its *equipment*. Merchants are involved in supplying instruments in both a general and a specific sense. Brass instruments, piano, harmonium and various string instruments (including banjo, predecessor of the electric guitar in *juju*) have been items of trade from Europe to West Africa since at least the nineteenth century. Horn gramophones, and 78 rpm records – featuring, from the 1930s, West African artists and songs – were stocked by the larger stores in West Africa's main urban centres. In addition to dealing in items of musical merchandise some merchants sponsor bands by providing their equipment. Few modern bands can start without such a sponsor, and few survive disagreement with their business benefactors. A comparable process of prestige investment in expensive instruments is encountered in the case of wealthy Christian congregations importing pipe organs. Demand was sufficiently great in Nigeria, and elsewhere in West Africa during the 1960s, to support an enterprising Lagos-based firm of organ builders, Fayemi and Jones.

Although doubtless only a small part of the business of most trading houses, musical commodities convey considerable symbolic force, well exemplified by one informant's childhood recollection of

leading out the dancers for a 'traditional' village festival in upcountry Sierra Leone with his prosperous trader-uncle's wind-up
gramophone balanced on his head. The German explorer Nachtigal
thought it worth the trouble of transporting a harmonium across the
Sahara – no easy load for a camel – as a present for the Sultan of
Borno.[18] Such transactions came to sum up the growing asymmetry
in trade between Europe and Africa during the nineteenth century.
Where seventeenth-century Europeans had marvelled at the skill of
west African craftsmen – the Portuguese, for example, commissioned complex art work from Sierra Leonian ivory carvers –
nineteenth-century Europeans saw the region primarily as a source
of *raw* materials and untutored labour (the practice of agriculture
was rarely thought of as a skilled art). The instruments of the
labourer – both musical and practical – were crude and of no
account. Drumming was noise. By contrast, the rapid evolution of
the modern piano in the mid-nineteenth century was a triumph of
the industrial manufacturer's skill, and its increasingly powerful
repertoire (*vide* the music of Schumann, Chopin and Liszt)
consonant with the new might of industrialism. Mrs Melville,
writing about Freetown in the 1840s, recorded the following:

One evening . . . I opened the pianoforte, and was trying what effect the
voyage and climate had had upon its keys, when I heard a servant slowly
and deliberately ascending the staircase. Instead of passing on to the pantry
. . . the bearer . . . stopped at the drawing room door, and after a profound
reverence advanced a few paces, bearing in his hand a sort of musical
instrument, upon which, without uttering a single word, he began to play
with much apparent self-complacency. He continued for a few minutes . . .
until I put an end to the performance by asking to look at the rude lyre,
which he evidently regarded with great veneration, and with an aspect of
the most solemn gravity he placed it in my hands as if delivering up a
valuable treasure. It was a simple triangle with a few strings stretched
across, and gave not an unpleasant though rather monotonous note.[19]

In another passage she is caught between seeing European music as
civilised (and civilising) compared to the 'savagery' implicit in
African music, and the Freetown white community's preoccupation
with the threat of Creole cultural competition:

But then in the street, at the other end, the practising of the military band
generally commences, and you might fancy that a barrel-organ, or hurdy-
gurdy somewhat out of tune, were playing under your windows, as the sable

musicians favour you with nothing except the same hackneyed old airs over and over again . . . In the evening, too, we have the everlasting *tom-tom*; at times diversified by the ominous stroke of the Mandingo kettle drum, a hollow booming sound, which, in spite of its sameness, somehow or other contrives always to convey to my mind the idea of dark deeds of savagery and treacherous warfare. Then there is the dull inharmonious singing of the natives . . . certainly the majority of the population seems to delight in uncouth, noisy, and what we should term ridiculous sounds.[20]

The notion of musical 'progress', an increasingly important ideological element in European music criticism in the nineteenth and early twentieth centuries (cf. the compositional ideals of 'progressive' composers such as Wagner and Schoenberg) is deeply embedded in broader ideas about material progress characteristic of an industrialising society. Mrs Melville's reaction to African music reflects this in a simplistic way, understandable in an amateur. In the Foreword to his *Twenty-Four Negro Melodies*, Op. 59 (1904), Samuel Coleridge Taylor, son of a Freetown Creole, develops a much more sophisticated view of the nature of the gap in progress between African and European music:

The Negro Melodies in this volume are not merely *arranged* – on the contrary they have been amplified, harmonised and altered . . . The plan adopted has been almost without exception that of the *Tema con Variazioni*. The actual melody has in every case been inserted at the head of each piece as a motto. The music which follows is nothing more or less than a series of variations built on the said motto. Therefore my share in the matter can be clearly traced and must not be confounded with any idea of 'improving' the original material . . .[21]

Thus it is important to *preserve* the integrity of the original material, but, at the same time, to fit it to the needs and tastes of European audiences it must be developed through the application of 'evolutionary' compositional procedures.

Music not based on instruments subject to laws of manufacturing improvement is then, conversely, constructed in an ideologically 'opposite' sense as 'traditional' and 'timeless'. This 'timelessness' in African musical tradition (sharply contrasting with the emphasis on measure and rhythm in musical practice) came to be much emphasised as a point of ideological transaction by forces of both conquest and resistance within the colonial period. Coleridge Taylor, aligning himself, in the same Foreword, with the African nationalists committed to the notion of 'racial self-improvement' via adoption of European-style educational institutions and standards, develops his argument as follows:

One of the most striking points regarding this African music is, in the author's opinion, its likeness to that of the Caucasian race. The native music of India, China and Japan, and in fact all non-European music, is to our more cultivated ears most unsatisfactory in its monotony and shapelessness. The music of Africa . . . is the great and noteworthy exception. Primitive as it is, it nevertheless has all the elements of the European folk song and it is remarkable that no alterations have had to be made before treating the Melodies. This is even so with the example from West Africa (a song of Yoruba origin, 'Oloba') – a highly original number. One conclusion may be safely drawn from this – the Negro is really and truly a most musical personality. What culture may do for the race in this respect has yet to be determined, but the underlying musical nature cannot for a moment be questioned.[22]

African music, then, is like the resources which Chamberlain, Kingsley, Morel and others were so keen to see exploited by British commercial enterprise: valuable enough in its own right to attract international attention, but 'unprogressive' – society would achieve much greater things when transformed by the impact of 'superior' techniques.[23]

Music and ideological struggles in West Africa under colonialism

European pioneers of 'African' ethnomusicology enthusiastically took up the issue of the authenticity of tradition. An important element in Hornbostel's ethnomusicological research (and more recently that of Tracey) was to conserve 'traditional' (and therefore genuine) music against the impact of alien influences.[24] This is presented primarily as an archival project, i.e. the protection of sources against 'syncretist' adulteration. At another level it is, in effect, an assertion that change is an unusual, even improper, process within African music. It would be easy to argue a crude functional link between this kind of scholarly work and the needs and requirements of European colonialism in Africa – especially British schemes of Indirect Rule based on 'tribal' authenticity, latterly legitimated (e.g. in Cameron's reform of Indirect Rule in Nigeria in the 1930s along lines indicated by properly 'scientific' ethnographic survey) by appeal to the racist notion of innate 'natural' forms of social organisation and government characteristic of specific, local, fractions of African society. But in all probability the reasons are more complex, and to do with a move within European culture to construct the 'primitive' and 'traditional' as antidotes to the less desirable aspects of industrial progress. The alienated conditions of 'primitivism' and 'progressivism' have been thoroughly diagnosed by Adorno in the music of Stravinsky and Schoenberg respectively, and owe nothing as such to the empirical realities of contact with Africa.[25] The 'dark continent' in this case is an artefact of a 'progressive' economy in which the relentless march of industrialism turns the old to scrap. Indeed it may be argued that the 'new imperialism' of the late nineteenth century is itself to be explained by such fears – as an economically irrational, quixotic venture by elements within European society standing to lose most in economic power and political influence as a result of industrial progress.[26] Although it is unlikely that economics lay too far beneath the surface of imperialism, it is clear that 'tradition' and the 'timelessness' of 'feudal' and 'tribal' Africa were important constructs in the personal motivation of many colonial administrators, and participation in 'authentic' African cultural life a valuable psychic reward. This is readily apparent in the following account by Constance Larymore, wife of one of Lugard's first Residents in Northern Nigeria, of their departure from Hadejia in 1902:

As we dismounted, the horsemen formed up into a gigantic double circle, ourselves, the Emir, his head men, and a few of our own people in the centre. When the last farewell had been said, my husband asked that the Limam might offer prayers for our safe journey, and – perhaps – another meeting some day . . . The cavalry dismounted and stood beside their horses, the Limam stood up, his towering white head-dress and earnest dark face turned to the morning sun, his solemn clear voice pouring out the prayer in sonorous Arabic, every word distinct in the great silence; thousands of heads and hands around following every gesture, our own included, for, at that strange moment creeds seemed very far away, and the one Father of us all, to whom such earnest words were being addressed on our behalf, the sole reality. It was a sight, I suppose, such as few people have ever witnessed, and it made a very deep and lasting impression on us. I had a lump in my throat when, as I turned to mount my pony, the stately old Emir laid his slender brown hand, with a beautiful amber rosary twined among his fingers, on my arm, and said gently: 'You will come back to us; surely God will send you back.'[27]

From an African point of view, the three positions of complete musical Europeanisation, austere traditionalism and some form of 'progressivism' each had their proponents, strategic strengths and weaknesses and ideological possibilities. An organisation such as the Lagos Philharmonic Society (1873), with the possibility of facilitating access to the British governor and his officials, might prove especially advantageous to a creole trader group whose businesses were predominantly 'backward linked' to Manchester, Liverpool and Hamburg rather than upcountry. Thus concerts and choral festivals became a feature of Lagos social life in the late nineteenth century, and local newspapers were not lacking in music critics.[28] The Lagosian musician (and, later, missionary to Ijebu Ode), R. A. Coker appears to have been active in organising concerts over a considerable period in the late nineteenth century (e.g. the Lagos Handel Festival of 1882) and may also have composed.[29]

Lagos and Freetown social life based around the replication of 'European' cultural forms appears to have reached a peak of intensity at this period, with a plethora of mostly short-lived literary, dramatic and musical societies. Both the intensity of these activities and their lack of durability may reflect the depressed condition of trade in the 1870s and 80s, if, as is our hypothesis, these societies provided social underpinning for certain types of trading interests – interests in effect readjusting to a spate of 'bankruptcies' and other fluctuations characteristic of a period of trade uncertainty. P. Dele Cole notes that late nineteenth century Lagosians looked back on the richer, more stable, social life surrounding Governor Glover in the 1860s with considerable feelings of nostalgia.[30]

Another factor in the late nineteenth century situation, revealing the fatal flaw in Europeanising cultural strategies, was an increase in the competitiveness of European trading houses, particularly as hazards to the health of Europeans – notably malaria – began to yield to scientific analysis. In lobbying the colonial administrations of British coastal possessions to underwrite the military and political risks of penetration further up country, the European trading community drew upon a set of late-Victorian hypotheses about Africans usually termed 'scientific racism'.[31] From this standpoint, African peoples occupied a lower rung than Europeans on the evolutionary ladder. Nevertheless it was supposed that 'savagery' had a certain natural nobility, the full heat of racist venom being reserved – and this brings into focus the real target of the body of ideas concerned – for the creole trader families of Lagos and Freetown, who, it was presumed, aimed to thwart 'scientific' principle by disguising a 'natural' condition under a thin veneer of European dress, manners and culture.

Such racism was neither gratuitous nor necessarily a determinative influence on the course of subsequent events. It is more appropriately viewed as an index of the extent to which creole groups were effective in using their understanding of both European and African culture and society to 'navigate' a complex social landscape upon which rival European groups had designs, but for which they had as yet neither the knowledge, the political clout nor the fire power to control directly.

A further threat to European control of West African trade networks was posed by the arrival of the first groups of 'Syrian' traders in the region. Willing to tolerate poor living standards, and working with low overheads, they proved effective pioneers of new trading opportunities inland. This competitiveness provoked an analogous racist response from the British, giving rise to a specifically West African colonial form of anti-semitism, in which the Syrians were seen as inherently corrupt and corruptors of local social order, well-captured in Graham Greene's novel, *The Heart of the Matter*, set in Sierra Leone.[32]

In the end racism proved irrelevant, since its objective was achieved through other means. In effect, colonial governments short-circuited the struggle by using military and technological control to privilege European trading interests. Official concern came to be focused upon the problems of political legitimacy, and on devising effective schemes for low-cost local administration. For these purposes ethnicity was much more useful currency than race. On the other hand, from the West African point of view, the experience of racism directed at Europeanised groups was an immediate prelude to imperial conquest, and it is not surprising, therefore, that the refutation of this slander has been a focus of some potency in nationalist political struggles. Typically this has taken the form of a polarised response – in many cases with the same individuals occupying opposite poles during successive phases of their careers – of besting Europeans at their own game, and then rejecting the rules as irrelevant.

Music provides several interesting examples of this. Having learnt Christianity in a church where only Victorian hymns would be sung, the Nigerian independent Baptist Mojola Agbebi (1860–1917) subsequently rejected all forms of European music in worship.[33] Fela Sowande (b. 1902), having established a reputation as Nigeria's leading 'symphonic' composer[34] subsequently argued the case for grounding Nigerian musicology in the study of African religion.[35] Akin Euba, composer of complex and successful scores in *avant-garde* idioms, has moved in the direction of works more accessible to mass audiences, in which 'western'-influenced 'intellectualist' procedures of composition are rejected.[36] The tension between the poles of 'Europeanisation' and 'authenticity' are also of creative significance in the music of Fela Anikulapo-Kuti. A musical onslaught on the police and militarism (e.g. 'Alagbon' and 'Zombie')[37] is a well-known aspect of this popular musician's work, but he has reserved his greatest venom for Nigerians whose pursuit of 'westernisation' carries with it no awareness of the history of racist abuse and betrayal by colonial authorities to which the creole communities of West Africa are heir. For example, note the words to his song 'Mr Follow Follow', and the sleeve note cartoon which shows a blindfolded 'Mr Africa' hanging on to the shirt tails of a European 'Colonial Master' as they leap over a chasm marked '1958' – the run-up to Nigerian Independence – with the predictable result that 'Mr Africa' falls and starts to drown.[38] He now rejects the anglicised element in his Saro family name, Ransome-Kuti, but at the same time, because his appeal is to a cosmopolitan cross-section of Nigerian youth, sophisticated in terms of 'street sense', he has moved away from songs in Yoruba to a greater use of 'pidgin'. As his songs become more politicised, and concerned with a vision of Nigerian society which is both 'alternative' and 'authentic', so he appears more determined to capture, on his own terms, an international audience.[39] Much of the strength of his art comes from the fact that these contradictions reflect real political dilemmas of decolonisation. It is music grounded in more than a century of Lagos history.

Highlife

Irony and ambivalence, stemming from vulnerability to the charge of living between two worlds – a charge then refuted by the character of a music which demands to be taken on its own terms –

are key elements in other West African popular music styles, specifically *highlife* and *juju*.

Highlife developed in the 1920s and 30s, first in Ghana then in Lagos and western Nigeria, and has had an enduring impact on popular music in eastern Nigeria and other areas of anglophone West Africa. It is a music especially associated with the economic boom conditions of the period between 1945 and Independence in the main towns of the coastal zone of anglophone West Africa, the ambience being well captured in Cyprian Ekwensi's novel about Lagos, *People of the City*.[40] The central character, Amusa Sango, is both musician and journalist, a significant conjunction, since highlife, along with other West African popular styles, inherits a West African tradition in which musicians are purveyors of news, history and social and political comment, in addition to their role as entertainers. Typical songs of this kind – although perhaps only arguably classifiable as highlife – are 'Double decker buses' by Ebenezer Calendar (celebrating the introduction of such buses in Freetown in 1950) and 'Cost of living gets so high it is cheaper now to die' by Earl Scrubbs. Calendar and Scrubbs were Freetown musicians active in the 1940s and 50s (happily, Calendar still broadcasts regularly for Sierra Leone radio).[41] A third song from this period illustrative of the link between highlife (and similar music) and popular journalism, is a gruesome musical tale re-counted by the Lagos-based Igbo band, Israel Nzemanze and His Three Night Wizards, concerning the body of a baby wrapped in a parcel and left on the Idi Oro bus.[42] This last is the equivalent of the mass-market entertainment journalism found in papers such as *Lagos Weekend*.

Ekwensi's novel also brings out the influence of American jazz – especially Louis Armstrong's trumpet style – on West African musicians.[43] This particular influence was strengthened by the 'Hitler War', which took many West African servicemen overseas (to Burma especially) and brought British and American troops to West Africa. The lead melody voice in a highlife band is typically trumpet – Armstrong himself endorsed the playing of 1950s highlife star Zeal Onyia – and choruses are commonly scored for trumpet-saxophone or trumpet-saxophone-trombone, underpinned by guitar and drums. Big-band styles were especially important in Ghana, and major bands of the sixties and early seventies (e.g. the Ramblers) sported extensive reed and brass sections.

Many of highlife's roots are to be found in Ghana. Local musicians operating around the trading forts of the Gold Coast were playing European tunes from an early date. By the time of the so-called 'Great War' various dance styles had emerged in which both local and imported tunes would be played on a mixture of local and imported instruments. Groups associated with palm-wine bars favoured the guitar, concertina and harmonica in particular (ancestral to today's 'guitar bands'). More prestigious events – merchants' 'at homes' and garden parties – made use of the keyboards and brass instruments supplied by their wealthy sponsors. Brass bands became an important adjunct to the expression of civic pride and most towns of note in southern Ghana thought it indispensible to have one. For instance, Koforidua, fifty miles north of Accra, set up its first brass band in 1910.[44] The wealth generated by Ghana's cocoa industry during this period, and the resulting nationalist self-confidence which led to Ghana freeing itself from colonial rule earlier than any other country in Black Africa, helped sustain the growing importance of big-band highlife as prestige entertainment. In fact the term 'highlife' itself seems to have come into use when 'prestige' bands and orchestras started to add versions of currently popular local dance tunes to their repertoire of European marches, polkas, waltzes, etc. According to Yebuah Mensah, leader of one of these early bands, the Accra Rhythmic Orchestra:

The term 'highlife' was created by the people who gathered around the dancing clubs, like the Rodger Club, to watch and listen to the couples enjoying themselves. Highlife started as a catch name for the indigenous songs played at these clubs by early dance bands . . . the people outside called it the High Life as they did not reach the class of couples going inside who not only had to pay a then relatively high entrance fee of 7s 6d but also had to wear full evening dress, including top hats.[45]

The first of these orchestras in Ghana for which we have detailed evidence was the Excelsior Orchestra, formed in 1914 by a group of Ga musicians in Accra to play ballroom music for an elite audience.[46] Instruments included piano, a full string section, flute, clarinet and percussion. Judging by the items from the programme of an engagement at the Old Wesley School, James Town, in November, 1920, the orchestra's staple fare included marches ('Colonel Bogey'), 'minstrel' songs, jazz numbers ('The Jazz Craze') and novelty items (e.g. 'Possum's Picnic', a banjo solo). The only highlife listed was a number called 'Look Trouble'.[47]

In the early twenties another group of Ga musicians, some from the ranks of the Excelsior Orchestra, came together under the title The Jazz Kings and played at dance halls and cinemas in Accra and Sekondi. Their shows would open with a silent film, followed by a vaudeville section, and end with the band playing foxtrots, quicksteps, rumbas etc., and a few highlife numbers.

The 1930s witnessed the emergence of a number of similar bands, one of the most notable being Lamptey's Accra Orchestra. Lamptey, a teacher, had been a member of the Excelsior Orchestra, and began recruiting his own band from pupils in the school fife band. The Accra Orchestra had approaching fifty members, covering a most impressive range of instruments:

Brass section:	Trumpets, trombones, cornets, euphonium, tubaphones and sousaphones.
Woodwind:	Flutes, piccolo, clarinets, oboe, bassoons and baritone saxophone.
Strings:	Violins, violas, 'cellos, double basses and guitar.
Percussion:	Trap drums, clips, bottle and Pati.
Miscellaneous:	Swanee whistle and musical saw.

Similar developments appear to have been taking place in Lagos and other large Nigerian towns at about the same time and some cross-fertilisation is probable. It is known, for example, that the Ghanaian band, Cape Coast Sugar Babies, toured Nigeria twice during the 1930s, visiting Lagos, Ibadan, Kano, Jos, Onitsha, Port Harcourt, Calabar and Benin City.

Meanwhile down-market versions of, or equivalents to, highlife were continuing to proliferate. One of these was a choral version of highlife known as *konkomba*, popular in both rural and urban areas. *Konkomba* groups substituted human voices for unattainably expensive brass instruments (though keeping the brass band's percussion section), they adopted uniforms and performed complicated drill-like dances in keen competition with rival groups.[48] *Konkomba* appears to have originated in Ghana in the 1930s but versions developed in Nigeria not long afterwards. Guitar bands, responding to the demands of palm-wine tavern/street corner society in the expanding cities of the coastal zone in West Africa, were also creating styles and idioms parallel to, influenced by and influencing the more up-market highlife bands. Ghanaian guitar band leader Kwame Asare was among the earliest recording artists in West Africa, cutting some records for Zonophone in 1928. Guitar bands, based around one or more acoustic guitars (and sometimes other plucked stringed instruments, such as mandolin and banjo) and a range of 'new' but local percussion instruments (e.g. the conga-like *gombe* drum and square frame *samba* drum), were popular with Yoruba and Igbo audiences in Nigeria, and in Sierra Leone. Tunde King and Okonkwo Adigwe are two other notable figures in the development of guitar bands. King – a banjo player – led a band with a heavy emphasis on percussion (hand drums, maraccas and *samba*) and a mastery of Yoruba 'palm-wine' styles. It is possible that he was the first to use the term *juju* in this context, to cover the range of these styles.[49]

Juju music

One of the historical threads in *juju*'s make-up appears to lead back to Lagos' 'Brazilian' community, Yoruba repatriates from Brazil, settled in Lagos from the 1840s where they constituted an important and distinct trading community.[50] It was the 'Brazilians' who first introduced techniques for processing bitter cassava into *gari*. *Gari* became a staple of major importance as the population of Lagos expanded during the late nineteenth century, and commercial production spread along the lagoon waterway system as far east as Ikale and the edge of the Niger delta. This lagoon waterway was the first stage on the main eastern 'road' through Yorubaland during the latter half of the nineteenth century – important at a time when more direct routes to the major inland Yoruba cities were blocked by civil war and Ijebu resistance to colonial expansion. The eastern road was the route through which Lagos traders supplied the *Ekitiparapo* with arms for their war against Ibadan.[51] Subsequently it became an important axis for the spread of Christianity into eastern Yoruba country, through the efforts of African missionaries like Bishop Phillips of Ondo and the Revs. Manuwa and Liadu in Itebu.[52] Later, this route constituted an alternative to the colonial railway, which went north to Ibadan and Oshogbo via Abeokuta, because it provided direct access to the ports of the western Delta – at a time when cocoa cultivation was being developed well to the east of the line of rail – and the option of cheap, if slow, water transport to Lagos from a series of creek ports, such as

Agbabu, in southern Ondo province. European traders were in a dominant position along the railway but African traders enjoyed a measure of autonomy along the eastern route, and therefore some advantage in securing trade generated by the cocoa boom in eastern Yorubaland in the 1920s and 30s.[53]

This freedom for manoeuvre by African enterprise was matched by social, political and cultural developments; the axis from Lagos through Okitipupa to Ondo and Ijesha being especially noted for the proliferation of and spread of independent African churches. The marshes of southern Okitipupa have even seen a number of experiments in utopian socialism, inspired by *Aladura* beliefs, the best-known being the settlement of the Holy Apostles of Aiyetoro on the Atlantic coast south of Mahin.[54] Aiyetoro survives today as a trading company involved in creek and lagoon transportation and the supply of frozen fish to Lagos.

Peel[55] has shown that the first *Aladura* churches appealed particularly to the 'middle grades' in large organisations especially those – the railway, post office and large trading houses – most directly stemming from the development of the colonial trading economy and bureaucracy. Clerks, messengers, postmen, store-keepers, etc. are conscious that the organisation controls them, yet, equally, they have an individualist, entrepreneurial conception of the idea of progress. With ultimate control of such workers' lives and prospects in the hands of European senior management, the *Aladura* church was an important forum for asserting freedom from that control in spiritual matters, and offered scope for exercising gifts suppressed by work routines, and opportunity for these skills to be socially recognised. Extempore prayer and prophecy, and the closely related gifts of musical expression and dance, are central in *Aladura* worship.

Some parallels can be drawn between 'performance' in Yoruba expressions of African Christianity and in *juju* music. In particular, *juju* song texts often conceive of 'progress' as the manifestation of the power of the individual, and the major threat to progress the machinations of ill-disposed individuals, along the lines essayed in *Aladura* theology. The present day rags-to-riches image of the music – *juju* musicians have far surpassed the old highlife bands in instrumental sophistication – epitomises these hopes (and fears). But this is not just because successful *juju* bands now employ a sophisticated barrage of modern electronic instruments undreamt of by the trumpet-playing hero of *People of the City*, but because of the way in which these instrumental transformations have been achieved. The essential 'spiritual' values of the music – especially in the use of 'talking drum' language – are conserved despite, perhaps even through, the instrumental changes taking place. Thus, for example, over the years the *gbedu* drum has been replaced by string bass and then by electric bass, and yet, despite the use of tonic-dominant cadence formulae to structure transitions from solo to chorus in the modern *juju* song, the bass's main function is not to imply a harmonic structure but to play as a drum. Much of the effectiveness of *juju* music resides, therefore, in its emphatic rejection of the 'traditional'/'modern' dichotomy. In the hands of the skilled *juju* musician even the latest electronic instruments can be taught to 'sing' in Yoruba.

Yoruba culture, *juju* music asserts, is a modern culture. It is also entrepreneurial in spirit – a medium for innovation (as opposed to those classical traditions in which value inheres in the ability to perform a set corpus of works to timeless standards of perfection). The *juju* musician thrives – and becomes rich – on his ability to innovate, or is condemned because he copies the 'systems' and formal devices of others (band leaders differentiate their specific styles with labels, e.g. 'miliki system', 'synchro system', etc., and launch new 'systems' to announce a new phase in a band's development).

A most valuable annotated discography by Matthew Ajibero[56] makes it possible to survey comprehensively the work of one major *juju* musician, Ebenezer Obey.[57] The recurring theme of Obey's songs is that his and his band's fame and wealth rest on a foundation of patient practice, individual genius, prayer and God's guidance; he thus warns 'enemies' against jealousy and rivals against easy imitation, 'lest they fall in the ditch'.[58] In any case, he notes in one song, he is not as wealthy as James Brown – a major influence in Nigerian Afro-Beat, and an object lesson (if only a marginal musical influence) to *juju* musicians – since Obey, unlike Brown, does not own a plane.[59] Obey is also skilful in his use of proverbs in the construction of morality songs. Familiar tunes, used as counterpoints to the main melody, create a similar effect. Praise songs, such as 'Alhaji Azeez Arisekola', a song for a prominent business man, and 'Constant Stars', for the club of that name, are frequent in his output.[60] 'Face to face' discusses the problems of chance and money in a philosophical manner, ending with an advertisement for a well-known Nigerian pools house.[61] The themes of 'love' and sexual conflict, and political critique, are less common in Obey's songs (and *juju* music in general) than in highlife and styles such as Afro-Beat (the recent work of Afro-Beat musicians Fela Anikulapo-Kuti and Sonny Okosun has been predominantly political in tone).[62] Nevertheless *juju* music shares with other West African styles a general love of irony and humour. One of Obey's best-known songs tells the story of a man, his son and a donkey. When the man rode the donkey, the boy walking behind, people criticised his selfishness. When they both rode the animal he was criticised for cruelty. Finally, when they both dismounted and walked behind the donkey people thought them mad.[63]

Juju music has come to be particularly associated with wedding and funeral celebrations and large 'society' dances where wealthy patrons, praised in song, ostentatiously give away money by pasting currency notes to the foreheads of dancers and musicians with whom they are pleased – a practice known as 'spraying'. (In the song 'Olowo ma jaiye' Obey defends 'conspicuous consumption' as legitimate enjoyment of hard-earned wealth.)[64] Spraying belongs to a long tradition of 'prestige giving' by those attempting to reinforce their political power in trading communities by extending their network of patron–client relationships. All West African musicians are conscious of their part in this system (in 'Ere ni tiwa' Obey argues, somewhat disingenuously, that whereas other musicians sow the seeds of social division by praising some prominent figures to the discredit of others, his own musicians work for the good of society as a whole).[65] Musicians are often feared and despised (and vulnerable to jealous slander) because they are in a unique position to 'see through' and publicly ridicule a patron who has displeased them. The musician enjoys a special kind of power through the independent 'popular' life his music leads, which carries it far beyond the contexts for which it was originally intended. Over-stated praise – not immediately apparent upon first performance – may serve to ridicule an overreaching patron as effectively as a far more obviously satirical text.[66] In short, a musician with the public ear is in a position to patronise his patron. A successful musician may also disburse patronage in the more usual sense. Obey, for example, makes a special point of his generosity to the members of his band, and of his commitment, as a Christian, to general charitable works. He has also, on occasion sponsored aspiring musicians outside his own organisation. Modern West African bands are capital intensive, and only the most successful own their own equipment. Most are indebted to a sponsor, with the attendant risks – conflict between sponsors and musicians leads to the rapid demise of many bands as equipment is reclaimed.[67]

In the face of such uncertainty, institutional sponsorship would appear attractive. Although many social activities are organised by large businesses on 'house' lines – and West African workers' unions have tended to be 'house' rather than 'trade' based – business sponsorship for musicians is haphazard and relatively unimportant (especially by comparison with the organisation of 'leisure' undertaken by mining corporations in southern Africa, or indeed the organisation of football by business houses in West Africa). Thus there is nothing to compare with the sponsorship of semi-professional brass bands, common from the middle of the nineteenth century onwards in industrial areas of the north of England. Nor have radio and television stations found it necessary or worthwhile to organise 'house bands' on the lines of the various BBC 'light music' bands of the 1940s and 50s. (The relationship between radio stations and musicians in West Africa appears to be based on the notion that musicians are sufficiently rewarded by the free publicity when their records are played over the air; regular royalties are uncommon, though fees are paid for live performance.) In anglophone West Africa, therefore, it has fallen to the police and armed forces to be the major institutional patrons of music. Apart from a handful of posts for academically trained musicians in universities and the media, the army and police force are the major source of regular 'salaried' employment for instrumentalists. They also organise training, and until recently have been the only major alternative to the apprenticeship system as a route to instrumental competence. In Nigeria, the various army and police bands play military music for formal occasions, but readily transform themselves into dance bands playing highlife, *juju*, etc. for social occasions and commercial recording purposes. This is not inappropriate since it is probable that among the roots of Ghanaian highlife is to be found the impact of army bandsmen on local musicians.

One of Sierra Leone's most popular singers, Big Fayia, is an army sergeant. His deeper, Mende, songs are full of poetry and philosophical irony, but his Krio songs are equally effective in a lighter vein. One example, 'Blackpool', is a 'football song' (a genre cultivated by *juju* musicians as well, as with 'Green Eagles' by I. K. Dairo and 'Africa Cup Winners Cup 1976' by Idowu Animashawun) in which the soloist is much occupied in listing the patrons, officials and players of Mighty Blackpool, one of Freetown's most prominent football clubs.[68] In another Big Fayia song, 'Rosaline', an angry boss, faced with the danger of his junior poaching his girl friend, blusters 'A go kill you te te you die', to be answered by a satirical chorus of 'Yes, Sirs' – something of an anthem for armies of apprentices and household servants under similar mock military discipline.

The police and military in West Africa have created their own corpus of songs as a means of establishing regimental identity. Echoes of this music are to be found in highlife and *juju*, and the dominance of the army in Nigerian political life from 1966 to 1979 was reflected in musicians' fondness for assuming 'military' titles – Obey, hedging his bets between traditional civil authority and the armed forces, became 'Chief Commander' – but the European marches, operetta and oratorio selections played at garden party and state occasions appear to have left little trace, and their stylistic overflow into West African popular music is, perhaps, smaller than might be supposed given the background and contacts of a number of the highlife pioneers. Harmonic procedures discernably adopted from European music – like the strong, some would argue over-strong, cadencing typically used to mark out the sections of a *juju* song – owe more to missionary hymnals, and deliberate 'churchy' connotations are carried over into the melody of, for example, the popular 1950s highlife, 'Unity', or the *juju* song 'Baba mode' by Sunny Ade.[69]

Music and networks

The brokerage, creation and maintenance of control over trade routes and networks, and the sustenance of volatile business values such as 'confidence' and 'reputation' are, in the absence of a dominant industrial sector, important among the notions and experiences which shape the daily lives of many West Africans (and a majority of those living in towns). In these circumstances music brings people together, confirms rumours, underlines or destroys reputations, and helps focus individual fears and aspirations in a market economy threatened by the witchcraft of sudden, inexplicable, changes of fortune. (Obey's songs 'Irinse lo jona Obey o jona', 'Babu lukudi' and 'Edumare a dupe' all deal with rumours surrounding trips to London, the second being a specific refutation of the charge that he travelled to acquire money-making 'medicine', *lukudi*.)[70] Music also helps reinforce the identity of groups forming around particular house routes or brokerage interests. Such identities may be assumed for purposes of social as well as economic 'trade'. Thus if Hausa butchers identify themselves in their music, so a Yoruba wedding or funeral party may adopt the uniform of *aso ebi* and commission a 'regimental' song. At times the social and economic motives are totally intertwined (in the Masonic lodges of the Freetown creole business community, for example).[71]

The prolonged life of merchant capital as dominating force in West Africa development is reflected in the hyper-mobility which affects the lives of the great mass of the people. Nearly all adults are seasoned travellers, and many adults, even in remote localities, have spent considerable periods of their life working away from home. Sometimes travel is undertaken for trade, study, or to learn a craft; in other cases it is out of interest and a sense of adventure. Much West African migration can be characterised as a series of temporary moves to employment in the so-called 'informal' sector (with low-level brokerage activities, e.g. railway station and lorry park touting, a useful starting point), while residence away from home may be treated – initially at least – as a periodic phenomenon especially associated with youth. Even formal sector employment may involve an unusually high degree of geographical mobility. The spatially diffuse operations of government administration, the railway, armed forces and major trading companies require frequent staff transfers, often over long distances. Colonial patterns of residence, with the great majority of the workforce temporarily lodged in government or company quarters, have persisted into the post-colonial period. In this paper we have in effect identified West African popular music, and differentiated it from more settled styles, largely in terms of its consonance with the shifting, cosmopolitan, volatile life-styles of traders and other migrants.

The gramophone, and more recently the radio and tape-recorder, are important symbols of the 'returned migrant's' material success. (Record dealers are often located close to lorry parks, and in Umuahia, in eastern Nigeria, the main street of record dealers

adjoins a major level crossing close to the railway station. Traders in
Lagos even peddle hi-fi equipment to traffic-jammed motorists at
motorway intersections during the rush hour. Obey's 'Idi Oro ni
yen'[72] is a song devoted to analysing Lagos' traffic problems, and
traffic congestion is a theme which has attracted other Nigerian
composers, including Fela Anikulapo Kuti.)

   Distance also adds an important dimension of meaning to the
music itself. In the 1950s, Zairois guitarist Mwenda Jean Bosco[73]
had a hit in Sierra Leone with a song recorded by Gallotone in
South Africa. Since the words meant nothing to a West African
audience the song acquired various local names. Some people
remember it as 'CO 89', its Gallotone record number. Others,
however, refer to it as 'Magbosi' (a village on the main road to the
east some seventy miles or so from Freetown). Apparently, during
road repairs, a lorry broke down at this point, blocking the road to
all traffic. Stranded passengers danced the night away to this record
played on a wind-up gramophone, and the song acquired the name
of the village as a result. Thus a song recorded over 3000 miles away
became a firm part of travellers' lore in Sierra Leone. Finally, as if to
refute the image of Africa as a continent of isolated villages and
untravelled villagers, aware of little outside their own backyard, the
Zairois band leader 'Dr Nico' composed a long quotation from this
Bosco song into a piece, 'Cherie Julie Nalingaka',[74] recorded in
conjunction with his west African tour of 1969 – an event still talked
about by musicians in Sierra Leone. In effect, then, an important
part of the appeal of popular music in West Africa is the range of
references upon which it is based, and the delight an audience takes
in decoding these influences and quotations. Listeners are reminded
of the way they have come and the route they may hope to travel.
The issue is not (as some critics suppose) 'whence came *merengue* to
Sierra Leone' but how Sierra Leonean musicians construct meanings
out of a series of Caribbean references. The basis for an answer lies
in two hundred years of regular interaction between the creole
communities of Freetown and the Caribbean, and would involve, in
its proper elucidation, a detailed consideration of factors such as the
rise and wider intellectual and political impact of pan-Africanism in
West Africa and the West Indies. Thus the Christian, European
and Caribbean references in music such as highlife are important
because they point down the cultural paths first pursued by creole
trading communities in the nineteenth century, paths which

continue today to have both social and economic significance for the communities concerned.

Styles such as *sakara, apala* and *fuji*, not discussed in this paper, are equally eloquent of the links between the coast and savanna communities, their consonance with the political and intellectual evolution of various Islamicised trading communities and brotherhoods being, perhaps, not dissimilar to the links we have attempted to delineate between *juju* music and the ambience of *Aladura* Christian groups.[75]

Conclusion

In this paper we have argued against the notion that West African popular music is a socially neutral synthesis of alien and indigenous influences criticisable on the grounds that it is culturally 'of two minds'. If organisations such as the colonial army and Christian missions have exercised influence on highlife and *juju* it is because their use of music is also strategically appropriate to the enactment of social and economic life in a wide range of civil and secular organisations. We argue, further, that merchant capital has been a major influence over both performance contexts and the construction of musical meanings in West Africa. We expect, as a result, that it will be possible to demonstrate important differences between the way in which popular music has developed here and in say, southern Africa, where industrial capital is in a much more dominant position.[76] Our major concern, however, has been to argue that seen in historical perspective the music under review assumes enhanced status as a cultural achievement.

Notes

1 An earlier draft of this paper drew helpful comments from John Peel. The revised version remains provisional. Our main concern is to sketch the outline of an alternative to syncretist explanations. We have been especially anxious to avoid the assumptions underlying such terms as 'semitribal' and 'neotraditional' applied to the music in question and to steer clear of the style of argument we term 'borrowings and retentions analysis', cf. Gerhard Kubik, *The Kachamba brothers' band: a study of neo-traditional music in Malawi*, Institute of African Studies, University of Zambia, Manchester, 1974; John Storm Roberts, *Black music of two worlds*, Allen Lane, London, 1973; Paul Oliver, *Savannah syncopators: African retentions in the*

Blues, Studio Vista, London, 1970. 'Borrowings and retentions' analysis is part of the legacy of Tylor's anthropology in ethnomusicology, see W. Dwight Allen, *Philosophies of music history: a study of general histories of music 1600–1960*, Dover, New York (2nd Edn.), 1962 and A. M. Jones, *Africa and Indonesia: the xylophone as culture indicator*, Brill, Leiden, 1964.

2   West African propensities to trade were a frequent focus for defamatory attacks by Europeans on Sierra Leonian Creoles. Agriculture was 'good' but trade 'corrupting'. See, for example, J. Peterson, *Province of Freedom*, Faber, London, 1969, for discussion of the competition between European and Creole trading interests and its ideological by-products.

3   Paul Richards, 'Ideas, environment and agricultural change: a case study from western Nigeria', Unpublished PhD Thesis, University of London, 1977.

4   Source printed in Christopher Fyfe, *Sierra Leone inheritance*, Oxford University Press, London, 1964, p. 68.

5   See, for example, John Levi, *African agriculture: economic action and reaction in Sierra Leone*, Commonwealth Agricultural Bureaux, Slough, 1976. An example of the crucial significance of debt management to the political economy of a West African trading community in the nineteenth century is to be found in Timothy C. Weiskel, *French colonial rule and the Baule peoples*, Clarendon Press, Oxford, 1980, pp. 110–111.

6   For discussion of the incorporation of 'strangers' into West African social life see W. A. Shack and E. P. Skinner (eds.), *Strangers in African society*, University of California Press, Berkeley and London, 1979.

7   Among A. G. Frank's writing see especially *Dependent accumulation and underdevelopment*, Macmillan, London, 1978.

8   A conclusion of a study of foodstuff marketing in western Nigeria, W. O. Jones, *Marketing staple food crops in tropical Africa*, Cornell University Press, Ithaca and London, 1972.

9   M. O. Filani and P. Richards 'Periodic market systems and rural development: the Ibarapa case', *Savanna*, V, 2, 1976, pp. 149–62.

10 Abner Cohen, *Custom and politics in urban Africa*, University of California Press, Berkeley and Los Angeles, 1969 and 'Cultural strategies in the organization of trading diasporas' in *The development of indigenous trade and markets in West Africa*, ed. C. Meillassoux, Oxford University Press, London; P. D. Curtin, 'Pre-colonial trading networks and traders: the Jakhanké' in Meillassoux, *op. cit.*; D. Northrup, *Trade without rulers: pre-colonial economic development in south-eastern Nigeria*, Clarendon Press, Oxford, 1978. Cf. B. Belasco, *The entrepreneur as culture hero: preadaptation in Nigerian economic development*, Praeger, New York, 1980.

11 Northrup, *ibid.*

12 Richards, *op. cit.*

13 B. Gyllström, *The organization of production as a space-modelling mechanism in under-developed countries: the case of tea production in Kenya*, Gleerup, Lund, 1977.

14 See, for example, the discussion in ch. 6 of A. G. Hopkins, *An economic history of West Africa*, Longman, London, 1973.

15 On the history of 'highlife' see J. Storm Roberts, *op. cit.*; Edna Smith, 'Popular music in West Africa', *African Music*, III, 1, 1962, pp. 11–14. Frank Aig-Imoukhuede, 'Contemporary culture', in *Lagos: the development of an African city*, ed. A. B. Aderibigbe, Longman Nigeria, Lagos, 1975; and the entry under 'Highlife' (by A. A. Mensah) in the new edition of *Grove*, 1981.

16 T. Ajayi Thomas (sleeve notes for Shade JRFM 2, *Great juju and sakara music*) states: 'Juju music . . . has come a long way. It has been around uncared for (even when Banjo was played in it) until an adventurous recording artiste introduced accordian, electric lead, rhythm and bass guitar into it. Immediately, popularity came to it . . .' This is a reference to I. K. Dairo. (See also J. Storm Roberts, *op. cit.*) Sierra Leonian musicians were making use of accordian in the 1940s – e.g. the famous singer Sallia Koroma, cf. K. Little, 'A Mende musician sings of his adventures', *Man*, XI, 1948, pp. 26–7.

17 *Festac 77*, Sunny Alade Records SALPS 14, issued by Sunny Ade's band to commemorate the Second World Black and African Festival of Arts and Culture (1977) was a notable example of what West African musicians sometimes refer to as 'expensive sound' (cf. Shade FMLP 002, *The great and expensive sound of the Supersonics*, a 1960s Lagos highlife band). The equivalent in European musical parlance would be 'opulent scoring'.

18 Shaykh Umar of Bornu was disappointed to find that the instrument would produce 'only a few hoarse notes' after its long journey. G. Nachtigal, *Sahara and Sudan v. II: Kawar, Bornu, Kanem, Borku, Ennedi*, translated and edited by A. G. B. & H. J. Fisher, C. Hurst, London, 1980. The Fishers add, in a footnote, that Rohlfs had presented a 'harmonica' to the ruler of Kawar and another to the Crown Prince of Bornu in 1866, and that Barth had also found this instrument an acceptable gift for dignitaries. Rohlfs carried a *Klavierharmonium* on his 1878 expedition, but this was destroyed when his camp was plundered at Kufra. According to Percy Scholes (*The Concise Oxford Dictionary of Music*) the harmonica first came into use in the 1830s.

19 Elizabeth Helen Melville, *A residence at Sierra Leone*, John Murray, London, 1849 (Cass Reprint Edition, 1968).

20 *Ibid.* Henry George Farmer, *Memoirs of the Royal Artillery Band: its origin history and progress*, Boosey and Co., London, 1904, notes that after 1785–87 'it then became "good style" to employ black men to play these instruments' (i.e. percussion instruments in British Army regimental bands) 'but matters were overdone in this particular, and some bands actually had one third of its members performing upon percussion instruments. They had the good sense, however, to

introduce more wind instruments to reduce this preponderance of noise' (pp. 50–52).
21 Samuel Coleridge Taylor (1875–1912), *Twenty-four Negro Melodies, transcribed for the piano* . . ., Op. 59, Oliver Ditson and Co, Boston, 1905. Composer's Foreword, dated 1904.
22 *Ibid. Oloba* is no. 7 in the set.
23 See, for example, the discussion in I. F. Nicolson, *The administration of Nigeria, 1900–1960*, Clarendon Press, Oxford, 1969, of the 'economic development lobby' in early colonialism in Nigeria.
24 E. M. von Hornbostel, 'African Negro music', *Africa*, I, 1928, pp. 30–62; Hugh Tracey, 'The state of folk music in Bantu Africa', *African Music*, I, 1954, pp. 8–11. For a recent discussion of 'syncretism' see B. Nettl, 'Some aspects of the history of world music in the twentieth century: questions, problems, and concepts', *Ethnomusicology*, XXII, 1978, pp. 123–36.
25 Theodor Adorno, *Philosophy of Modern Music* (trans. A. Mitchell and W. Bloomster), Sheed and Ward, London, 1973.
26 Nicolson, *op. cit.*, is an entertaining commentator on the pseudo-mediaeval pretensions of some of Northern Nigeria's 'indirect rulers', cf. Charles Temple, *Native races and their rulers*, Capetown, 1917.
27 Constance Larymore, *A Resident's wife in Nigeria*, Routledge, London, 1908.
28 On cultural life in nineteenth century Lagos see P. D. Cole, 'Lagos society in the nineteenth century' and Frank Aig-Imoukhuede, 'Contemporary culture' in A. B. Aderibigbe (ed.), *Lagos: the development of an African city*, Longman Nigeria, Lagos, 1975 and M. Echeruo, *Victorian Lagos*, Macmillan, London, 1976.
29 Aig-Imoukhuede, *op. cit.* Fela Sowande, 'Nigerian music and musicians: then and now', *Nigeria*, XCIV, September 1967.
30 Cole, *op. cit.*
31 E. A. Ayandale, 'Background to the "Duel" between Crowther and Goldie on the Lower Niger, 1857–85' and 'The Colonial Church Question in Lagos politics, 1905–11', both reprinted in *Nigerian Historical Studies*, Cass, London, 1979.
32 The balance is redressed in H. L. van der Laan's scrupulous scholarly study, *The Lebanese Traders in Sierra Leone*, Mouton, The Hague, 1975.
33 E. A. Ayandale, 'A visionary of the African Church: Mojola Agbebi (1860–1917)' in *African Historical Studies*, Cass, London, 1979.
34 Among Sowande's works for concert orchestra are a *Nigerian Folk Symphony* and the *African Suite* for strings (1944). The fifth movement of the suite is based on a 'highlife' tune, *Akinla*, popular in Ghana in the 1930s but said to have originated in Liberia.
35 Sowande returned to Nigeria in 1953, and subsequently was appointed to an academic position in the University of Ibadan. A series of lectures on the background to African musicology, organised by Sowande at the Institute of African Studies in 1968, began with a paper, by the Rev. D. Olarinwa Epega, on *Ifa*, the Yoruba system of

divinatory wisdom. In a foreword to this lecture Sowande argued that African musicology cannot be adapted from European models. It must be derived from indigenous principles expressed in African religion.

36 Compare for example the String Quartet (1957) with his work on the music for Wale Ogunyemi's play *Obaluaye* recorded in 1974 (Associated Record Company ARC 1101).

37 *Alagbon Close*, Makossa EM 2313, 1975; *Zombie*, Creole CRLP 511, 1977.

38 Much of the record sleeve art work on his recent LPs, including the Mr Follow Follow cartoon, is by Ghariokwu Lemi.

39 Lindsay Barrett 'Fela conquers Europe', *West Africa*, 3323, 6 April 1981. Fela Anikulapo Kuti's political philosophy is in the tradition of Nkrumah's attempts to mobilise youth (e.g. the Young African Pioneers). 'Youth' in this sense is as much a class as an age category, i.e. youth = proletarian. Urban populism, and a style of politics which dramatises irreverence for authority, has a history stretching back to the 'warboys' and 'freed slaves' in Europe and North America in the 1950s). Barrett reports that at the Paris concert in March 1981 Fela achieved considerable rapport with a politically aware audience of European youth by linking his concern that 'Western technology . . . is an evil to be avoided in Africa' with their concern for the dangers of nuclear energy.

40 First published 1954. For a discussion of Ekwensi as a writer of popular urban fiction see Adrian Roscoe, *Mother is gold: a study in West African literature*, Cambridge University Press, Cambridge, 1971.

41 *Double decker buses*, Decca R?, *Cost of living* . . ., Decca R 531.

42 Israel Njemanze and His Three Night Wizards, Decca R 428 and 429. Musicians are 'powerful' people and lead dangerous lives. Like the *juju* pioneer Ayinde Bakare, Njemanze died in suspicious circumstances.

43 Louis Armstrong visited Ghana in 1956, and toured Africa in 1960.

44 Samuel Charters includes a recording of a village brass band in Ghana in the 1970s on his record *African journey* (Sonet SNTF 667, 1974). According to Storm Roberts (*op. cit.*) the Basel Mission introduced brass bands into Ghana.

45 Interview by John Collins.

46 Echeruo, *op. cit.* describes mid-nineteenth-century British 'finishing schools' for the daughters of wealthy Lagos merchants in which ballroom dancing and piano lessons were included in the curriculum. Klevor Abo (personal communication) tells us that Ewe merchants in the Keta area of southeastern Ghana sponsored orchestral and choral concerts (including Handel oratorios) during the early colonial period. *Messiah* and Coleridge Taylor's *Hiawatha's Wedding Feast* are well-known, especially to the older generation, in merchant society in a number of centres in the coastal zone of anglophone West Africa.

47 Collected by John Collins.

48 *Konkomba* (or *concoma* in Storm Roberts, *op. cit*) is not unlike the East
    African *beni* dance phenomenon described by Terence Ranger, *Dance
    and society in eastern Africa*, Heinemann, London, 1975. According to
    Storm Roberts (*op. cit.*, p. 246) it developed in the Kumasi area in the
    1940s, and Edna Smith, *op. cit.* reports that most Ghanaians con-
    sidered it to be a forerunner of highlife. The origin of the name is not
    clear. J. H. Kwabena Nketia, *The music of Africa*, Gollancz, London,
    1975, citing Tait, *The Konkomba of Northern Ghana*, Oxford University
    Press, London, 1962, notes that 'among the Konkomba of northern
    Ghana, it is the duty of young men to dance at the burials of elders of
    their clan, of related clans and even of contiguous districts, if they are
    sent by their leaders, for dancing at the burials is a symbol of clan
    membership as well as an expression of interclan relationship' (p. 208).
    Northern Ghana 'exported' labour to the cocoa districts centred on
    Kumasi. Southern cocoa farmers participated in 'regional cults'
    organised around shrines in the far north, e.g. in the Tong Hills
    (Richard Werbner, 'Totemism in history: the ritual passage of West
    African strangers', *Man* (N.S.) XIV, pp. 663–83, 1980). *Konkomba*
    dancing, may, however, have little to do with the 'northern con-
    nection'. In Sierra Leone the term *kongoma* applies to a large
    lamellaphone used to supply a bass rhythm. Aig-Imoukhuede, *op. cit.*
    notes that *konkoma* music preceded *agidigbo* as musical fashions in
    Lagos in the 1940s and early 1950s. *Konkoma*, he states, was
    introduced by Ewe and Fanti migrants from Ghana. *Agidigbo* is named
    after 'the big box-type *sansa* with metal lamellae which provided the
    background rhythm' (p. 214). Street dancing – dance parades from one
    end of Lagos island to the other – known as 'steaming', was also
    popular in Lagos during the colonial period (to the accompaniment of
    the Calabar Brass Band). Aig-Imoukhuede describes the music as a
    rhythmically freer variant of the military marching music of the Hausa
    constabulary.

49 The best account of Lagos popular music in the colonial period, and of
    the origins of *juju* music is to be found in Aig-Imoukhuede, *op. cit.*

50 Of a total Lagos population in 1881 of 37,458, 'Brazilians' numbered
    3,221 and 'Sierra Leoneans' 1,533. Just over 30 per cent of the city's
    population was directly engaged in commerce (Cole, *op. cit.*). On the
    role of 'repatriates' in Lagos and Yoruba society in the nineteenth
    century see Jean Herskovits Kopytoff, *A preface to modern Nigeria: the
    Sierra Leoneans in Yoruba, 1830–1890*, University of Wisconsin Press,
    Madison, 1965, and S. A. Akintoye, *Revolution and power politics in
    Yorubaland 1840–1893*, Longman, London, 1971. On the interaction
    between West Africa and Brazil see Pierre Verger, *Trade relations
    between the Bight of Benin and Bahia from the 17th to the 19th Century*
    (translated by E. Crawford), Ibadan University Press, Ibadan, 1976.

51 S. A. Akintoye, *op. cit.* (especially ch. 3) and S. A. Akintoye, 'The
    Ondo road eastwards of Lagos c. 1870–1895', *Journal of African
    History*, X, 4, pp. 581–98, 1969.

52 The Rev. E. Moses Lijadu, an Egba working as a missionary for the CMS in the area south of Ondo, established a network of self-governing and financially self-supporting congregations in the Okitipupa area known as the Evangelist's Mission. Confrontation between Lijadu's group and the CMS (under Bishop Phillips) in Ondo came to a head in 1902, and the Rev. R. A. Coker (the musician) travelled from Ijebu Ode to mediate in the dispute. An amicable settlement was reached, after which Coker describes a 'social entertainment' at which 'Mr Lijadu came out and gave an improvised Yoruba Ode in a charming Recitative form dealing on the peace obtained . . .' (Coker to Harding, 30 October, 1902, CMS (Y) 2/2/4, National Archives Ibadan). By 1905 there were vigorous congregations, well supported financially by local merchants, in Igbotako, Igbo Egunrin, Siluko, Makun and Aiyede, precursors of an especially intense development of independent African church activities in Ikale and Ilaje in the 1920s and 30s.

Music in the Lijadu Family Papers (National Archives, Ibadan) includes *Congregational Anthems*, and a variety of dances (polkas, waltzes, the fourth figure of the Lancer), ballads and 'salon' pieces (e.g. *Home, sweet home* and selections from *Les Cloches de Corneville*). In 1899 Lijadu was in correspondence with various British typewriter suppliers over the possibility of supplying him a typewriter modified to the Yoruba alphabet (LFB 3/3/1, National Archives, Ibadan). The late nineteenth century was a time for 'particular concern over the preservation of Yoruba proverbs and songs' (Aig-Imoukhuede, *op. cit*, p. 218). Lijadu was a keen contributor to such developments, e.g. his *Aribiloso* (1886) and *Ifa*. The point we wish to make is that the span of Lijadu's interests is no more puzzling, or in need of explanation by way of the concept 'syncretism', than, say, the interest of the early English radical in the French Revolution and Anglo-Saxon social formations. Nor was the process one of 'modernising' a traditional culture – if anything it was 'tradition' that was under construction.

53 Further details are to be found in Richards, *op. cit.*
54 Stanley Barrett, *Two villages on stilts*, Chandler Publishing Co., New York and London, 1974 and *The rise and fall of an African Utopia*, Wilfred Laurier University Press, Waterloo, Ontario, 1977.
55 J. D. Y. Peel, *Aladura*, Oxford University Press, London, 1968. *Aladura* churches sometimes have choirs and bands which record religious songs in a style related to *juju* and *highlife*, e.g. *Celestial Church of Christ*, EMI NEMI (LP) 0003 (n.d.); *Hallel'Yah group of Nigeria*, Alawada Records ARLPS 12 (1976). African popular musicians are very often from the same urban 'middle rank' social background. Storm Roberts (*op. cit.*) comments as follows:

The social background of modern African pop musicians is interesting. They spring neither from the elite (though they may become members of the elite if successful) not, on the whole, from the peasantry. The famous Congolese musician Rochereau was a minor

civil servant in education, and Jacques Kibembe, who founded the
Orchestra Sinza, was a bicycle repairman. Docteur Nico, another
prominent figure in music, was a technical college teacher. (p. 254)

56   Matthew Idowu Ajibero, 'Yoruba music on gramophone records: a
      comprehensive annotated discography of Chief Commander Ebenezer
      Obey's Juju music', Unpublished dissertation, Bachelor of Library
      Science, Ahmadu Bello University, Zaria, 1978.
57   Chief Commander Ebenezer Obey (Ebenezer Oluremi Olasupo
      Fabiyi), was born in Idogo nr. Ilaro, Egbado Division, Abeokuta
      Province (now Ogun State), 3 April 1942. After leaving Secondary
      Modern School in 1958 he worked as a Pools Clerk with the Oriental
      Brothers Pools Company in Lagos, playing part-time with a number of
      bands, doubling all instruments except brass. After six years with the
      band of Fatayi Rolling Dollar he formed his own band, the Inter-
      national Brothers, in 1964. Consistently one of the most successful *juju*
      musicians in Nigeria from the late 1960s, he has suggested recently
      that he may now retire from the commercial scene and concentrate on
      making 'Christian' records. (Biographical details from Ajibero, *ibid.*
      Two Fatayi Rolling Dollar tracks have been re-released on Shade
      JRFM2.)
58   For example, *Abanije enia*, Decca WAPS 338 (1976); *Eiye to ba fara
      wegu*, Decca WAPS 408 (1977); *Inter-Reformers atunda*, Decca WAPS
      148 (1974). (Throughout, we have used the sometimes non-standard
      Yoruba titles of songs as they appear on the record labels, and in
      Ajibero's discography.)
59   *Esa ma miliki*, Decca NWA 5882 (1970).
60   Prayer: *Baba fona han wa*, Decca WAPS 378 (1977); *Maje ki a
                       pade agbako*, Decca WAPS 408 (1977); *Oluwa gbe mi
                       leke*, Decca WAPS 358 (1976).
      Money: *Ma se ohun rere nile aiye mi*, Decca WAPS 148 (1974).
      Witchcraft: *Kini ati ma se aiye yi si*, Decca WAPS 358 (1976).
      Proverbs: *ABD olowe*, Decca WAPS 108 (1973); *Eledumare a
                       segun elegan*, Decca WAPS 358 (1976).
      Praise songs: *Alhaji Azeez Arisekola*, Decca WAPS 408 (1977);
                       Constant Stars, Decca WAPS 308 (1975); *Kabiyesi
                       Oba Lipede*, WAPS 58 (1972).
61   *Face to face*, Decca NWA 5883 (1970).
62   Merchants and the professional elite, major patrons of *juju* music, have
      less use for the uncompromisingly dramatic style of urban politics
      pursued by proletarian 'youth'. Sonny Okosun – a musician who tries to
      extend his appeal to both groups – is explicit about his *aladura*
      commitments (in part his particular success is to suggest a parallel
      between *aladura* and *Rastafarian* beliefs at the same time as his music
      skilfully blends Afro-beat and *reggae* elements). The sleeve notes for
      Papa's land, EMI NEMI (LP) 0232 (1977), quote from Isaiah 60 and
      Psalm 91 under the heading 'The might Jah assured me' and state that the
      album was born as the result of a prayer meeting at the meeting house of

the Eternal Order of Cherubim and Seraphim, Pearse Street, Surulere. Choruses on this record were sung by the Lagos Royal Choir, The Enugu Postmen Singers and the Ishan Cultural Singers, a mix which would have appealed no doubt, to Moses Lijadu.

63 *Babo oni ketekete*, Decca WAPS 98 (1973).

64 *Alowo [sic] ma jaiye*, Decca WAPS 78 (1973). *Juju* musicians tend to find most of their employment in social engagements such as wedding and funeral celebrations, where the sponsors control access through a guest list, rather than in 'nightlife' engagements in clubs and dance halls, where access depends on payment of a gate fee. 'Praise song' and the furtherance of social and political reputation is much more important in the first, as opposed to the second context (bearing in mind the nature of the occasion and the composition of the audience). Cf. William Weber, *Music and the Middle Class*, Croom Helm, London, 1975.

65 *Ere ni tiwa*, Decca WAOS 98 (1973).

66 M. G. Smith, 'The social functions and meaning of Hausa praise singing', *Africa*, XXVII, pp. 26–44, 1957.

67 Naomi Ware Hooker, 'Popular musicians in Freetown', *African Urban Notes*, V, 4, pp. 11–18, 1970.

68 *Blackpool*, Taretone TTL 101 (1977); *African Cup Winners' Cup 1976*, Take Your Choice Record Stores TYC 61–L (1976); *Green Eagles*, Star IKLPS 12 (1976); *Rosaline*, Taretone TTL 101 (1977). On the history of the Brass Band movement in Britain see A. R. Taylor, *Brass bands*, Granada Publishing, St Albans, 1979. Little research has been carried out into the topic of army and police bands in West Africa. A. Haywood and F. A. S. Clarke, *The history of the Royal West Africa Frontier Force*, Gale and Polden, Aldershot, 1964, say little beyond noting that the RWAFF march was *Old Calabar*, that various battalions used their own additional marches, and that the *Hausa Farewell* was a medley of bugle calls 'believed to be based on Hausa tunes played when men went to war' (p. 495). There are enough references in the archives to suggest, however, that the topic would repay systematic investigation. For example, IBADIV 1/1 931 (Handing over notes, D. O. Ibadan), National Archives, Ibadan, refers to the Ibadan Native Authority Police Band in 1937, which had twenty members under the direction of Sgt. Turner (at a time when the total strength of the force was only 'eighty available men'). It could be hired at 10/6d per hour in Ibadan and £1 1s. elsewhere. The musicians received 1/3d and the rest went into a fund for instruments and music (of which quantities were on order from Boosey and Hawkes).

69 *Unity*, Melodisc MLP 12–131; *Baba mode*, Sunny Alade Records SALPS 14 (1977). *Unity* was the work of Abiodun Oke (Brewster Hughes) and the Nigerian Union Rhythm Band, an offshoot of Ambrose Campbell's West African Rhythm Brothers (1946). According to Storm Roberts (p. 249) Campbell's musicians were skilled players on Nigerian instruments who were then trained to play European instruments.

70 *Babu lukudi*, Decca WAPS 338 (1976); *Edumare a dupe*, Decca WAPS 338 (1976); *Irinse lo jona Obey o jona*, Decca WAPS 168 (1974).

71 Abner Cohen, *The politics of elite culture: explorations in the dramaturgy of power in a modern African society*, University of California Press, Berkeley, Los Angeles and London, 1981.
72 *Idi Oro ni yen*, Decca WAPS 278 (1975).
73 David Rycroft. 'The guitar improvisations of Mwenda Jean Bosco', *African Music*, II, 4, pp. 81–98, 1961; and III, 1, pp. 86–102, 1962. *Kuturizana/Watoko Wawili*, Gallotone CO 89 (1955).
74 *Cherie Julie Nalingaka*, African 360.020 (1970).
75 In his sleeve note to *Alhaji Chief Kollington Ayinia and his 78 Fuji Organisation: me kun nu nji-ya*, Olumo ORPS 201 (1980), Lanre Akinbo writes: 'Kollington has made himself an enigma by first introducing "bata" and recently jazz band set, a queer landmark indeed; all to add glamour to his Fuji. And that is why this is Bata-Disco Fuji.'

This is comparable to the 'new instrument' ethos of *juju* music. For a discussion of innovation in the music of a northern Nigerian urban community see David Ames, 'Urban Hausa music', *African Urban Notes*, V, 4, pp. 19–24, 1970.
76 Cf. The entry (by David Coplan) on music in the *Cambridge Encyclopedia of Africa*, edited by Michael Crowder and Roland Oliver, Cambridge University Press, Cambridge, 1981.

Popular music in Indonesia

It is impossible to avoid being impressed by the richness and variety of musical experiences in Indonesia today. Not only is this richness and variety impressive, but the omnipresence of musical experiences overwhelms even this American who is accustomed to weekly concerts, daily TV and radio jingles and soundtracks, supermarket muzak, the chimes of a fully programmed bell-tower, or the music that cascades from the radios of passing cars. In this essay I want to present one kind of survey of the repertory of Indonesian song recorded on cassette tape during the past ten years and distributed and sold, at the least, throughout the island of Java, Indonesia. The designation Indonesian in the construction 'Indonesian song' means, for the most part, songs with texts in the Indonesian language, not in any one of the 250 regional languages and dialects of the Island nation. This designation also means songs with other musical ingredients – instruments, timbres, or melodic, rhythmic, and formal organisation – which came to Indonesia within the past fifty years, or which are not directly derived from any one of the many regional types of music from Indonesia's past. I am focusing on the island of Java, because almost all of the two years I have been in Indonesia I spent on that island, particularly in the central area, the district known as Surakarta.

Java, which is approximately the size of New York state, has a present population of over eighty million people, and the absence of urban concentrations of population, other than Jakarta with its eight million and Surabaya with its four million, guarantees that there are few places now on the island where one does not find communities of people. In fact, the conception of a return to nature, an outing away from others, or even a search for the natural world, does not exist for Javanese. *Alam*, the closest Javanese word to the English 'nature', is a part of the Javanese idea of human experience which defines the existence of the natural. All of the world is received and mediated through human experience. The natural world exists through human action in it. It is not a category of experience which is external to human thought and actions.

The closest one comes in Java to a return to nature or, better, a withdrawal from society, is the practice of meditation known as *Semadi*. This practice involves a withdrawal from consciousness of one's surroundings – external matters (*lair*) – and a focus on the inner world of one's thoughts and feelings (*batin*). The spiritual discipline of which *Semadi* is a part, is called *ngelmu batin* (sometimes *ngelmu luhung*). Intense concentration of this type is said to produce several benefits to the individual. Among these is a suffusion of power from outside the individual, an experience sometimes described by the metaphor *rasa tumlawung* – the hearing of a great sound, resounding from afar.

One of the results of meditation can be the attainment of power, both through personal invigoration and by the social acknowledgement of personal powers. The powerful person can be capable of what might be regarded as reckless or rash acts, behaviour which might be called anti-social in other individuals or by societies with other beliefs, but the person with power is also charged with social responsibilities – to keep the peace (*tentrem kerta-rahaja*), to teach proper behaviour by example (*laku*) and in language (*basa*), and to establish and maintain just order in society.

In this brief presentation of some of the aspects of Javanese society three points can be stressed. First, nature without people is an environment that is disorganised and hostile. One does not achieve purification by retreat into an environment devoid of people. Second, purification of spirit, body, and mind can be achieved by meditation and concentration. These processes will achieve personal power. Third, powerful people have social responsibilities. A breakdown of public order means a breakdown or weakening of power in a leader. These points will return in my discussion of a genre of song known as *pop* in Java today.

The varieties of music in Java are many. Each major type of music has many genres – stylistic, formal or contextual subtypes. The major type of music in times past for most Javanese was, of course, gamelan. In some ways it is improper to leave the impression that gamelan is a single type of music, for in times past there were many different configurations of gamelan ensembles, repertories, and styles of performance appropriate to different contexts. In recent times the world 'gamelan' has emerged as a name for a category of almost all the musical ensembles and repertories that were performed in these different contexts. There are at least ten types of ensembles known by this name, and many different groups of performers, repertories and styles of performance for each type of ensemble. There are also, in Java, several different types of ensemble composed of instruments from musical traditions of Western Europe and America. In addition there are ensembles in which some of the instruments from gamelan are mixed with western or electronic instruments. There are gamelan concerts, 'jam sessions', and contributions to the accompaniment of at least ten basic types of dramatic or ceremonial events. A list of types of gamelan music in Java would occupy a full page. A list of types of song would occupy another.

Strong traditions of song on Java existed in times past, in at least four different languages and twice that number of dialects. These songs were sung unaccompanied or accompanied by one of the instrumental ensembles. The traditions of unaccompanied singing in central Java were the only means in the Javanese past to communicate written texts. Almost all texts were written in poetry, and poetry was meant to be sung. The most recent name for the genre of poetry metres and melodies used for these purposes is *tembang* (*sekar*, in another language level). In *tembang* verbal meanings were not only embellished in song, but song influenced the perception of verbal meaning. Alliteration, assonance and tone were important aspects of meaning. This proper intonation of words was not limited to song alone but extended to spoken language. The tone of words was a measure of the relationships between people. This dimension of tone was built into the vocabulary of speech, but had melodic implications as well.

The practice of singing *tembang* in the communication of texts of letters, stories, prayers and teachings was for many centuries an integral part of Javanese life. It is hard for us to imagine a state of mind which sees melody in all writing. It is hard for us to imagine a state of mind which places such a high degree of importance on song in such everyday processes as letters, chronicles or teachings. Yet this state of mind was present in Java as little as fifty years ago, and it now continues to influence the perception of new genres of Indonesian song in Java.

Faced with the rich display of musical experiences in Java, it is difficult to develop a set of categories for musical experience there. One obvious generalisation places *tembang* and gamelan ensembles and repertories into a broad category called 'traditional', and the ensembles and repertories of western origin and western–Javanese mix into another called 'modern'. This easy categorisation presents several difficulties.

First, several types of gamelan continue to be vigorous parts of life in present-day Java. Significant changes have taken place in the repertories and social–cultural functions of these types of gamelan. Obvious changes have occurred, such as mixing of gamelan instruments with electronic and acoustic instruments which originated in other areas of the world. Less obvious changes include the adoption of new roles for gamelan, such as concert performance, with a passive audience and a staged ensemble, and the abandonment of old roles, such as processional accompaniment or meditative discipline. Some gamelan were played, in the past, in religious and educational contexts, or in demonstrations of political and religious power. These events were often accompanied by entertainment and enjoyment, but this entertainment was a consequence of the fulfilment of other social–cultural functions, which were woven into the fabric of daily life. Gamelan performance was an educationally and politically classless activity. There were, certainly, court orchestras consisting of instruments produced at a higher social cost than village instruments, but even as late as the twentieth century, very few musicians who performed in the courts were aristocrats. Moreover, most music-making occurred in villages. Many villagers participated in these performances, assuming roles in ensembles based on abilities. Most of the others understood well the workings of gamelan and song.

There were also elaborate, long and complicated pieces (*gendhing ageng* and *bonang*) composed in the courts of the nineteenth century, but these represented a small number of the pieces performed. Most pieces were straightforward subjects for development by means of the standard techniques of gamelan performance in one of its many varieties. These techniques were understood by most Javanese, and executable by a large number of those who understood. Thus gamelan and the processes of music-making are still parts of the musical background system by which Javanese now interpret music.

A second difficulty in creating a set of categories for music based on the traditional–modern matrix is that the system must account for the important place of *tembang* in the Javanese past. Recent theories on the organisation of gamelan have stressed the importance of *tembang* to the development of even those gamelan repertories which seem, on the surface, so strongly rooted in pure instrumental play. *Tembang*, it is maintained, have been sources for the creation of almost all pieces in the repertories of most types of gamelan ensembles. Thus *tembang* can hardly be ignored in a system of categories for present-day music in Java.

The system of categories that I want to explore in this paper differentiates between older types of Javanese music, those types of gamelan and *tembang* which developed through the past centuries, and newer forms of music in present-day Java. I will concentrate on the newer forms, and will explore a set of categories for this new music that was suggested to me by an Indonesian student in Surakarta, Central Java. This set is not absolute; it is meant to be flexible and able to be revised. But I think it is a good place to start in understanding the great variety of forms of contemporary Indonesian musics. At least it is better than the system which proposes two general categories, traditional and modern. It is also more appropriate to Java than a system which divides music into the categories traditional and popular.

Indonesian commentators generally regard the last decade as the most lively and fruitful for Indonesian music in recent history. Several factors are responsible for this development, but the strongest factor is probably the development of cassette technology. Cassette playback capabilities arrived in Indonesia in the early 1970s, and provoked an immediate mushrooming of the Indonesian recording industry. The phonograph had been available since the 1920s, but it was not widespread. By the 1950s the Indonesian phonograph industry was producing recordings of many types of gamelan from Java and Bali, and a few types of music from the other Indonesian islands. This industry was almost entirely state controlled by the 1950s, and the state recording industry, Lokananta, continued to produce phono-records through the 1970s. But in the 1950s most phonographs needed electricity, and the Indonesian electricity industry was not yet fully developed. Records and players were costly, and were not durable in Indonesian climates. The medium of phono recordings was limited to the well-to-do and their servants, a very small number of urban Indonesians. Cassettes, on the other hand, have been relatively cheap in Indonesia from the beginning: $0.50 in 1970 for a fully-recorded, sixty-minute issue, and still only $1.75 in 1981 – a slight rise in real price over ten years. This is still too expensive for Indonesians in the lowest income group, who earn about this amount for one day's work, but it makes the recorded cassette, new or second-hand, available for purchase by more than half the Indonesian population. Cassette tape players are indeed costly for most Indonesian families, but probably almost all extended families have one or have access to one. The absence of the need for electricity means that cassette recorders have found their places in those towns and villages which are the most isolated in Indonesia from the cities where recordings are made and cassette-recorded musics are nurtured. Radio had been in many of these places long before: portable radios in large numbers had preceded cassette machines by about eight years. Until 1978 almost all radio stations were run by the Indonesian national government. State radio time was generally divided among gamelan, certain genres of western music, and certain newer genres of Indonesian music. The proportion and representation of western and new Indonesian genres depended somewhat on current government policy toward these genres. During the period from 1960 to 1975 this policy changed several times, first permitting, then restricting, then permitting again certain genres of western music and imitative Indonesian new music. By the mid-1970s, government stations had adopted a guarded *laissez-faire* policy on airtime for new musics. The proportion of gamelan had decreased from the 1960s, and each piece of western music was screened to determine if its content was 'offensive' or 'potentially disturbing' to audiences.

Meanwhile the cassette market had expanded to provide an alternative free-flow of musics. Several of the earliest Indonesian cassette releases were successful enough to prompt a dramatic growth in new cassette recording studios and reproducing factories. These early hits of course sold well in the largest cities of Java, but they also filtered into the towns and larger villages of the island. They were mostly Indonesian language songs with instrumental backgrounds consciously fashioned after the musics of the west which had been popular in the 1960s and 1970s. They came to be known by the general name *pop* in Indonesia. When the success of these *pop* releases and accessibility of the cassette medium were seen by other circles of musicians and music marketers, these circles quickly entered into cassette production. By the mid-1970s, marketplaces were filled with a wide variety of types of music which had existed unrecorded or only on phonograph records until that time. Lokananta had begun to phase out its phonograph recording division, in the face of stiff competition for sales of recorded music by the many private companies that had emerged. Many of the first cassettes in the early 1970s were pirated editions of phono-recordings already in existence. The practice of pirating continued in the 1970s and 1980s, predominantly in various genres of western music. Pirating of Indonesian cassettes has declined. Owing to the low cost of Indonesian issues, there is less profit in pirating these.

By 1981, it is estimated, at least eight million newly-recorded cassettes were issued per month in Indonesia. There was an average of twelve new titles of new and older Indonesian musics, with first pressings of between 60,000 and 500,000. Only in the area of older Indonesian music are any efforts made to keep early recordings in stock. Lokananta is the major manufacturer of these recordings. It is estimated that 25 per cent of the new cassette releases are of the older musics of Indonesian regions: gamelan and the like.

Perhaps 96 millon cassettes per year is a small number for a country of 155 million, but the importance of the cassette to musical life in Indonesia goes far beyond these numbers. Very quickly in the 1970s after cassette technology was introduced, almost all performers of Indonesian music who had been recording on phonograph records were supplanted by a new group of musicians who recorded on cassette. There were factors in this change other than the access to technology. The growth of television went hand-in-hand with cassettes. Some Indonesian critics of recordings and television suggest that phonograph recording artists were not able to master the ability to mouth the lyrics of songs on television. But the accessibility and cheapness of recording technology for cassettes also permitted a young generation of performers to emerge. The kids who were singing and playing Indonesian blues, rock, jazz or country in their homes or small halls for friends were able to make rough masters of their groups and sell them to eager cassette producers. An easing of restrictions by the government during the past fifteen years, and gradual changes in economics and social attitudes in Indonesian urban centres has led to the development of a wide variety of new genres of Indonesian music. While these genres were mostly localised or limited in appeal, and even as late as the beginning of the 1970s, public performances were few, by the end of that decade performances of new music groups accompanying dance or in concert were quite frequent in urban centres. Many were attended by thousands.

Pop is one of the three basic categories of new music in Indonesia today. The other two are *kroncong* and *dangdut*. Table 2.1 lists these categories, their alternate names, and sub-genres in each category. Types of early *kroncong* have been discussed in several scholarly articles written in the past twenty years (Becker; Kusbini; Heins; Kornhauser). The historical roots of *kroncong* extend to the

Table 2.1: Three categories of new music in Indonesia

---

1 Kroncong:
   a. Sub-genres and alternate names: stambul, kroncong asli, langgam kroncong, kroncong beat, kroncong pop
   b. Regional variants: langgam jawi, kroncong madura, campur sari

2 Dangdut:
   a. Sub-genres and alternate names: orkes melayu, dangdut rock, dangdut pop, irama melayu, dangdut biasa
   b. Regional variants: dangdut sunda, dangdut jawa

3 Pop:
   a. Sub-genres and alternate names: pop ringin, pop tengah, pop berat, pop umum, pop rock, pop contemporer, pop country, nostalgia, pop anak-anak
   b. Regional variants: pop daerah (regional pop); pop jawa, pop sunda, pop minang

---

seventeenth-century songs and string ensembles of communities of Portuguese sailors, traders and their servants, on the north-west coast of Java. *Kroncong* developed a wider popularity as it became, in the twentieth century, a street and restaurant music that appealed to Europeans, Indo-Europeans, and a small number of city-dwelling Indonesians. It was the first of the three types of new music to grow into a pan-Indonesian phenomenon, when it was carried to urban centres throughout Indonesia, broadcast on radio and recorded on phonograph in the middle decades of the twentieth century. Still, the appeal of the music was limited to a small group of Indonesianised urban dwellers of Java and some other islands.

Kroncong benefited from a Japanese ban (during their occupation) on the other mass-mediated new music, particularly western and westernised-Indonesian music. After the war, *kroncong* emerged with a much larger constituency than before, for it had gained by its perception as a music for all the ethno-linguistic groups in Indonesia – an Indonesian national music – but it never really achieved broad acceptance by the majority in any of the dozen major ethnic groups in the island nation.

Little is known about the style of *kroncong* pieces before the beginning of the twentieth century. By the middle of this century, almost all *kroncong* were songs, or instrumental arrangments of songs, in seven-tone pitch and interval tunings, usually very close to equal-tempered western major and minor. These songs were in the Indonesian language, with instrumental parts consisting of florid, free-metre introductions on flute, violin or guitar, followed by full ensemble accompaniment of a solo vocalist. The accompaniment was in a texture that can be described as punctuated counterpoint, which had many affinities to the textures of several of the gamelan traditions of Java and Bali, but also reflected many characteristics of western, 'Latin' string music and song. Early accompaniment probably consisted of one or two guitars, but by the mid-1930s, a basic ensemble consisted of guitar, violin, banjo, ukulele, 'cello and bass viol. These instruments were often supplemented, or individual instruments replaced, by transverse flute, viola and celesta. The harmonic progressions of each of these early songs followed one of several stock forms. In the *kroncong asli* sub-genre, the harmonic centres move in four-bar units, mostly through some arrangement of I, II, IV, and V chords, or their minor equivalents. The songs are in simple quadruple metre.

It is not known what were the languages of the texts of the earliest *kroncong* songs. By the twentieth century, probably all songs associated with *kroncong* ensembles were in Indonesian, but by the middle of this century, several regional types had arisen, each using the ethnic language of its region. The influences of regional traditions went further than language alone. A portion of the *kroncong* repertory known as *langgam jawi* consists of songs with *kroncong* ingredients mixed with ingredients derived directly from Javanese gamelan and *tembang*, notably the introductory *tembang* for Javanese gamelan pieces and the adoption of pentatonic slendro and pelog pitch and interval tunings. The latter masks but does not eliminate western harmonic progressions.

The words of early *kroncong* songs told of love lost and love found, yearning for someone far away, the felicitous effects of *kroncong* songs and rhythms on sad and lonesome hearts, the beauty of the countryside, the sweetness and smoothness of the melodies and rhythms of the songs. Occasionally, songs were composed with topical, social importance, but these are not characteristic of the genre. The text that I have translated comes from a song in the *kroncong asli* (original *kroncong*) style. This sub-genre is said to be the closest in form and content to the earliest Portuguese-related songs. Other sub-genres exist for groups of songs that have different stanza or melodic structures, different instrumentation, or slight variations of the *kroncong* rhythmic structure. Regional varieties use languages other than Indonesian, as in the Javanese *langgam jawi*, or instrumentation which commits the ensemble to one particular Indonesian geographic region, as in songs which use Javanese gamelan instruments together with the regular *kroncong* ensemble. This last is known as *campur sari*, which means 'mix of flowers'. Only a small number, perhaps under 5 per cent, of new cassette releases, are *kroncong*.

Translation 1

> *Kroncong asli*: 'Moritsko' (*Keroncong Asli, Kenangan Lama*: Lokananta AC1–021, 1975?)

> When you hear this, it is hoped you will be happy. Ah, pluck the guitar while singing, so that the listener will be happy. Eee . . . kronkong moritsko is kroncong from long ago. Whoever hears it will experience heart-throbbing.

The roots of *dangdut* can be traced to several of the stylistic attributes of *kroncong*, as well as to Malay-Arabic singing accompanied by *orkes melayu* ensembles or by frame drums and flutes, found in northern Sumatra and the west coast of the Malay peninsula as early as the eighteenth century. Early forms of this music were relatively isolated in the back streets of Jakarta and the towns in the areas of its origin. By the middle of the twentieth century, some of the *orkes melayu* ensembles were performing music that was a mix of ingredients from Indian film music and Arabic secular dance music, with a dash of western light pop. Texts were usually in Indonesian, but occasionally in Arabic.

In the early-1960s, perhaps aided by the suppression of certain forms of Indonesian *pop* and western rock, *dangdut* began to develop a strong following, which grew in the 1970s, aided by the establishment and success of the Indonesian cassette industry. Very early in its period of acceptance, *dangdut* came to be associated with a rather restrained type of social dance, a slow rhythmic undulation in time with the dominant stress pattern in the metre of *dangdut* songs. The most prominent aspect of this pattern, a low-pitched drum stroke on the fourth pulse, followed by a high-pitched stroke on the first pulse of each four-pulse measure, became the ono-matopoeic name for the entire genre. Probably the most important aid to the growth of *dangdut* popularity was its function as a dance music. By the end of the 1960s, mass public dancing at festivals and fairs was becoming possible. *Dangdut* was an accessible, pleasing type of musical accompaniment.

In the beginning of its popularity, almost all of the words of *dangdut* songs pertained to love affairs. Early instrumental ensembles consisted of Indian flutes and *tabla* (the *dangdut* drum), acoustic guitar, mandolin, tambourine. Electric guitars, pianos, electric organs, and a western trap drum set soon complemented or replaced instruments in the early ensemble. Since 1975, radically new directions, new themes in words and additions to the ensemble have developed. The strongest impetus for both kinds of innovation came from one of the two most popular *dangdut* musicians, Rhoma Irama. He introduced a set of rock and roll drums and a slight rock and roll edge to the *dangdut* rhythm of many of his songs. He added a synthesiser to his ensemble, and loosened the form of songs to accommodate changes in texture away from the usual *dangdut* fare. But perhaps the most dramatic change perpetrated by Rhoma Irama is in the themes of his *dangdut* lyrics. He initiated light social criticism and commentary in the texts of his songs. This was mixed with large doses of moral teachings that drew from Islamic doctrine.

Rhoma Irama's social criticism is subtle, when measured in relation to the most political of 1960s American protest rock, but is sufficiently clear to have provoked official disapproval of several of his songs of the mid-1970s. (See Frederick for more on Rhoma Irama, and the history of *dangdut*.)

The *dangdut* text that I have translated is from a more recent Rhoma Irama cassette release. It is both a mild commiseration with the working poor of Indonesia, who are forced to stay up and work all night to make enough money for substance needs, and an admonishment to young people not to waste their time and ruin their health.

Translation 2

> *Dangdut rock*: 'Begadang' (*Rhoma Irama, Begadang*: Yukawi, 1978
>
> Don't stay up all night if there is no reason for it; but of course you can stay up all night if there's a need to do so. If you stay up too much, your face will become pale from a weakening of circulation; if you often experience the night air, all sicknesses will come easily to you. Care for your body: don't stay up every night.

By the end of the 1970s, about 50 per cent of new cassette tapes were *dangdut* releases. There were indications that in the early 1980s the percentage was falling (see *Tempo*, 20 March 1982, p. 26). Yet the broad appeal of *dangdut*, reaching all social levels and ethnolinguistic groups of Indonesians, will be difficult to match. Regional variants in *dangdut* style are, as in *kroncong*, characterised by texts in regional dialects. A recent development in Javanese *dangdut* is the performance of *dangdut*-like rhythms on the Javanese gamelan drum set, accompanying otherwise ordinary Javanese gamelan pieces. This practice, known as *klenengan dangdut*, is not widespread, and can be seen as an attempt by a few gamelan performers and merchandisers to capitalise on the popularity of *dangdut*.

The last 20 per cent of the Indonesian cassette market consists of music that falls into the basic category of *pop*. Though a smaller percentage of the cassette market than *dangdut*, *pop* has many more stylistic subdivisions in indigenous cataloguing systems. Yet a common thread ties together all the varieties of *pop*: almost all *pop* songs sound recognisably western in ways that almost all *kroncong* and *dangdut* songs do not. Some recent *pop berat* (heavy pop) and *pop country* records have included regional instruments, such as Balinese and Javanese gamelan and *angklung, suling,* and *tongtong,* but although several of these fusions were well-received, even popular, such experiments are occasional, and have not had a noticeable effect on the bulk of *pop* music. This remains, in all its various forms, committed to mixing and developing all aspects of western popular music – forms, instruments, tunings, harmonic changes, dynamics, timbres, and aspects of word-content such as syllable count of line and number of lines in a stanza. In some case, even the themes of lyrics are directly connected to the themes of songs from western popular music, though it is clearly in lyrical texts that genres of Indonesian *pop* are tailored to meet Indonesian (and sometimes regional rural) needs and interests. It would seem, then, that in most of the ingredients of musical content, Indonesian *pop* is derived from western music. Yet there are two grounds, other than lyrics and language, on which to debate this assertion. First, western musical instruments and repertories have been in Indonesia since almost 400 years before the rise of *pop*, as a consequence of the presence of Europeans. During colonial times, the quality of this music was usually low, but it was there, and it served as a musical resource for Indonesian musicians. Various forms of this western music were even performed by Indonesian musicians. By the middle of the twentieth century, there was a symphony orchestra in Jakarta staffed entirely by Indonesian musicians. Today, in several large cities of Indonesia, and various places around the world, Indonesian musicians are highly regarded performers of cocktail jazz and western light pop, Bing Crosby or Doris Day style. *Kroncong* was an early hybrid music that benefited from the earliest contacts with western music.

Second, western music has been in Indonesia in mixed and indigenised forms, for example, in the religious music of the Christianised peoples of Sulawesi and Ambon, for nearly as long. Secular forms of indigenous music, with synchronised western attributes, existed in these places, and elsewhere in Indonesia, as dance music. In Christianised cultures, this music served as an alternative to indigenous dance music, which was often branded as immoral by the missionaries.

The roots of *pop* can be traced to the hymnody and secular song of these Christianised peoples. Indeed, many of the first *pop* singers and instrumentalists were from these ethno-linguistic groups. Since the 1960s these early varieties of *pop* have continued, though they have become only several of many varieties. I will now briefly discuss several of the most important of these varieties, as they are catalogued into sub-genres by an Indonesian student and aficionado of Indonesian new music (Hatch, 1981). Most of the sub-genres of *pop* in this system are defined on the basis of judgements of their musical complexity: the rhythms, form, pitch contours, tunings. In the area of words, the judgement can be based on the language (Indonesian, regional dialect or mixed languages), the ease of comprehension, and the theme of the text.

Some *pop* performers play and sing songs entirely in one of the sub-genres. There are others whose repertoires and styles include songs from several sub-genres. These singers and groups, the generalists of *pop*, are as many as the performers in any one of the genres. They include the singers Titlek Puspa, Melky Goeslaw, Bob Tutupoli and Broery Pesulima, and the group Bimbo.

Pop ringin (light pop) is a category of songs with lyrics, melodies and rhythms relatively easy to comprehend, and so received by people from all educational levels of society. In the first half of the 1970s, when the social censorship of *pop* first eased, and when cassettes began to reach large numbers of Indonesians, young people from all educational classes liked this type of *pop*. It was, admittedly, the only type around. Yet its appeal was broad because the ingredients of its songs were uncomplicated – their pulse structures were clear and continuous, their metres simple, their melodies smooth, repetitive and clear, their timbres sweet and smooth; their words were everyday Indonesian, and their themes accessible. The prominent *pop ringin* group in the late 1960s and early 1970s, indeed, the only widely-known *pop* group of that time, was the Koeswoyo group, known in the 1970s as Koes Plus. This group styled many of their songs after pieces in the early repertory of the Beatles such as 'She Loves You' and 'I Want to Hold Your Hand'. Singers who later became well known *pop ringin* singers are A. Riyanto and Rinto Harahap. Many of the all-purpose singers of *pop* concentrate their repertory on *pop ringin* songs. As an example of the texts of *pop ringin* songs, I have translated a piece written and recorded by Koes Plus in 1979. In the mid-1970s, Koes Plus turned from *pop ringin* to produce a Javanisation of Indonesian *pop*. They performed and recorded songs which had Javanese texts, but in all other ways were similar to the *pop ringin* repertory of their past. This set off a rush by other groups and tape companies to produce *pop* music in several of the regional ethnic languages. As a class, these types of *pop* are known as *pop daerah* (regional pop).

Translation 3

'Melapas Kerinduan': (*Koes Plus '79*: Purnama RL–323, 1979)

Young lovers feel like they own the world. They're always together everywhere they go; they always pay attention to each other, setting free their longings. When they go out together, to enjoy themselves, they hold hands and sing of their love. True happiness, true happiness, falling in love. I think all are the same when they experience this. I even fell in love when I was still young.

It is impossible to find a single singer or group which performs songs entirely in the *pop tengah* (middle pop) category. The songs in this category are somewhat more difficult to understand and assimilate than *pop ringin* songs. Often the texts include difficult words, perhaps from a regional dialect of Indonesian, or proverbs in riddle-like formulations. The melodies are generally straight-forward and the rhythms and metres usually simple. Initially high school students were the primary listeners for this group of songs but, over the past eight years, most have switched to the music of Guruh Soekarno Putra or other practitioners of *pop berat*.

Pop berat (heavy pop) includes many varieties of Indonesian new music, because the formation of the category is based on an overall impression of the complexity of various ingredients, rather than a few characteristic ingredients. Thus the music of Guruh Soekarno Putra, which includes pieces mixing Balinese gamelan, rock band, synthesiser and piano, and the music of Harry Roesli, which includes rock operas and the closest that Indonesia comes to heavy metal, both fall into this category. It includes songs that have difficult or complex words; texts that contain social criticism or mix archaic language, regional ethnic dialects or obscure references with colloquial Indonesian; rhythms or metres that are complex, dis-jointed, interrupted or mixed; melodies with disjunct contours, mixed tunings, harsh timbres, mixed timbres or quotations from regional ethnic music. The primary constituency for this type of music is high school and university students; young people of the upper middle economic class. An early exponent, Harry Roesli began to be widely known in Java in 1975. Shortly thereafter, Guruh Soekarno Putra began his swift rise to the top of popularity in this category of *pop* and, for a time, in all of Indonesian *pop*. Guruh is the youngest son of the former leader of Indonesia, Ir. Soekarno. Raised in the presidential palace, Guruh spent much time with palace musicians, and played some Balinese music. In the mid-1970s he interrupted a course of study in a Dutch university to return to Indonesia. There he organised a rock band, and by the late 1970s his was the most popular of *pop* groups.

Indonesian music critics have called his 1977 release *Guruh Gypsi* – a cassette in which he mixes old and new Indonesian music – the most important work in Indonesian music of the 1970s (*Tempo*, 3 January 1981, p. 42). This work fused pentatonic gamelan with diatonic western instrumental music. The lyrics mixed Old Javanese, Balinese and Indonesian languages – prayers, *mantras* and social commentary. But the mix was fluid enough to be acceptable to a wide spectrum of the public. Subsequent works by Guruh moved further and further in the direction of 'establishment' *pop*, expensive musical dramas and pageants and songs extolling the glories of Indonesia in times past.

By the end of the 1970s, Harry Roesli and Guruh had stimulated an interest in *pop berat* music, and many other musicians had begun to play music of that type. Many of the members of the audience for Guruh's work had shifted their attention to the music of these newcomers, two of whom, Keenan Nasution and Chrisye, had performed with Guruh in his early cassettes and stage shows. Others, like Yockie S. and Fariz R. M. were influenced by the more conventional pop of Guruh, performing *pop berat* songs which can be called Indonesian jazz-rock. Throughout their careers, these *pop berat* musicians have worked intermittently together, in various combinations, as well as having issued single cassettes under their own names. The texts of their songs have moved in the direction of light social criticism: comments on poverty, corruption and luxury, the war in Timor, and the virtues of rural life. They have also produced songs that show concern for the decay of the environment in Indonesia. These have been trends in the songs of musicians in each category of *pop* and in the *dangdut rock* songs of Rhoma Irama and, to a certain extent, each musician feeds on the work of the others in the development of themes in his or her songs. Yet these developments in the themes of songs also reflect the influence of deep cultural attitudes toward the function of song in Javanese society, and the roles and responsibilities of leaders – albeit musical leaders – in Indonesian cultures. These points are even more clearly demonstrated in the repertory of musicians in the *pop country* category.

By the mid-1970s, *pop country* had emerged as a type of Indonesian music with widespread popularity throughout Java, though at that time it was known mostly in stage shows. The earliest well-known performer of *pop country* was Leo Kristi, a singer, guitarist and song-writer from Surabaya who, by 1976, had a large following in urban centres throughout Java. By 1978 several other major performers had emerged in this category, including Franky and Jane, Ully Sigar Rusadi, Moogi Darusman and Ebiet G. Ade. Ebiet's music, mostly songs written and sung by him, accompanying himself on the guitar, achieved the most widespread following, displacing Guruh's music as the most popular of *pop* (*Tempo*, 8 March 1980, pp. 42–5).

Many styles characterise the category *pop country*, but most *country* musicians have as part of their repertories some songs which draw heavily in styles of performance – instrumentation, vocal and instrumental timbres, harmonic changes or rhythms – from 1960s American commercial folk and folk-rock, and various types of 1960s and 1970s American country and western music. From these areas of American music, the most influential musicians seem to have been Joan Baez, Bob Dylan and John Denver. Yet Indonesian *pop country* musicians also perform music which has close stylistic connections to one or more kinds of western rock, and often pieces which have strong country or folk ingredients also reflect the influences of rock and easy listening music from the west. Influential rock groups include the Rolling Stones and the Beatles. Single cassette releases by *country* musicians will usually mix styles in back-to-back selections.

Probably the most striking characteristic of Indonesian *pop country* is the theme of the lyrics. It is here that one might find a clearer definition of the category than in stylistic characteristics of the music. Most *country* musicians perform songs about national and regional social issues. The work of some of these musicians, notably Ebiet, deals with private or individual issues such as love or family life as well but, compared to other forms of *pop*, and to *kroncong* and *dangdut*, *country* songs more often discuss issues important to regional and national society. These issues are discussed without a slant toward a particular ethnic attitude, except where an ethnic tradition presents a theme that might fulfil a national social need. This can be regarded, in itself, as a particular cultural attitude, perhaps best described as a modern, rationalised or westernised ethic, but it is not identified as a part of a particular ethnic tradition.

Translation 4, is from *Berita Cuaca* (Weather Report), a 1981 cassette release by Gombloh, a *country* musician from Surabaya who had become well-known throughout Java by the beginning of the 1980s. With his group, Lemon Trees Anno '69, he has released eight cassettes, of which *Berita Cuaca* is the sixth. The jacket of this cassette shows a photo of Gombloh, superimposed on a colour painting of a desolate landscape, trees denuded by fire or drought, land parched and sky ominous. On the branch of one tree is draped the deformed face of a clock (probably inspired by Dali's 'The Persistence of Memory'), and behind the tree is a flagpole from which flies, undaunted, the Indonesian national flag. The imagery is mixed, but the idea that stands out is that a unified Indonesian people can/will overcome the problems in Indonesian society. This theme is projected in the lyrics of the title song for the cassette, the first song on side A. The musical components are styled after the Rolling Stones' 'You Can't Always Get What You Want': a children's chorus opens and closes the song, and there are similarities in the harmonic changes of the song and in the instrumentation of the accompanying ensemble. But the similarities end there. Gombloh's use of the chorus is meant to evoke images of wisdom and innocence, and the entire song projects hope and positive, constructive energy. The words are Indonesian, salted with colloquial and poetic or old Javanese words. One of the latter references, 'peaceful-prosperous' (*tentrem kerta-raharja*), ties the song into the regional Javanese dramatic form *wayang*, a repertory of all-night shadow-puppet dramas, accompanied by gamelan, usually performed at community gatherings of religious significance. The 'country of long ago' could be one of the mythical kingships of the *wayang* plays, as well as one of the historical kingships of

Indonesia's past. The desolation of the land today is contrasted with the richness of times past, and a prayer is offered for a return to prosperity and fruitfulness of the land.

Translation 4

Pop country: 'Berita Cuaca' (*Berita Cuaca*: Chandra, 1981)
1 Everlasting, my surroundings, everlasting, my village, where my god deposited me; children sing at the time of the full moon, singing a prayer for the land.
2 Peaceful my brothers, prosperous my land; I remember my mother telling a story, a tale about the glorious archipelago of old; peaceful, prosperous, then.
3 Why is my land anxious these days; the hills stand naked; trees and grass do not want to sprout again; birds are afraid to sing.
4 I want my hills to be green again; the trees and grass wait impatiently; I pray this prayer every day; and now, when will this heart be relieved.
5 Same as 1.
6 Same as 1, first line; We will sing in the full moon then, singing a verse to our state.
7 Be peaceful my brothers, be prosperous my state; I remember my mother telling a story, a tale about the victory of the country long ago; it was peaceful, prosperous, then.
8 Same as 6.
9 Same as 7.
10 Same as 6, fade out . . .

The song which follows 'Berita Cuaca' is another prayer, this one entirely in Javanese, and linked to two stanzas from a nineteenth-century Javanese poem, *Wedhatama*. This poem was written in the palace of a Javanese prince, Mangkunegara IV, of Surakarta. It contains teachings on leadership and the spiritual, mystical discipline of *ngelmu batin*. By the middle of the twentieth century this poem had become well known to educated Javanese. The sung forms of several stanzas are among the few examples of *tembang* that remain popular today. (For more on *tembang* and the early forms of the *Wedhatama*, see Hatch 1980.) Gombloh places the first and the twelfth stanzas of the first canto of the poem in juxtaposition with a

Javanese *mantra* (ritual prayer) of Buddhist heritage. This mantra, 'hong wilaheng sekareng bawono langgeng', is important in *wayang* stories, as well as in Javanese poetry, where it serves to introduce religious texts. The text of Gombloh's song, named after the mantra, is Translation 5. Gombloh sets the two texts with separate musical accompaniments, but both are closely connected to types of American hard rock. The texts are set with close attention to congruence of text meanings and melodic flow. Rhythms follow syllable stress patterns and line count follows rules of poetic form. But most of these Javanese words are not part of colloquial Javanese. They are part of an archaic poetic language. Their use is meant to convey an image of the power of the past, to create an aural connection to older religious values and perhaps to place those values and their ethnic identity into a modern setting, a multi-ethnic Indonesian popular identity.

Translation 5

Pop country: 'Hong Wilaheng Sekareng Bawono Langgeng'

1   Turning away from desire, because of the pleasure of educating children; conveyed in the beauty of song, embellished and well-formed; oh god, the practice of esoteric knowledge which belongs to the everyday world is the religion which is the possession of the wise.
2   Whoever gains the blessing of god soon becomes enlightened, able to exercise esoteric knowledge, the ability to obtain knowledge about dissolving, the dissolution of being; one like that can be called old; old in the sense of passions quieted, aware of the two in one.
3   The sounding of the song of the eternal world; song of the jambe flower; song of the grasses.
4   Same as 2.
5   Fade out on 'hong wilaheng' (the sounding . . .).

These two songs – Translations 4 and 5 – are only a small slice of the repertoire of Gombloh both in relation to the number of his songs and to their range of styles and themes. And Gombloh is only one of at least a dozen well-known *pop country* musicians in Indonesia today. Their songs, and those of other performers of *pop, kroncong* and *dangdut*, represent the major part of the present-day rich musical life of that country.

References

Becker, J. (1975), 'Kronkong, Indonesian popular music', *Asian Music*, VII, 1, pp. 1–19.

Frederick, W. (1982), 'Rhoma Irama and the Dangdut style: aspects of contemporary Indonesian popular culture', *Indonesia* XXXIV, October, pp. 103–30.

Hatch, M. (1980), 'Lagu, Laras, Layang: rethinking melody in Javanese music', Ph.D. dissertation, Cornell University.

—— (1981), Unpublished notes from conversations with the Suripto family (Surakarta, Indonesia).

Heins, E. (1975), 'Kroncong and Tanjidor: two cases of urban folk music in Jakarta', *Asian Music*, VII, 1, pp. 20–32.

Kornhauser, B. (1978), 'In defense of Kronkong', *Studies in Indonesian Music*, Monash University, Clayton, Australia.

Kusbini, (1972), 'Kroncong Indonesia', *Musica* (Jakarta) I, pp. 19–42.

Tempo (weekly newsmagazine, Jakarta), 1975–83.

Recordings

Berita Cuaca, Candra, 1981.
Guruh-Gypsi, Musica, 1977.
Keroncong Asli, Kenangan Lama, Lokananta ACI-021, 1975.
Koes Plus '79, Purnama RL-323, 1979.
Rhoma Irama, Begadang, Yukawi, 1978.

Part 2

Tradition and acculturation

Editor's note

Acculturation is a term used by anthropologists to describe one aspect of social change, and ethnomusicologists have long used their descriptive skills to show how one system of musical rules and values adapts (accultures itself) to another. The importance of this approach, as the papers in this section show, is its focus on music's role in expressing and shaping people's cultural *identities*. The question becomes, under what circumstances do people feel empowered (rather than limted) by musical conventions? What happens to collective musical identities when they are institutionalised by commercial or state agencies and policies?

Alenka Barber-Kersovan approaches these questions from the perspective of cultural studies. She reads cultural forms for their social significance, interprets popular music by uncovering the meanings carried (more or less symbolically) by its aural elements. Methodologically, this means describing pop forms by reference to how they feel to their audience – and Barber-Kersovan deftly deploys autobiography to this end. Theoretically, the cultural studies argument is that the explicit aims and intentions of music-makers are less significant than the meanings read into their sounds by their consumers (although, as Barber-Kersovan suggests, one important way Slovenian young people consumed post-Beatles pop was by creating it: local musicians' attempts to copy what they heard as the essence of rock and roll resulted, for technological as well as cultural reasons, in music expressive, rather, of their own situation).

The appeal of particular (international) sounds to particular (local) audiences can be explained in terms of *homology*: music represents the experience and (imaginary) identity of certain social groups not because it is necessarily created by them but because its aural qualities are heard as 'homologous' to their values. This is the link between musical object and musical subject, between text and pleasure. In claiming some pop genres for themselves this way, using them to mark the boundaries of group solidarity, Slovenian youth subcultures had to label sounds, to describe and define their differences from other music publics. And one feature of popular musical change is the struggle over labels. Barber-Kersovan shows how in the Slovenian context the ideological meaning of 'rock' shifted from youth cultural radicalism to mainstream entertainment: a shift which has to be explained by reference to what was happening to Yugoslavia rather than to what was happening to rock. In exploring this theme, Barber-Kersovan doesn't abandon the concept of acculturation, but she does show how messy it is.

Judith Cohen comes to a similar conclusion from a different starting point. Her interest is in what happens to a people's music when they migrate. Her case study is the small community of Sephardic Jews in Montreal, but it is worth remembering that migration – the compulsory diaspora of Africans – has had a much greater impact on popular music history than even the cultural imperialism of the Anglo-American entertainment industry. Cohen's own interest is in music's role in shaping people's collective identity (Barber-Kersovan puts more emphasis on individual values), and she writes out of the tradition of folk studies, as someone engaged in collecting songs (and the information surrounding them), and tracing their history and influence. But even from this traditionalist perspective it is apparent that in using music to provide a continuing sense of their identity, Canada's Sephardic Jews have not chosen to freeze one (random) musical moment of their history to represent themselves (although, ironically, modern recording technology makes possible and encourages precisely such a preservation of sound). Rather, their tradition is understood as a matter of continuous invention: to be a continuing source of value, Cohen argues, music has to adapt to changing circumstance.

Tradition and acculturation as polarities of Slovenian popular music

A village festival in Vanca vas

The roof of the new fire station outside the village had just been completed and the newly tarred drive was to serve as the dance-floor. An improvised bar was squeezed alongside the unplastered wall. Tables and benches were placed in the field in front of the building. The wooden stage, which had been thrown together in a hurry, was about to collapse under the heavy machinery of the rock band, while hundreds of watts roared out of the loudspeakers. It was not yet two o'clock in the afternoon and the festival seemed to be in full swing. The first guests had drowned the unbelievable heat in cold beer and were chatting away cheerfully. Some couples were already trying their skills on the dance floor. At the entrance two youngsters were dealing with entrance tickets: 100 dinars for male adults, 80 dinars for female adults, 50 dinars for youngsters between fourteen and eighteen. For girls and kids entrance was free. The children came alone or accompanied by grown-ups, for what could possibly happen to them at a village festival in Vanca vas? They took over the dance floor, were constantly under the feet of the grown-ups and enjoyed themselves chasing around and imitating the adults.

The rock band, three guitars, drums and keyboards, were lads between eighteen and twenty-five, wearing jeans, T-shirts and long hair, looking exactly as a rock band is supposed to look. The guests, on the other hand, were mostly in their Sunday bests. They were elderly men in black suits with black ties, elderly women, wearing wide nondescript skirts and dark tops, with their hair hidden under scarfs, pulled down hard over their foreheads. Younger guests were more modern, even fashionably dressed. The women were showing their décolletés in light summer dresses and sported colourful make-up to stress the festive nature of the occasion.

So, this festival was meant for everybody in Vanca vas: for young and old, for the farmers from the village and the surrounding neighbourhood, for those who worked in the town nearby, for the gypsies from the gypsy settlement as well as for the schoolchildren and the students who were spending their summer holidays at home. In order to make everyone happy and get them all going, the band started off with a few fast waltzes and polkas, followed by a cocktail of popular songs, rock numbers, folk dances and pieces written in a folky style, compositions by members of the band and even the Strauss dynasty did not come off too badly.

There were a number of good reasons for this festival. The weather had been very good that summer and the crops had been harvested in time, even before the festival of the village patron saint. Also the brick-work on the fire station had been finished. The festival sponsors were the voluntary firemen who obtained permission from the local authorities. The village socialist youth organisation was responsible for setting up the tables and benches, hiring the musicians and helping the inn-keeper to take care of the guests' bodily welfare. Everybody was in great spirits and despite the fact that it was too loud, the music was accepted comparatively well. 'There isn't any other', said the old village Don Juan and carried on dancing his waltzes and polkas to the pulse of the electrical beat.

'The music you make yourself'

The village festival in Vanca vas should serve as an example of the rich and heterogeneous informal musical life in Slovenia, which ranges from village dances to chanson and punk concerts, sophisticated jazz sessions and evenings with esoteric acoustic music. All these events are based on what can be best referred to as 'music you make yourself'. This phrase is not a technical term nor does it define any specific musical form, content or style. It is simply how musicians themselves refer to their music in order to stress its high personal value and to express their freedom in the reshaping of existing musical material as well as the growing tendency to find their own musical utterances through production of new musical numbers. Thus 'music you make yourself' clearly implies a creative aspect, which is closely tied to its second significant feature, the amateur character of music-making. This does not mean that there is no money involved in this music. It should not be understood in the sense of low quality either, for some performances in fact do reach a professional level and much of this music appears in one form or other in the media as well. 'Music you make yourself' is amateur not only because the limited possibilities of public performance in Slovenia prevent musicians from taking it up as a job, but predominantly because of its explicit value as a hobby. It is something you can pick up or drop whenever you want to. Eventual economic profit is of course welcome, but money itself does not serve as the primary source of motivation. 'Music you make yourself' is derived from more subtle psychological mechanisms, which have been activated by the requirements of an industrial and mass media dominated society as a creative response to its positive as well as negative effects.

Tradition and acculturation

According to the general rule that no-one can create in a vacuum, all creative objects must result from the reshaping of existing ones or their elements. This applies also to the 'music you make yourself'. It is based on musical patterns from two main sources, the transformation of the indigenous musical idiom on the one hand and the reshaping of musical forms originating from non-Slovenian backgrounds on the other. Thus 'self-made' music can be theoretically dichotomised into forms derived from Slovenian *tradition* and those which were submitted to the process of *acculturation*.

When speaking about *traditional music*, it should be understood that we do not mean genuine folk song, but those musical forms which are referred to by Slovenian media as 'domestic popular music', 'newly composed Slovenian folk music' or 'popular folk music'. All these terms indicate an attempt to stress the distance from genuine folk music as well as connections to it. Despite the fact that transitions between both are fluid and influences reciprocal, they differ in form, content, manner of presentation and transmission as well as in the role they play in the life of an individual or a community.

We understand *acculturated musical forms* as referring mainly to Anglo-Saxon music such as beat, rock or punk, although popular music of other European countries, especially Italy and Germany, has also occasionally been a subject of acculturation. These musical forms have spread to Slovenia during the last three decades and have been predominantly transmitted via the mass media. The process of acceptance on the part of the consumers went through several stages, but not until recently did these musics attain the degree of familiarity which enabled them to serve as models for reshaping.

Historical survey of traditional musical forms

The emergence of musical forms which are closely related to tradition is habitually placed in the year 1953 and associated with the Brothers Avsenik.

The ensemble of the Brothers Avsenik, which served as an ideal to almost all its followers, originated from close contact with the lively tradition of the folk musicians from the region of Begunje. Being natives of Begunje themselves, the brothers Avsenik had been associated since their youth with Kleman, musician from Polovce. This listened to his tunes and observed his manner of playing. So, as is usually the case with transmission in folk music, the traditions were carried over from the older to the younger generation. If the pupils were more skilled than their teachers, they themselves created music on the basis of what they received. Something similar seems to happen with the Brothers Avsenik and that might be the secret of their enormous success. There is some hidden element in the tunes they play which makes one remember the tunes of the folk musicians. It is no wonder that the process was repeated. The Avseniks' tunes were imitated by musicians in the country – consciously by some and unconsciously by others and so they were returned to where they come from – to the folk music tradition.[1]

The brothers' first radio recording in 1953 launched a highly successful international career, which by 1978 had resulted in around 6,000 concerts, 500 different records, and sales of over 23,000,000.[2] Indeed, the group's output was rather greater than the annual production of the Yugoslav record industry (most of their records were produced by German manufacturers). They were awarded one diamond and one platinum record, two gold cassettes and twenty-one gold records as well as a gold plaquette for creativity in the field of popular music by the Yugoslav composers' association.[3] Outside the country numerous Avsenik fan clubs were formed in order to cultivate their image and to organise trips to Slovenia.

What was the secret of their international breakthrough? The ensemble is supposed to have created music which was new in terms of temperament, language and costume presentation, and in 1975 the West German *Phonoakademie* awarded them the European Oscar for originality, spontaneity and authenticity. Behind the light-hearted and carefree music-making of the happy waltzes and polkas there is, in fact, a high degree of musical know-how since all members of the ensemble except one (Slavko Avsenik) are graduates from an academy of music, and what is important, then, is that the group is taken to be best represented by Slavko Avsenik, that is, by the only non-professional musician. His success is constantly referred to by other Slovenian musicians, not in the sense that he also had to 'fight his way up from the bottom', 'this is the sort of success even we could attain', but in a different identification mechanism, based on Slavko's personal qualities: 'Slavko is such a simple man, he does not really care about his success', 'he is so homely', 'he is just one of us', 'Slavko Avsenik is so Slovenian'.[4]

This understanding of the ensemble as homely and Slovenian is reinforced by the fact that Slovenians are a very small nation numbering not more than 1,800,000 souls and Avsenik's music is seen as a means of preserving national identity. The Slavko Avsenik ensemble holds a firm place in the pattern of values which can be called 'Slovenian' and at the same time endorses the well-known foreign stereotype in the formula: 'Yugoslavia is Tito, Avsenik und Slivovicz'.

Though the Avsenik ensemble did play an important role in the formation of musical forms closely related to tradition, it cannot be considered as the decisive factor in this. A more important aspect seems to be the emergence of a psychological readiness on the part of a broad spectrum of the population to accept this music and to develop it further. In this respect the radical social and political changes in the first post-war period should be mentioned, since they accelerated the process of industrialisation and a great wave of migration from the countryside into the towns. Having been wrenched from their original surroundings, the newly-installed citizens found themselves in a struggle between rural and urban norms; the old life-style had partially to give way to new cultural patterns:

This also means that a great deal of that background, which could be described as manners and customs and which constitutes the spiritual origin of folk music, was lost. But despite this loss, some of the traditional forms seemed to be more tenacious than the life patterns of specific social groups they were based on. This tendency to preserve does not mean unchangeable continuity of fixed forms and content, but predominantly a typological constancy.[5]

The adoption or rejection of a new cultural model is always carried out in relation to existing value systems. Since media density in the fifties was pretty low, the only known musical utterance for a part of this new urban population was folk music. Being bound to local manners and customs it possessed a certain exclusiveness and remained largely incomprehensible for the non-initiated. On the other hand, the music of the Brothers Avsenik and similar ensembles had a kind of folk constancy in its veiled bondage to the soil (which was so stylised that it was no longer understood as 'peasant' in the negative sense) and the music was accepted not only in urban but also in rural environments. In the early fifties and at the beginning of the sixties this type of sound thus underwent an enormous development and new ensembles sprouted up like mushrooms after rain. Even during the second half of the sixties, when enthusiasm began to fade and the ensembles began to repeat themselves, the record industry continued to promote such folk song. If quantity of musical material is anything to go by, the following statistics are interesting: approxmately 8,000 titles of newly composed folk music have been taped during the last three decades, while the Ethnological Institute of Ljubljana is in possession of 30,000 tunes of 'real' folk music, as the complete cultural heritage of the nation.

Historical survey of acculturated musical forms

The musical forms based on traditional folk idiom are seen as an integral part of Slovenian culture in a broader sense and as such, apart from negative evaluation of some ethnologists and cultural purists, receive full moral and institutional support. The same cannot be said for their acculturated counterpart. In the last decade Slovenia has found itself confronted with a new form of musical behaviour just as if a virus had been invisibly active and was now bursting out as an epidemic. This phenomenon reached such proportions that by the late seventies the public realised that the headlines of the past, such as 'An appeal to pure reason: or on the concerts of electricians', or 'Our race is being barbarised to greater and greater extent', were not mere literary utterances from isolated pessimists, but serious attempts to point out the new socio-cultural behaviour of the younger generation. The rock phenomenon, previously an object of interest for youth psychologists and music teachers, suddenly became a big social and political problem and a favoured conference topic even for those who had not felt competent to deal with it before. It became clear that the problem was not simply a matter of music.

The development of acculturated musical forms in Slovenia can, in fact, be divided into three phases:

(a) The fifties: *The dream of the big strange world*
During the first post-war period, especially before the political break with Moscow in 1948, the attitude towards American cultural influence was not particulaly friendly. Jazz, for instance, was for a time in severe danger of being banned. This negative attitude softened gradually, although the reactions to the provocative slogan 'American' – which in fact covers everything coming from the western hemisphere – is still far from being free from prejudice. In spite of all this, memories of my childhood are flooded with all kinds of things 'American', and blue jeans and Coca Cola are as much a part of Slovenian everyday life as are the supermarkets, maxi-markets and the monstrous Holiday Inn spoiling one of the nicest streets in Ljubljana. Whether these and similar phenomena are labeled as 'Americanisms' and 'cultural imperialism' or not, does not really change the fact that this culture did have a certain influence on ours and that its influence was the profounder, the further back we turn the wheel of history.

The fifties were described by an ex pop fan as follows:

Before 1960, our range of musical experience was rather limited. It included the Italian *canzona*, the German *Schlager*, the Slovenian *popevka*, the American musical and jazz. Since we did not sympathise with America for a long time, American hits were seldom played on local radio, and even if they were, one hardly ever heard any rock and roll. However, listeners began to make more and more requests for American music which deviated from central European hits like 'O sole mio',' Marina', 'Oh, mein Papa' and soon conquered even our parents, who bought the first rock and roll records. The record companies, Yugotan and Discos, in fact issued some singles by P. Boone, E. Presley, P. Como, H. Belafonte, L. Armstrong and F. Domino. The reaction of our parents encouraged us to buy something similar, only with a faster rhythm. Anything one could not buy in

Yugoslavia was brought back by parents from their business trips abroad.
We and our parents were all mad about the same singers at that time, the
only difference being the speed of the music. We cannot speak of any pop
idolatry before the Beatles. Our enthusiasm did not reach beyond the
playing of records and listening to various radio programmes, very often
together with parents. That was all.[6]

Further elements which encouraged the acceptance of pop music
came from films which were of particular appeal to the younger
generation. Rock music, dances, typical problems of young people,
popularity, self-confidence and the easy-going attitude of Western
youth had their effects. Films with Conny Froebes and Peter Kraus,
for instance, were of the kind one dreamt about ten times a night. At
first, these were just dreams because the movie heroes were
unattainable and came from a strange, unreal world. The cultural
model was too far removed from the cultural matrix to be accepted.
The image of youth, whose task was defined by society as 'learning,
learning and more learning', was reinforced in the family by the
necessity to be good, honest, helpful and modest. The role of young
people was defined without any contradiction and, in fact, did not
differ from the role of the grown-ups. However, deviation from this
role, projected on the screen and transmitted through music, was a
tempting prospect. The desire for self-determination, felt by the
young generation, went hand in hand with the desire for nice
clothes, rock and roll shoes, make-up, chewing gum, hot dances and
adventures with a happy ending. This complexity of desires was
slowly developing into a readiness to translate the dreams some day
into reality. For years the pop virus had a silent and invisible
presence. Nobody realised what changes were taking place among
the younger generation, and the seed, once sown, was growing and
growing, leading to a fundamental change with which the whole of
society would be trying to cope some twenty years later.

(b) The sixties: *growing up with the Beatles*
Then the Beatles came; not suddenly and overnight so as to achieve
an absolute victory, but slowly seeping into the consciousness of the
youngsters. In the beginning the reaction was one of ignorance,
scepticism and even rejection. It was not just the music which
provoked the scepticism and it was not just the music which caused
the Beatles to be accepted. From the complex phenomenon 'The
Beatles' some small, sometimes even irrelevant elements resonated

with the existing value systems. The grown-ups at first observed the phenomenon with an indecisive helplessness, followed by a negative reaction. Supported by impatient attacks over the media, the first acts of repression were carried out. In the beginning they were concentrated against external characteristics as, for example, in the big struggle for long hair. What pop music could not achieve on its own was achieved by the negative reaction of the grown-ups: namely, an increasing attachment to the Beatles. What in the beginning had been a hand-to-hand skirmish was developing into a real battle with smaller or larger, institutionalised or non-institutionalised group formations, who initially acted in many different ways and were independent of one another. They were bound to the life and behaviour pattern of a specific youth group and adapted to the group norms.

The variety of the Beatlemania phenomenon, its absorption by already existing groups and their continuing independence of each other, was due to the lack of a national scene, in which behaviour patterns could have been adapted on a larger scale. Domestic radio stations opened their doors slowly to new influences. The first Beatles record was not issued in Yugoslavia until 1967 and by 1968 the Beatles had been shown only twice on television. In the first half of the sixties there were no mass pop performances and it was not until 1965 that the first foreign beat band had a concert in Slovenia. The first important domestic band did not emerge until 1967, the year of the establishment of the first discotheque. So, young people were forced to build up their behavioural patterns according to the possibilities available. One of the most popular forms of musical event then were the so-called 'house parties', at which some twenty to thirty youngsters gathered in private flats in order to dance and listen to records. And, paradoxical as it may seem, the schools were not only the most ardent opponents of long hair, but also the first public institutions to organise rock dances and concerts. Otherwise, the family radio and record player were the centre of interest.

Not all youngsters succumbed to the Beatles, girls in particular held back to some degree, but initial enthusiasm was followed by group compulsion, and soon one could not ignore the phenomenon, unless one wanted to be isolated. Passive adoration and endless discussions were followed by more active identifications. Not only the controversial length of the hair, the black pullovers and the roll-neck shirts, but also the general attitude and the music itself became subjects of imitation. Possession of a guitar doubled individual prestige, which multiplied further if one played in a band. It became very important to know members, even better to help a little bit around the stage. If none of this was possible, it helped a lot if you pretended; this was because members of a band enjoyed a special social status, demonstrated in public by even longer hair, even more colourful gear and so on. All this, of course, had consequences and the first domestic stars were born. Everyone knew the names, likes and dislikes of the members of the 'Kameleoni', for instance, in the same way as they knew about the Beatles.

Playing in a band was not easy. The difficulties started with the purchase of equipment. The Yugoslav music instrument industry was very slow to react to the new youth culture and it took years before it was able to meet the most modest demands. So acoustic guitars were converted into electric ones, microphones and amplifiers were homemade; instead of cymbals, cheese boxes were used and Dixan drums (Dixan was a washing powder). The imagination of young people was boundless in their desire to identify as closely as possible with their idols.

Although these first musical experiments were in one way a complete disappointment, since they were a long shot from what was offered on records at that time, they nevertheless aroused a lot of enthusiasm. In terms of technical equipment and musical realisation, Slovenian bands were far from matching the Beatles, but they were within reach. The members of a local band were human beings made of flesh and blood, guys from the next class, with whom one could identify without any difficulties, and in the second half of the sixties the Slovenian rock avalanche began to roll slowly and irresistibly. On all fronts things began to change. One could feel the sudden upheaval of the standard of living through which new ways of life were created. The media included more popular music in their programmes and the time lapse before an international hit was first broadcast by the local media was no longer a matter of years, but of months or even weeks. The record industry showed an increasing interest in issuing recordings by foreign stars as well as by native musicians. The music instrument industry slowly came to understand that they had better catch up with the market demands. Nevertheless, dressed in a complete Beatles outfit one was still exposed to numerous malicious remarks in the street and it was not uncommon for one to be followed by an anti-Beatles gang and even to be robbed of the precious splendour of one's hair. From this kind of incident and from repression at school, attacks by printed media and remarks from parents, the protest inherent in the Beatles package started to take shape. What initially might have been protest in a vacuum found its desired battlefield in these negative reactions. Questioning the establishment, and engaging in generational conflict, brought Slovenian youngsters closer to the student upheaval of other industrial nations. Pop music became an indication of social unrest and tension between young and old; this discord intensified and culminated in the occupation of the Philosophical Faculty in Ljubljana. The centre of the ferment was a student culture determined to develop new forms. In a colourful spectrum, ranging from experimental theatre to poetry and photography, music also played its part. The students supported everything 'new': popular music, jazz, *avant-garde* art music as well as non-European music. In 1969 all these efforts resulted in a public medium, the student radio station *Radio Student*. Set up and run by students, it was designed to serve all those who saw themselves as young, modern, unconventional and demanding. What had started as an insidious but private hobby now became a part of Slovenian culture in general.

(c) The seventies: *Saturday Night Fever*
The seventies are characterised by Tuksar[7] as an era of increased and diversified communication. British records were issued under license and there was a big increase in their consumption; groups such as the Rolling Stones made their first visits; pop music critics appeared as did the first scientific studies of musical mass culture. However, the most important characteristic of this decade was the emergence of a pop and rock climate dependent on the specific conditions in Yugoslav industrial society and reflected in the indigenous musical forms such as 'Yugorock', as well as by a pop audience with specific psychological and sociological properties. In 1973, the first spontaneous 'pop boom' festival was organised in the capital as if to prove that the acculturated musical forms of behaviour had taken on a mass character. By 1975 the 'Hop-pop' festivals had spread to smaller towns. During the same period continual efforts to organise local concerts were evident. In 1976 Radio Ljubljana organised the first rock selection in order to promote this kind of music. With the group Pankrti in 1977 everybody started to talk about punk.

There is just one full decade between the first Beatles and the first punk generation, but the differences between the phases are enormous. At the beginning of the sixties youngsters were prepared to walk a couple of kilometres to the home of a friend whose parents happened to possess a record player in order to hear their favourite hits. The most important feature of pop fandom then was the listener's active search for pop music, this consuming a large amount of time, money and energy. Today mass media are in every family home, and pop music belongs to everyday life. Though young people still listen to Radio Luxemburg and Österreich 3, more attention is paid to the local radio stations. Despite the fact that youngsters still read foreign newspapers, most information is now acquired from the domestic pop music press. The 'house party', which was at that time the venue for musical rituals, has now lost its popularity. Concerts, mass performances and discos have replaced small group experiences; individually structured forms of musical behaviour have been replaced by coordinated forms.

In the sixties, youngsters distinguished between *VIS* (vocal instrumental band) and *non-VIS*; only *VIS* really counted. Today there is a huge variety of groups, styles and manners of presentation. The spectrum ranges from singer-songwriters to all sorts of electrical and acoustic bands, from classic rock to punk. If in the sixties the highest maxim was to come as close as possible to one's idols, today it is most important to be as individualistic as possible. Moreover, not everything coming from abroad is necessarily evaluated as positive just because it is foreign; certain concerts by foreign groups have actually had to be cancelled because of a total lack of interest – not everything enjoying an international reputation is well received simply for that reason. The spell of the dream of the big strange world has been broken. Young people are no longer prepared to be dominated by foreign influence without a second thought or to imitate without reflection. The domestic scene has enough musicians able to stand up to comparison with foreigners, and their possible weaknesses can anyway be ignored thanks to the corrective mechanisms of the concepts 'domestic' and 'Slovenian'. For being understood as such assures a positive response on the part of the public and critics.

The first generation of pop fans took over foreign patterns of behaviour as a moral maxim. The Beatles were understood as the 'positive institution of that time', as the 'weavers of dreams of one generation', offering the *Leitmotiv* of youth: Beatlemania was a game with a pattern on to which the most positive wishes of the youngsters were projected. Thus, if the image of their ideal became uncertain, reality was corrected and the Beatles were assimilated into the moral model of the youngsters themselves. Even today, when they are in their thirties, the representatives of the first Beatles generation are sure that the Beatles had a positive influence in forming their personalities. When they describe themselves as sensitive, strong-willed and critical, but by no means destructive or individualistic, they relate these properties to their experiences with John Lennon *et al.*

The evaluation of pop music today gives us a completely different picture. Since it is continually present in the media, pop has lost its exclusive character. It is not the *Leitmotiv* of a generation any more, but simply 'pop music', suitable for any situation and a medicine for every single disease. Pop music no longer has only one central value; it is multifunctional. It can be background music, a possibility for enjoyment, a fashionable attitude, a means to self-realisation, identification and communication as well as a way to express discomfort when everyday life puts too much pressure on. The moral maxim the Beatles represented was summed up by the first Beatles generation in the phrase 'It might be our way'. Now this slogan is replaced by 'Saturday Night Fever'. Not only has the music changed, the attitudes of young people have also changed. Youngsters are not dreamy romantics any more, but hard realists. They do not try to escape to Fairyland but to evaluate soberly and objectively the boundaries of freedom. If they retire from society, this retirement is temporary, a purification session, after which they return to reality, strengthened and ready to cope with tomorrow.

Tradition and acculturation as polarities and fluid transitions of Slovenian popular music

The theoretical division of the various forms of 'music you make yourself' according to cultural models certainly has some advantages. It enables us to sketch historical surveys of traditional and acculturated musical forms, taking into consideration the changes of both individuals and society. Besides serving as a point of departure for text analysis, it proves useful for the construction of characteristic psycho-social personality patterns of musicians; it also offers a comparison between the creative object and the creative subject. Though musical offerings are rich and various, individuals mainly consider just one kind of music to be valuable enough for imitation and recreation. The choice of this favourite music is far from being random because the general pattern of music has to correspond with the general personality pattern of the consumer in order to be accepted. On the other hand there is a great resemblance between the message and the messenger as well. Individuals never reshape the universe objectively, but always in the way they perceive it, on the basis of their experiences and expectations.

A detailed comparison of characteristic psycho-social personality patterns of musicians with the music they make corroborates these assumptions. Traditional musicians do differ from representatives of acculturated musical forms according to a number of socio-economic, educational and cultural factors. Traditional musicians can be described as coming from rural, rather than urban environments, having a lower socio-economic status, and poorer living conditions, with less education and exposure to the media, with firmer ties to family and village or geographical region, to traditional rituals and religions. The following attitudes can be considered as typical:

We are very Slovenian Slovenians . . . We love the mountains and climb Triglav almost every year. Our badge is red, white and blue just like the national flag and we always perform in national costumes . . . What should be considered as Slovenian in our music? Simply the fact that we are singing about our country. I think that we feel much more Slovenian than the rockers do. Some of them write in English as if they were ashamed of their mother tongue. I doubt that these people would be willing to protect our country if it were necessary, since they seem to surrender to foreign influences so easily.[8]

The representatives of acculturated musical forms show a quite different psycho-social pattern. They come from urban, rather than rural environments, have a higher social and economic status and better living conditions, are more highly educated and more media literate, with loose family ties and tighter peer groups, more likely to be non-conformist and to be in favour of social change. Their views on what Slovenia is about and how their music fits into the social reality is thus in sharp contrast to the traditionalists' opinions:

Slovenian punk exists. And Slovenian narrowness, stupidity, national dogmatism and insane self-satisfaction exist as well. So Slovenian punk exists in order to mock and satirise it. Not to perform national nihilism, but to achieve a form of internationalism, in which typical features of a specific society would not be denied. The Slovenian complex and the implicit nationalism is a danger for the country and has no relation whatsoever to contemporary socialist society.

But in spite of these differences between traditional and acculturated musical forms, the assumption that they have nothing to do with each other is wrong. In both cases they were developed according to the following sequence of events: changes in socio-economic and cultural environment causing changes in the life of individuals; increasing readiness by a large part of population to accept a new cultural model; imitation of this model and the internalisation of its elements to a degree which makes creation of similar objects possible; acceptance of these newly created objects on the part of society, and promotion through cultural organisations and the mass media. And this common pattern of evolution does not exclude mutual relations. On the contrary, current developments in both forms of music are to an ever greater degree dependent on the musical situation as a whole.

As I write there is still a dominance of traditional over acculturated musical forms in terms of both consumption and production. There are approximately 400 traditional ensembles currently active in Slovenia and 200–300 individuals and bands using acculturated musical forms, but the tendency is in the direction of acculturation. The first Beatles generation came from a very thin social stratum of privileged youngsters, enjoying supreme socio-economic status and good educational opportunities, and though acculturated musical forms are still preferred mostly by those young people who are not yet absorbed into the workforce, they are slowly losing their elitist character. Social as well as geographical and educational boundaries seem to be fading and the number of youngsters showing interest in pop music and creating on acculturated patterns is increasing. Recall the example of the village festival in Vanca vas: acculturated music had found its way to a community where it would not have been imaginable some fifteen years ago.

Since their beginning both musical forms have been open to various influences; in practice they do not stand independently side by side, but are subjected to mutual encouragement and even various forms of amalgamation. It seems that acculturated musical forms have exerted much greater influence on traditional forms than vice versa. Examples in which the verse of a traditional song (as *Schnaderhupferl* verse) is hidden behind the hard rock beat, are rather rare. In towns, at any rate, a rock band does not have to perform waltzes and polkas as in the case of the village festival in Vanca vas. On the other hand, traditional ensembles do now perform pop numbers almost without exception, and it should be stressed further that traditional ensembles have been influenced even more significantly in their manner of presentation. In order to be able to compete with the sound level of acculturated bands, almost all traditional ensembles have undergone a process of electrification. Acoustic performances are rare and are mainly used for attaining some special effect.

The description of the village festival of Vanca vas was chosen from the colourful spectrum of informal musical life in Slovenia for a special purpose. It should serve as an extreme example of the amalgamation of different cultural influences, affecting all levels of behaviour. Let us demonstrate it by focusing on just one single element: the multifocal role young people played in the event. Though almost all of them were members of the socialist youth organisation, much of their behaviour, (for example, the haggling over the price of entrance tickets) reminded me of the traditional local brotherhood. On the other hand the same young people expressed their musical preferences (not to the unreserved approval of everybody else involved) by hiring a rock band. Old and new ways of life, indigenous elements and those coming from elsewhere, original Slovenian habits handed down through generations and partially adopted foreign patterns of behaviour were merged in the cheerful atmosphere of the village dance. Tradition and acculturation in Slovenian popular music are polarities at a theoretical level: the practice itself is dominated by reciprocal influences and fluid transitions.

Notes

1   Z. Kumer, 'Godcevstvo in sodobni instrumentalalni ansambli na Slovenskem', *Pogledi na etnologijo*, Partizanska knjiga, Ljubljana, 1978, pp. 375–6. My translation.
2   K. Zupan, 'Cetrtkov vecer domacih pesmi in napevov', RTV Ljubljana, na, broadcast 20 April 1978.

3   C. Novak, 'Neokusno, osladno kicasto', *Komunist*, Ljubljana, 28 November, 1977, p. 9.
4   Quotes from my own interviews.
5   W. Deutsch: 'Zur gegenwärtigen Lage der Volksmusik in Österreich', *Österreichische Musikzeitscrift 33*, XII, 1978, p. 641.
6   This quotation and other material on the first and second pop generation was partially derived from interviews which were collected by Damjan Ovsec for his – to my great regret – still unfinished study on the influence of the Anglo-American pop music on two generations of grammar school students. I would like to thank Mr. Ovsec for letting me use his material.
7   B. Tuksar, Prisutnost pop i rock glazbe u jugoslovenskom muzickom zivotu', *Zvuk 3*, Zagreb, 1978.
8   Triglav is the highest Slovenian mountain and serves as a symbol of Slovenia.

The impact of mass media and acculturation on the Judeo-Spanish song tradition in Montreal

The past three decades have seen the establishment of a substantial Sephardic community in Montreal, with several thousand people from Judeo-Spanish speaking families from Morocco, and others from Greece and Turkey. Although some older Moroccans can still sing traditional Judeo-Spanish songs, this repertoire, in Montreal as elsewhere, is not being passed on to the younger generation. This paper is intended to examine what is being learned and transmitted, placing Judeo-Spanish songs in the context of other Sephardic music, and putting the important factors of mass media and acculturation into historical and geographical perspective.

From their beginnings in mediaeval Spain, Judeo-Spanish songs have been largely a product of mass – if not electronic – media and of acculturation. Well before the expulsion of the Jews from the Iberian peninsula in the late fifteenth century, rabbis were grumbling about the popularity of troubadour songs in the Jewish community; across the Pyrenees in Occitania a thirteenth-century rabbi, Jacob Anatoli, singled out women and young girls as the chief offenders.[1] Later on, the exiled Spanish Jews continued to receive musical input from Spain through the Marranos. At the same time, the music of their new environments in North Africa and the Ottoman Empire began to find its way into Sephardic traditions. The historian Joseph Nehama writes of seventeenth-century Salonica: 'La musique profane . . . s'augmente de tous les airs du voisinage . . . En dépit des rémonstrances des rabbins . . . les chansons à boire sont nombreuses.'[2]

Writing of the gradual adoption of Turkish musical forms, he goes on:

C'est par-ci, par-là, un petit air qui s'infiltre, un de ces airs que l'on est accoûtumé à entendre tous les jours, sur les lèvres des voisins grecs, bulgares, valaques, turcs, arabes et même persans . . . Le public ignore généralement qu'ils viennent du dehors. Il les croit siens puisqu'ils volent de bouche en bouche . . . avec la faveur des antiennes sympathiques.[3]

The combination of religious traditions, the Spanish heritage and local musical practice eventually evolved into the genres which are now considered to be 'traditional' Judeo-Spanish song: *romances*, the narrative ballads, whose texts and form can be traced to mediaeval Spain; and songs accompanying the calendrical and life cycles. As sung in Morocco and in the eastern Mediterranean, the songs often share texts and themes, indicating their common origins, but the two areas use not only different melodies but also different musical systems.[4] Neither tradition can be said to be a direct heritage of mediaeval or Renaissance Spain. But while the music of the songs has been profoundly influenced by local forms, and cannot be traced to early Spanish music, (and some songs are translations or adaptations of Mediterranean texts), an important number of *romance* texts can be easily traced to mediaeval Spanish *poetry*. They have not been preserved intact, but in several cases actually altered to conform with Jewish ethics and philosophy. The most obvious example of this is a 'dechristianisation' tendency; concepts of honour and the treatment of aggressive and punitive violence have also been adapted over the centuries by the women who are the main bearers of this tradition. The *word* is of paramount importance in Judaism, and it would seem that while music, the vehicle for them, may freely borrow from outside, words and ideas need to be brought closer to appropriate internal concepts.

Besides the genres mentioned, the eastern Mediterranean communities in particular evolved a lyric song tradition which draws deeply on Turkish and Greek music. In its twentieth-century form, this tradition is less beloved of scholars than the *romance*, but more widely anthologised and performed; it has, in fact, come to be nearly synonymous with the phrase 'Sephardic music' or '*Ladino song*', for the general public.

By the early twentieth century, especially in the eastern Mediterranean, the *romance* was already being sung less frequently. Women in their sixties have told me that their mothers and grandmothers sang, but that they themselves did not learn the repertoires. In Morocco, young people attended schools run in

French by the Alliance Israélite Universelle, and there were other
more complex reasons for the *romance* to cease being the 'code
carriers', as Benmayor puts it, of Judeo-Spanish *Sephardim*.[5] In the
eastern Mediterranean, chapbooks containing printed versions of
romance texts were produced and circulated, notably by Y. A. Yoná;
these popular pamphlets also contained paraliturgical and lyric
songs. But at the same time, *Sephardim* were finding musical
inspiration in contemporary urban forms. The Turkish *gazel* and
Greek *rembetika* music were performed by well-known Sephardic
singers, who also sang Judeo-Spanish songs in the same style. The
čalgi, the small orchestra of violin, *santur* and drum, was a
standard instrumental accompaniment. But French, Italian and
Latin American music, as well as light classical music, were in great
vogue, and a new repertoire emerged with words in Judeo-Spanish
written to popular tunes from these sources. A particularly popular
composer in this style was Leon Botón of Salonica; according to one
of my informants he worked regularly with Sadík 'El Ciego' ('the
Blind'), almost as a Sephardic Gilbert and Sullivan. Apparently
these two men were also experts in traditional genres and could
always be found leading the singing for weddings, circumcisions
and other community events. This same informant sang several
songs which she attributed to the team; later on, I located some of
them in a transliteration done by the Arias Montano Institute in
Madrid of a pamphlet produced in the early 1920s and attributed to
'Sadík el Gozós'. The *incipits* of these songs include such intriguing
indications as 'Foxtrot elle s'est fait couper les cheveux', 'Tango
t'en fais pas bouboule' and 'march socialista'. Songs may also
include key words such as *el Charlèstón* or 'sex appeal', and a song I
heard from a young Istanbul woman changed the month of *mayo* to
a hybrid French–Spanish *mai* – to rhyme with *tramvai*. One of my
favourite examples of this repertoire was sung to me by the same
informant to the tune of Maurice Chevalier's 'Valentine'. A more
complete version of this song appears in the Sadík pamphlet as a
duet between 'Pépé y Joc' to the 'són del hermoso güan-step
Valantina'. In it, Jacques says the ideal wife must play the piano and
violin, and be 'como flamma en la cama' (aflame in bed), but Pépé
accuses him of treating women 'à la légère' and wanting a 'kewpie
doll'.

Another genre of song which became popular during these pre-
World War II years was the Zionist song, often based on marching

tunes and composed in what was then Palestine. Other songs were topical, commenting on the current political scene or recounting the tragic story of the great fire which altered the face of Salonica in 1917. So far, these Judeo-Spanish popular songs have been sadly neglected by Sephardic studies.

The music of the Moroccan *Sephardim* also drew on a variety of sources. The first Alliance school opened as early as 1862, in Tetuan, and the French and Spanish Protectorates meant continuing close cultural ties with Spain and France. Several Spanish and French folk tunes became incorporated into the repertoire, as did Andalusian characteristics. At the same time, the women borrowed their North African neighbours' driving tambourine rhythms and piercing ululations (*barwalá*) to accompany Judeo-Spanish wedding songs. For the singing of *piyyutim* (hymns in Hebrew) the men used traditional North African combinations, such as *oud*, *kanun*, and violin (with adapted technique as in the Middle East). At the same time, especially in cosmopolitan Tangiers, many men also sang in choirs and learned western instruments and musical ideas. Though there is not to my knowledge a documented popular contrefact repertoire which would correspond to the one I have described in Salonica, parodies and light songs in *haketía* (Moroccan Judeo-Spanish) were popular and I have been able to record some very amusing ones from an informant in Montreal. These include a Judeo-Spanish wedding song sung to the tune of a Mexican *ranchero* and a paraliturgical song, the 'Debate of the flowers', transformed into a debate between Churchill and Roosevelt.

Yet another set of musical influences came from Israel. Not all the *Sephardim* emigrated directly to Canada from Morocco or the other countries mentioned; a good number spent some years in Israel first. Israel's incredibly rapidly developed folk music included local Arabic music, Yiddish love songs and East European dance tunes, and the ancient traditions of the Yemenites, as well as western popular music. The Judeo-Spanish lyric tradition described earlier was taken up by popular Israeli singing stars, sometimes in Hebrew translation and often with a fairly large western orchestra, perhaps accompanied by traditional percussion. This is widely accepted as a 'Sephardic sound', and has become popular outside Israel as well; Shiloah and Cohen classify it as 'neo-traditional' and call it 'pan-Sephardic'.[6] As anthologies of these songs appeared, trained cantors and even opera singers (Victoria de los Angeles is a famous example) began to perform them, and eventually they were adopted by early music groups thirsty for new repertoire and often labouring under the fond illusion that they were performing authentic mediaeval survivals.

When the present Sephardic community began to immigrate to Canada nearly thirty years ago, Canada's Jewish population was almost entirely Ashkenaz, and English-speaking. The *Sephardim* had to adjust to North American life while balancing their linguistic and cultural affinities between their correligionists, who spoke English, and the Francophone population, often culturally more familiar, but largely Catholic. The traditional genres of Judeo-Spanish song, were already giving way, as we have seen, to newer forms, and their preservation was even less of a priority as the community applied its energies to establishing a stable synagogue and community life and succeeding as professionals in a new country. There are still people who know the old repertoire, and I have collected over 250 traditional and new songs between Montreal and Toronto. But these informants are the minority, and a rapidly ageing one.

What is the musical involvement, then, of the Sephardic community here? In a brief, but perceptive article, Solly Lévy, himself a Moroccan Sephardi and performer of the Judeo-Spanish tradition, describes 'le monde musical des séphardim montréalais'.[7] This world extends from traditional *paytanim* (singers of *piyyutim*, of whom Lévy himself is a fine example) to 'la guitare "jazzante" d'un Jacques Amar', to some of the 'émules les plus prometteuses de Michael Jackson' (my own introduction to breakdancing was the performance of the Sephardic community centre's young team at Purim festivities two years ago). Moroccan dances are also performed by several groups and featured in community 'soirées orientales'; in fact, it has been suggested that it is only since coming to America that the Moroccan Sephardim have come to really appreciate them.[8] The Sephardic KINOR choir, founded by Levy over a decade ago, itself has an eclectic repertoire which includes Judeo-Spanish songs, Latin American songs and Mozart. For another, younger Moroccan singer, the French tradition of Brel, Ferrat and Brassens is the best vehicle for musical communication between her and her audience – she is not at home singing English, and Judeo-Spanish or even standard Spanish would not be generally understood. She occasionally performs Judeo-Spanish songs learned from her

parents, but they criticise her singing style as being non traditional
and conditioned by her French repertoire. Spanish and French
popular music influences are found in the original compositions of
Tangiers-born Jack Benlolo, who lives in Toronto and is one of the
few composers of songs in *haketia* in Canada – or anywhere. One
song, about the difficulties of immigration to Canada, is composed
to the tune of 'Dominique' by the late Singing Nun.

If Judeo-Spanish songs as such are rarely any longer, if at all,
transmitted through the family, they still circulate, partly through
LPs and cassettes, and partly through live performances. Almost all
my informants owned or have often heard recordings of the eastern
lyric songs, especially those sung by popular Israeli singers.
Younger informants of Greek and Turkish origin often re-learned
or even learned some of their repertoire directly from these records.
There are many fewer recordings of the Moroccan tradition, which,
in fact, is little known to the general public. Few of my informants
had heard the documentary record produced by Folkways recently,
but most had LPs or cassettes by Ester Roffé, a Moroccan Sephardi
living in Caracas. Roffé sings in traditional style but accompanied
by western instruments, and sometimes even background vocals.
Far from criticising these arrangements, my informants often feel
they enhance the songs and confirm their value.

From time to time there are live performances of Judeo-Spanish
Sephardic music given by people outside the community, and by
and large they are received benevolently. More stringent criticism is
often aimed at Gerineldo, a Montreal-based group composed of
three Moroccan Sephardim, and one Ashkenaz. Gerineldo's repertoire is gleaned almost entirely from field recordings. Several
biblical and historical *romances* are sung *a capella*; also in traditional
style, wedding songs are accompanied only by percussion and the
barwalá. *Oud* and *derbukka*, again traditional, may accompany the
paraliturgical material. Influenced by folk and early music treatments, the group also occasionally uses a recorder, and a mediaeval-
style bowed fiddle for historical *romances*. The group is liked, even
loved, and the Sephardic community attends its concerts and buys
its cassettes, but it has also received interesting criticisms – the
songs are 'not sung right'; the *floreo* is wrong'; the instruments are
wrong. The first objection is mostly a question of differing versions
– because the group's versions are so close to oral tradition, they
offer opportunity to this public for comparison. The second

question is more difficult; it refers to ornamentation, which is a central defining factor for many Judeo-Spanish Sephardim when judging performances, but very difficult to pinpoint. The instrument question is interesting because the group's traditional arrangements are sometimes accepted less readily than Roffé's western orchestra and harmonies, or even than the piano which it is now not unusual to hear accompanying *paytanim* performing in public. The group's mediaeval fiddle, though it has affinities with the violin and older North African bowed instruments, is a particular object of doubt. It is not a familiar instrument, and while scholars and early music specialists delight in searching for roots in mediaeval-Christian-Spain, the bearers of the Judeo-Spanish tradition do not. They are aware, certainly, that they have conserved a heritage for five centuries, and they are justifiably proud of it, but for centuries it has survived in part by adapting to local custom, and there is no reason to assume that late-twentieth-century mainstream culture should be an exception. It is true that Sephardim in Montreal and in several countries have been moved to tears and dancing by Gerineldo's performances, but it is also true that Roffé's use of western instruments makes a statement about the possibility of the survival of old songs in a modern culture, and about their intrinsic value.

Taking into account the age-old 'dialectique de . . . la tentation de l'extérieur et le retour aux sources', Lévy concludes that the musical life of *Sephardim* in Montreal is 'en pleine effervescence créatrice'. This observation by a member of the community reconfirms Benmayor's point that the *romance* tradition was not 'a product of an antiquarian yearning for roots' but had to do with maintaining identity. For centuries this identity was maintained partially through the traditional genres of Judeo-Spanish song, which, it must be remembered, was not a fixed form but changing and adapting from its beginnings. At present, it would seem that even the 'new' genres of Judeo-Spanish song may not be crucial for this purpose of identity; rather, it is maintained through liturgical music, on the one hand, and various contemporary forms, on the other, a development which fits in well with Nettl's notion of a stable amount of musical energy in a given group.[9] Meanwhile, the very forces of mass media and acculturation which helped render the tradition obsolete as an active everyday musical activity have produced systematic documentation of it; this has been used for both nostalgic and re-creative purposes and helped shape and disseminate a neo-Sephardic performance genre often practiced by non-Sephardim. In fact, the very concept of Sephardic music as a separate phenomenon owes much to the mass media and while one may justly mourn the passing of the old repertoire, and probably even its language, one must admire the flexibility and tenacity of those who created the tradition, maintained and adapted it through the centuries – and knew when to express their creativity in other ways: some genres may have diminished or disappeared, but not the exuberant musical energy which produced them.

Notes

1   A. Posner, *Literature for Jewish Women in Medieval and Later Times*, The Jewish Library, New York, 1934, p. 79.

2   Joseph Nehama, *Histoire dews Israélites de Salonique*, 7 vols, Libraire Molho/Fédération Mondiale Séphardite, Salonica, 1935–77, IV, p. 228.

3   *Ibid*, V, pp. 172, 226–7.

4   Israel Joseph Katz, 'La música de los romances judeo-españoles', in *En Torno al romancero Sefardi (Hispanismo y balcanismo de la tradición judeo-española)*, S. G. Armistead and J. Silverman, CMP, Madrid, 1982, pp. 243 ff. describes the main characteristics and differences of each.

5   Rina Benmayor, 'Social determinants in poetic transmission or a wide-angle lens for *Romancero* scholarship' in *El Romancero Hoy: Historia, Comparatismo, Bibliografía crítica*, 20 Colóquio Internacional, ed. S. G. Armistead *et al.*, Cátedra-Seminario Menéndez Pidel, Madríd, 1979, p.163.

6   Amnon Shiloah and Erik Cohen, 'The dynamics of change in Jewish oriental ethnic music in Israel', *Ethnomusicology*, XXVII, 2, 1983, pp. 240–41.

7   Salomon Lévy, 'Le monde musical des *Séphardim* montréalais' in *Samy El Maghribi*, Souvenir Programme, Rabbinat Sépharade du Québec, Montreal, 1984, pp. 12, 14, 22.

8   Jean-Claude Lasry, 'Une diaspora francophone au Québec: les Juifs sépharades', *Questions de Culture*, II, 1982, p. 128.

9   Bruno Nettl, *The Study of Ethnomusicology*, University of Illinois Press, Urbana, 1983, pp. 348–9.

Part 3

The problem of genre

Editor's note

What is obvious from the papers in this book so far is the importance of *labels* for popular music studies – whether the 'external' labels applied by scholars ('folk' versus 'popular', for example) or the labels used by musicians, record companies and fans within the popular music field, to account for different tastes and market choices. The question now is how musical labelling itself works. What is being labelled exactly? The musical score? Its performance? Its technological form – as tape or record? Its commodity form – as package? IASPM's second international conference focused on the theme, 'What is popular music?', and it soon emerged in discussion that the real difficulty was not defining 'popular' but defining 'music'. The issue was raised too of authority. Who makes labelling decisions stick? Who has the power to define a sound as folk or pop, punk or metal?

One continuing IASPM task, then, has been to try to systematise the rules according to which musicians and critics, salesmen and audiences, agree on genre labels. As the papers in this section emphasise, these rules can't be determined from the outside, whether by folk purists or subcultural celebrants. They are produced, rather, in the everyday social practices of music-making, music-selling and music-listening.

Bernard Broere addresses the problem of genre as an ethno-musicologist. His starting question is this: how have distinctly local musics been able to survive in colonial and post-colonial Colombia? His immediate problem is that conventional ethnomusicological distinctions between popular music and folk forms, on the one hand, and popular music and art forms, on the other, are difficult to draw, even with respect to pre-recorded, pre-commercial forms of local music-making. Musics in Nariño, his study area, are not labelled and distinguished from each other according to formal musical characteristics but in terms of use and context. Musicological data, in other words, has to be supplemented with sociological data, the musicologist's formal language with the musician's common sense. If music takes on its distinctive meaning in the very act of labelling, then the analyst has to understand the social processes through which such labels come to be agreed.

Franco Fabbri pursues this suggestion with reference to the commercial world of the Italian song. Fabbri has, in fact, made the most systematic attempt to formalise the rules of contemporary pop, outlining the bewildering variety of norms a performer or piece must follow to be recognisable in genre terms, showing how both musicological and sociological conventions must be placed in a wider framework of semiology – *every* aspect of a pop performance carries a genre meaning, from the pre-concert interview to the post-concert party, from the chat in the recording studio to the chat in the record shop. There's an element of cynicism in Fabbri's approach – the most sincere pop gesture is shown to follow the appropriate rules of sincerity, and Fabbri's own fascination with the recording studio, with the moment when genre rules are most explicitly articulated (and packaged), puts further emphasis on the commercial calculation of genre rules. But in the section of Fabbri's work published here, an applied example of his typological method, he also describes how a new pop genre, *canzone d'autore*, was created, and his delight in the way musicians offer new pleasures by breaking genre rules is infectious.

In answer to the question as to who makes the distinctions that matter, Broere, an ethnomusicologist, implies, 'the people', and Fabbri, a musician, suggests, 'musicians'! Motti Regev, a sociologist, is more concerned with music's institutional arrangements, and his investigation of how genre rules are established and maintained in Israel raises directly the questions of *power* and *value*. Regev's classification of Israeli pop thus echoes Fabbri's in its range of reference, but differs in its stress on an aesthetic *hierarchy*. Regev is interested in the contradiction in Israel between the commercial popularity of 'oriental music' and its low cultural prestige (as measured by institutional support – from radio stations, for example). Musical change, he argues, is not just a result of musicians' semiological games or listeners' subcultural needs, but reflects too the tensions *within* music institutions.

5 *Bernard J. Broere*

El Chambú – a study of popular musics in Nariño, South Colombia

Introduction

Until recently musicologists and ethnomusicologists have generally paid little or no attention to different types of popular music. Jaap Kunst, one of the first ethnomusicologists, emphatically excluded 'Western art and popular entertainment music' from this specialisation (Kunst, 1959). However, in 1927 Erich M. von Hornbostel had already published a short article on jazz in which he pointed to the vitality of this form of popular music (Hornbostel, 1972). Even so, it was his opinion that the traditional forms of music which still survived in the world should first be studied and collected before the influence of European culture would bring 'Tarabumdieh [*sic*] to all parts of Africa, and that quaint song about little Kohn to the South Seas' (Hornbostel, 1975, p. 270).

One of the few scholars supporting the study of popular music by ethnomusicologists was Willard Rhodes, who provided the following definition:

By popular music I refer to that sizable body of material which, while failing to qualify as a genuine folk or art music, represents by its widespread popularity a musical expression of the mass of people who produce, consume and support it . . . If we approach this material with an unbiased mind and the proper techniques for ethnological and musicological analysis, we may learn much about man through his music. (Rhodes, 1956, p. 4)

Such ideas met with little enthusiasm.

The International Folk Music Council (IFMC), founded in 1947 in the UK, recognised the importance of popular music studies, if only inasmuch as this would contribute a better understanding of 'folk music, extra-European as well as European' (Karpeles, 1956,

p. 18). However, even if times seem to be changing, there is still no
systematic study of popular music by ethnomusicologists. An
important exception to this negative attitude may be found in the
article 'Mesomusic' by the famous Argentinian ethnomusicologist
Carlos Vega (1898–1966), published in the only Latin-American
issue of the *Journal of the Society for Ethnomusicology* (Vega, 1966).

The main objective of my paper is to make a comparative analysis
of Carlos Vega's approach to the question, 'What is popular music?'
This will be considered in relation to some representative interpretations made by the people of the department of Nariño in South
Colombia, especially from the town of Pasto, with regard to their
own music culture and the criteria that they use to discuss it. The
bambuco 'Chambú' will be taken as an example of Nariño's popular
music. 'Chambú' is one of the most popular works of the Pastuso
composer Luis E. Nieto.

'Popular music' and 'Mesomusic'

In general 'popular music' and 'mesomusic' are terms used by
Latin-American specialists to refer to the same sort of music.

From one point of view, popular music ranges from music which
is popular in the widest sense – such as Beethoven's 'Für Elise' – to
commercial music which is pre-eminently urban, and outside the
western art music repertoire. The global spread of this music – and
its frequent popularity on this count – is due to the continuous
intermediary activity of commercial interests and the mass media.
Together they try to create the widest possible international market
for their products. Especially in Latin-America, which from the
beginning of the nineteenth century seemed in some aspects, not least
culturally, to have achieved liberation from the domination of foreign
powers, international popular music is considered by some specialists
as a direct threat to their pristine Mestizo cultures, which developed
as a result of the interaction of Indian, African and Iberian cultural
elements. This is the standpoint taken by most Latin-American
folklorists and folklore specialists regarding 'música populár'.

Isabel Aretz, herself a student of Carlos Vega, expresses this
problem as follows:

What is more important for us, is the fact that the hits in Europe do not alter
European culture, because its roots are already established. Our case is
different! Our fight is to see that Latin-America is not converted into an

appendix of Europe or of the United States, but that Latin-America has its own life . . . In this respect music plays a most important part because Latin-America is infinitely rich in this aspect of its way of life. (Aretz, 1977, p. 26).

Among the chief reasons for the threat to the existence of the Latin-American cultural heritage, Dr Aretz cites:

the role of local authorities in permitting popular music groups to perform at traditional feasts in the name of 'progress' because they fear that otherwise they would be considered backward; young people, who find traditional music 'old-fashioned'; cultural authorities, who neglect their own folk music and folklore, and only give importance to the 'great arts' (*ibid.* p. 262).

Clearly the first objective of specialists such as Isabel Aretz is to collect and study the existing musical folklore and as far as possible to protect this cultural heritage from what are considered undesirable influences. Even if alongside international popular mass media music there are also numerous forms of local popular music with their own regional context, the traditional 'música folclórica' is still chosen as the most important category because it is considered to be the most threatened form. Even if the popular music forms are susceptible to change, it is considered that there is insufficient time to study them, because 'música folclórica' takes precedence.

From the other point of view, 'música popular' for Carlos Vega was originally nothing more than a waste product, an adulterated residue left when 'música folclórica' was extracted from the conglomerate of the Latin-American music repertoire. This elimination process as he himself calls it, is described in the introductory essay 'The Science of Folklore' ('La scientia de folklore') to his *Panorama de la Música Argentina*, where he defines folklore as traditional popular knowledge and its product (Vega, 1944, p. 56). This introduction can be considered as a pre-study to his article on mesomusic.

In the first instance Vega makes a distinction between the cultures of the 'grupos etnográficos' (ethnic groups – the Indians) and the 'patrimonio popular' (popular heritage); this last category is divided into 'superior' (that is, the literate culture of the urban elites) and the illiterate culture of the people. Within this category he makes another subdivision between 'hechos folclóricos' and 'no-folclóricos', that is, folk elements and non-folk elements. He therefore concludes that everything which is 'folklore' is also 'popular', but not the other way round! Thus the context and the use determines whether an artefact or an instrument is folklore or not.

The same elimination process is applied to music. Thus, for Vega, not all 'popular music' is 'folk music' (e.g. hymns, marches and children's songs). He emphasises that 'música folclórica' does not need to be anonymous and that oral transmission is not necessarily a criterion for authenticity. The decisive factor for him is whether or not the music concerned is in keeping with the musical norms of the people (Vega, 1944, p. 67).

By rejecting 'anonymous origin' and 'oral transmission' as criteria for defining traditional folk music, Vega differs from many of his colleagues and contemporaries, as well as from the definition of the IFMC. Some thirty years later Vega's Colombian colleague Guillermo Abadía Morales supported his viewpoint for the simple reason that without Vega's definition folklore would never have a chance to renew itself (Abadía, 1977, p. 194).

On the basis of his view of the *history* of the musical life of Latin-America, Vega arrived at the following classification:

Música superior (art music)
Música de salón (light semi-classical music)
Música primitiva (tribal music)

The first two categories are of European origin. The second category became the basis of the 'música folclórica' of Latin-America because of its use and function in Latin-America. As Vega puts it, 'The folk music of today is originally the classical music of yesterday' (Vega, 1944, p. 78), the lower class having taken over the achievements of the higher classes. In Latin-America Spanish folk music was out of context and it was for that reason, he concludes that it did not survive.

It was this 'música de salón' which Vega later took as the starting point for his study on mesomusic. This category was called 'mesomusic' because of the position it took between art music and folk music, or, as Vega states: 'Mesomusic then, co-exists in the minds of urban groups along with fine-art music, and participates in the life of rural groups along with folk music' (Vega, 1966, p. 3). In his opinion, primitive peoples could not appreciate this music (*ibid.*

p. 16). In answer to the question, what does mesomusic comprise, he gives the following description: 'Mesomusic is the aggregate of musical creations (melodies with or without words) functionally designed for recreation, for social dancing, for the theatre, for ceremonies, public acts, class rooms, games etc. adopted or accepted by listeners of the culturally modern nations' (*ibid.* p. 3).

This music originated in Western Eurpe (Paris, Madrid), where this form of light music ('música de salón') was used and valued alongside 'música superior'. According to Vega, mesomusic differs from art music on the following counts:

> *form and structure*: simple, very often tripartite/ternary forms built from simple symmetrically constructed melodies based on diatonic major/minor tone scales;
> *harmony*: the supporting harmonies similarly simple in their progression; there are only short modulations to related tone centres;
> *rhythms*: the rhythms are always regular binary or ternary dance rhythms.

In this respect classical music is considered to be much more complex, and he comes therefore to the following analogy: '. . . mesomusic speaks 'in verse' . . . art music is more and more conceived 'in prose' (Vega, 1966, p. 5).

As examples of popular Latin-American musical forms which clearly originated in Europe, he gives the *contradanza* of Argentina and the *triste* of Peru/Ecuador. Extending this line of thought, it is also possible to include the Colombian *jota* as such a form. It is part of the repertoire of the *conjunto chirimía*, a form of Afro-Colombian music performed in the lowlands of the Chocó (Central Colombia). This dance was brought to Colombia in the sixteenth and seventeenth centuries by the Spanish conquistadors and later by the Spanish colonisers. It was taken over by the black population, descendants of African slaves. They adapted the *jota* to fit into their own musical patterns. *Chirimía* music therefore lost its real status as mesomusic and became 'música típica' (folk music) which had little in common with the Spanish *jota*. The *conjunto chirimía* does not use the chirimía, the Spanish shawm. The only traditional wind instrument used is either a bamboo transverse flute or a clarinet.

It seems therefore that contemporary mesomusic in Latin-America partly derives from a European origin. In many cases, however, the new context has led to the development of new forms of traditional folk music, as well as to a wide-ranging and varied repertoire of 'música popular'.

Just as with folk music, specific types of 'música popular' are limited to specific regions. The Colombia folklorist Lopez Ocampo names this phenomenon *criollismo*.[1] This adaptation of European elements to different circumstances and cultural patterns has also led to the development of new musical instruments or to a new use of instruments from other cultures. Thus, the European origin no longer plays a role in the new context.

It is not surprising, then, that outsiders, especially non-participating specialists, have the greatest difficulty in making a clear distinction between folk music and popular music. The *public* – that is to say, consumers or producers (including musicians and composers) – who know and value these types of music, have considerably less difficulties with these distinctions, especially when it comes to the music of their own area. This can be shown by examples of participant evaluation of music in the province of Nariño. The history and geography of this part of Colombia have played such an important role in this context, that these aspects should be discussed first.

Nariño – introduction to geography – history and people

The department of Nariño is situated in Southwest Colombia, bordering Ecuador and the Pacific Ocean. From a geographical point of view this area of only 33·270 sq km is greatly varied. East and Central Nariño lie in the Andes, rising to 5,000 m and intersected by high fertile valleys. Pasto, the department's capital town, lies in such a valley, 2,500 m above sea level. In contrast, the Western coastal area along the Pacific Ocean is lowland and partly covered with tropical rain forests. The transition between the highland (*sierra*) and the coastal area (*costa*) is extremely abrupt, consisting of an enormous formation of rocks, called Chambú, through which a small track, the only connection with the interior to the West, hacked out of the rocks, wrests its way downward in numerous hairpin bends. Chambú – meaning 'shout' (Bastidas, 1975, p. 87) – is for the Nariñese much more than a natural ridge between two different climatic and geographic areas. For them Chambú marks the borderline between two different population groups and their cultures. Because of the many lives lost while the road was constructed and because of numerous traffic accidents, Chambú also symbolises the threshold between life and death.

Nariño's population is about one million. The sierra is the ancient home of Indian groups. Only two of these still use their own language: the Coaiquer, who live near Chambú, and the Kementxa, on the borders of Alto Putumayo and Nariño. The majority of Nariño's sierra population consists of descendants of Indian groups, Quillacinga and Pastos, who have relinquished their original culture. Most of them are *campesinos*, peasant farmers with their own characteristic culture. *Mestizos* and *criollos* mostly live near the town of Pasto (300,000 inhabitants). The *criollos* have developed a flourishing cultural and scholarly life, centred at the local University and the Javeriano College, and based on old Spanish and traditional Roman Catholic norms. In contrast, the coastal area is inhabited by descendants of African slaves, mainly smuggled illegally in the nineteenth century after the slave trade was abolished. They work mainly in the timber and gold industries, as fishermen or as labourers in the harbour town of Tumaco. All these groups have their own culture and forms of musical expression, which continued to co-exist because of practical communication difficulties throughout the whole area. While it is often the case that intercultural tension and conflicts occur in such situations, the history of this area demonstrates that there was always a strong feeling of unity which was clearly manifested from time to time.

The area nowadays known as Nariño lies directly north of the Northern border of the former Inca empire, which ran right through the area of the Pastos Indians. The border dividing Colombia from Ecuador hardly differs from that old Inca border-line, so that the descendants of the Pastos as well as their culture still survive today on both sides of the border. This area was conquered and colonised by the Spaniards in the beginning of the sixteenth century. The town of San Juan de Pasto was founded in 1538. During the colonial period this area was ruled for two centuries as part of the vice-royalty of Peru, with Quito as its capital. From the beginning of the nineteenth century, a period when many Latin-American areas were created as independent states, it was in this region that fierce battles and conflicts were staged, whereby the ownership of Nariño frequently changed hands between Ecuador and Colombia. At the start of the liberation struggle, the people of Nariño sided with the Spanish, from whom they hoped to receive better treatment than from the liberators. After independence Nariño's inhabitants – Nariñense – often took a pro-Ecuadorean stand because of the cultural connections and because of their closer proximity to Quito than to Bogotá.

To most other Colombians Nariño's population is backward, especially because it is the department with the highest percentage of Indians. This inferior position is especially demonstrated by the lack of attention paid by the national government to the development of Nariño's infra-structure. Consequently the heterogeneous population of Nariño often presents itself as one people, Nariñenses, a unity which is officialy demonstrated at least once a year during Pasto's famous carnival *Negros y Blancos* (Blacks and Whites).

The following text about Nariño's department shows this regional nationalism:

Departamento de Nariño	*Department of Nariño*(trans.)
Centenela de la Patria en el Sur. Uno de los más bellos de Colombia. Con el Santuario más hermoso de América.	Southern sentinel of our Fatherland. One of the most beautiful of Colombia. With the most magnificent sanctuary in America.
Con gentes nobles, valientes y laboriosas. Con artesanías que recorren el mundo.	With courageous, noble and industrious people, and with crafts known throughout the world.
Tiene Volcanes, Nevados y Playas.	It has volcanoes, snowcapped mountains and beaches.
Hombres sabios y mujeres virtuosas.	Wise men and virtuous women.
Su historia es tan admirable, que su hijos han merecido el apelativo de espartanos.	Its history is so admirable that its offspring have earned the title of Spartans (from *Cultura Nariñense*, p. 84)

This is the backcloth to Nariño's popular music.

Nariño's music – some specialists' views

The Mexican ethnomusicologist Samuel Martí visited Colombia in the sixties to find out about the different types of music there, and came to the following conclusion: 'In this important town [Pasto] the only local music that you hear in the streets – and always as loud as possible on radios and juke-boxes – is the music of Ecuadorean origin' (Martí, n.d., p. 134). Martí's observation is important because he makes a distinction between 'Ecuadorean' and 'autochthonous music' (i.e. Colombian music). Perhaps he did not realise that both types are indigenous, as the history of the area shows.

The 'Ecuadorean type' of music performed in Nariño is indeed found in almost the same form in Ecuador, that is the region inhabited by Pastos *campesinos* and Otavalo Indians. Although in principle many different musical instruments can be used, the traditional folkmusic is performed mainly on flutes and drums. For the most part the melodies have a pronounced pentatonic flavour, with the first part often in major key, and the second part in the parallel minor. It is usually only the rhythm which gives the key to its origin: if it is a *bambuco* rhythm, then it is certainly of Colombian origin.[2]

While the *campesinos* value this music and keep it alive as one form of their own tradition – they speak of 'correct music' ('música correcta') – it is hardly appreciated in the rest of Colombia or in the northern Nariño. 'Música típica' is thought to be sad, monotonous because of its many repetitions, Indian, and even un-Colombian! Moreover there is a correct form of presentation in that each member of the *conjunto* (ensemble) has a fixed role to play in which aesthetic criteria have no place – roles such as 'performer of the melody', 'performer of the supporting harmonies', 'performer of the rhythms'.

The music of the string ensemble, *conjunto de cuerdas*, is another traditional style, considered to be typically Colombian. The *conjunto de cuerdas* consists of a *bandola* (sixteen-stringed Colombian adaptation of the mandolin), *tiple* (twelve-stringed guitar type), and one or more guitars which along with the *tiple* provide the harmonic background of the melody, which is usually played on the *bandola*. Sometimes a *requinto*, a smaller version of the *tiple*, is added, while the rhythm may be reinforced by the use of maracas or/and scraper.

The origin of the instruments and instrumentarium as a characteristic Colombian ensemble is undoubtedly Spain. In Aragon for example the traditional ensemble (*ronda*) consists of *bandurria, laúd* and guitar. This music, to be found in the regions around Bogotá (Cundinamarca, Boyacá), is usually based on the rhythm of the *bambuco* or the *pasillo*, the Colombian walse. The melodies are usually diatonic in major or minor with short transitions to parallel or similar tone centres. Regarding structure they also show the characteristics of 'mesomusic' listed by Vega. It seems clear that it was this music, which is so popular (especially in Colombia's highlands) that Martí was looking for in Pasto. One of the musicians he was probably seeking was the *requinto/bandola* player Luis E. Nieto (1898–1968) who was well-known in all Colombia and who became famous as a composer of works such as the march 'Cero-cero', later played in the United States and recorded on disc, and the *bambucos* 'Chambú' and 'Ñapanguita' (Martí, n.d., p. 134).

Nieto's work poses classificatory problems for the folklore specialist. This can be seen in the writings of Nariño's expert Roberto Mora Benavides. In an introductory chapter entitled 'The Folklore of Nariño' he makes a strict division between 'música popular' and 'música folclór'. His criteria for the latter category are:

> that the music has formed a living tradition for a hundred years;
> that the melody is accepted and known to the largest part of the social group concerned;
> that the author/composer is absolutely unknown.
>
> (Mora, 1974, p. 9)

In the chapter 'Musical Folklore' he presents the *bambuco* 'La Guaneña' as a typical example.[3] Surprisingly, he also presents Luis E. Nieto and his compositions 'Cero-cero', 'Ñapanguita' and 'Chamú' as 'the musical treasure of the treasures' of Nariño's traditional musical life! (*ibid*. pp. 121–2).

Once again one is forced to conclude that specialists have not succeeded in providing clear and valid criteria for differentiating between 'música folclórica' and 'música popular'. Taking as an example Nieto's 'Chambú', I shall now describe the classification made by the public and the norms they use for the various repertoires in Nariño.

Chambú

The *bambuco* 'Chambú' is not only important for Nariño's culture as a piece of music. According to the poet José Félix Castro, author of a short homage to Nieto (Castro, 1978), the text and melody of

'Chambú' inspired the writer Guillermo Edmundo Chavès to write his novel of the same name, a work which the famous Colombian literary critic and author Juan Lozano y Lozano rates as 'one of the best four or five novels of Colombia' (Bastidas, 1975, p. 86). The novel presents a realistic image of the life of this part of Colombia through the experiences of the main character Ernesto Santacoloma. It also provides a great deal of information on Nariño's history, including the origin of many place names (mainly Quechua), the countryside, in which Chambú has a central position, and the culture. In one section Chavès describes a *bambuco* performance, which takes place near the foot of the Chambú outcrop, where roadworks are underway, carried out by labourers mainly from Pasto. After dinner everyone gathers to watch the local beauty, called 'La Molinera' (the miller's daughter), dance one of the newest *bambucos* of Maestro Nieto, with one of the young labourers. Nieto, the famous Pastuso *requinista*, has come to the place with his five instrumentalists. The author notes that Nieto's *bambucos* and *pasillos* were famous all over Colombia, although he could not read music. The same was said of Nieto in real life: 'No sé nota, pero no se nota' ('I don't know notes, but they don't note it') (Castro, 1978, p. 4).

The dance described by the author is not the 'ballroom' version of the *bambuco*. On the contrary, the dance is performed according to strict rules, with M. Nieto acting as master of ceremonies, and during the performance symbolic gestures are made with hand-kerchiefs. The dance itself is a stylised expression of chivalrous love of a man for a woman, who continues to reject him for conventional reasons. The following *coplas* – short verses sometimes improvised – are an even more regimented form of communication whereby man and woman display themselves while keeping at a safe distance (Chavès, 1974, pp. 13–19). While this scene could seem to be reminiscent of the Spanish flamenco, Chavès did not have this in mind at all. Bastidas Urresty notes the great value Chavès attached to the intercultural process in America, i.e. *mestizaje*, which leads to a totally new type of person 'in the right balance of land and blood' (Bastidas, 1975, p. 89; Chavès, p. 81).

The fame of various compositions by Nieto, even outside Latin-America, indicates that this interpreter of 'música folclórica' – a music form strongly connected with a local group – was at the same time a 'popular composer'. This is because the traditional elements are not represented in the compositions themselves so much as in their performances, in the usage of the music – in other words, in the manner of playing, in the timbre of the musical instruments when played together, as well as in the context in which they are used. On this subject Abadía Morales also points out the important role played by musical timbres in giving 'personality' (*personalidad*) to a melody or a dance (Abadía, 1973, p. 121). That is to say, it is a matter of giving a performance an identity, and *not* of claiming that 'an authentic *bambuco* can never be played on an organ, or an autochthonous cumbia never on a harp or guitar' (*ibid.*). In practice this often occurs – apparently the public appreciated this kind of performance even more than the traditional version, whether it is 'authentic' or not. The public identifies the different musical genres according to the principle 'just listen and look'. One of the chief characteristics of a performance is *timbre*, while the melody takes second place, being adapted according to the instruments and the idiom of the musical genre used.

The composition 'Chambú' – which complies completely with Vega's criteria for mesomusic in structure, form and rhythm – is then rightly called 'popular', because it has become well-known in different presentations. Undoubtedly a second factor, which plays an important role as far as Nariño is concerned, is the *text*.

The text is as follows:

(translation)

Es Chambú de mi vida gigante roca que en sus picachos se recuestan las estrellas. Mas entre roca sales molinerita, la más bonita desprendida del peñón.	Chambú is the gigantic rock of my life; the stars take rest on its peaks. But between the rocks you emerge, miller's daughter, the most beautiful treasure removed from the rock.
Soy el minero mejor de Ambiyaco y Güelmambí, Molinerita querida todo el oro es para tí . . . Tierra, tierra de sol Chambú, tierra, paisaje azul Chambú, tierra bella, región que sueña en tí, mujer.	I am the best miner of Ambiyaco and Güelmambí. Beloved miller's daughter, all the gold is for you . . . Earth, earth of the sun, Chambú, earth, blue countryside, Chambú, earth, beautiful region which dreams in you, woman.

Soy el minero mejor	I am the best miner
de Ambiyaco y Güelmambí,	of Ambiyaco and Güelmambí.
Molinerita querida	Beloved miller's daughter,
toto el oro es para tí . . .	all the gold is for you . . .
Tierra, tierra de sol Chambú,	Earth, earth of the sun, Chambú,
tierra, paisaje azul Chambú,	earth, blue countryside, Chambú,
tierra tierra morena	earth, brown land,
donde vive el narinés.	where the Nariñense lives.

This love song of a mineworker for the daughter of a miller, paralleled in Chavès' novel, shows in the first place the love 'Nariñes' have for their land. The song does not refer to a particular part of Nariño, nor to a particular happening or time (as in the case of La Guanena). The text concerns Nariño as a whole, at all times, and its total population, which together constitute 'Nariñes'.

Thus the song acquires more than a regional or temporal character. It expresses a timeless feeling of unity with the land and provides a means of identity to those who identify with it. This is typical of many popular texts. 'Música popular' therefore is not bound to specific areas or groups, but is an expression of departmental identity. This is no doubt the reason why Benavides Mora counted Nieto and his works as Nariño's 'cultural patrimony' without being 'folklore'.

It is also important for the public to see who is performing the music and to a lesser extent where this is happening. In this respect a difference is made between performances of 'live music' for a specific context, and prepared performances for radio, TV or records, in which case 'música popular' loses its specific context and takes its place in the immense repertoire of mass media music.

The following typology of music types in Nariño can thus be made, using the public's criteria. Vega's classification is given for comparison.

Nariñense popular classification	*Vega's classification*
Música indígens: traditional music of the Indians; the Indians call it 'música autóctona' (autochthonous music) or deny they have anything comparable to our concept of music	*Ethnic music,* which is performed by 'primitive' groups.

Música típica: music of the *campesinos*.
Regarding idiom and timbre this is separated
into a 'Colombian' and an 'Ecuadorean'
repertoire. Melodies are nevertheless exchanged,
even if the instrumentarium does not always have
the acoustic capacity for playing the Colombian
type of music. The musicians are amateurs, who
are aware that they represent a specific tradition,
which they want to keep alive in the correct
manner ('música correcta'). The most well-
known dances are *bambuco* and *pasillo*. They are
performed at weddings, feasts and as relaxation
after work, for example after collective harvesting
(the *minga*). The performance takes place
following strict role patterns. Aesthetic
considerations play no part.

Folk music, which is
performed by rural
groups.

Música popular: not directly connected with
specific groups. Includes the same dance
types as 'típica', but in place of the traditional
presentation forms, aesthetic considerations play
a rôle. The presentation is arranged for the
instruments, which are sometimes traditional.
Local popular music often comments on the local
folklore and is sometimes considered as a form of
autochthonous identity.

Mesomusic: urban as
well as rural groups.

Música clásica, culta or académica:

Art music: urban elite.

Música costeña: music of the Afro-Colombians,
in fact a form of 'música típica'
in which some dances are derived from
European models.

Mesomusic: rural
groups.

The following categories are not mentioned by Vega, but because of
their characteristics belong to 'música popular' and 'mesomusic':
música moderna and *música folclorista*.

Música moderna: in this category the local people include Latin-
American dance music, especially of Caribbean origin, such as the
salsa. For their salsa Colombians made use of local dance music,
such as the *cumbia*, the *porro* and the *merengue*. In Nariño, 'música
moderna' (along with *bambuco* and *pasillo*) forms the most popular
dance music (*bailables*) in Colombia; it is widely disseminated via
radio and records.

Musica folclorista describes forms of traditional music, including 'música indígena', played by musical groups which do not belong to the social groups from which the music they play originates. In such ensembles traditional and modern music instruments are used, including instruments borrowed from extra-indigenous cultures, such as the Ecuadorean panpipe (*rondador*), the Peruvian notched-end flute (*kena*), the Peruvian/Bolivian panpipe (*siku*) and the *charango*, a mandolin type, especially popular among the Colla Indians of Peru and Bolivia. In Nariño this music is played by the group América Libre, among many others. This music genre is often used as a form of protest music, whereby the music ensemble becomes the mouthpiece of cultures and societies whose existence is threatened by current regimes. Unity and solidarity of heterogeneous groups are then symbolised by combining different instrument types, such as *kena* and *siku*, which otherwise belong to special ensembles. These instruments are used to perform music outside their own repertoire. Timbres and melodies then become signs of solidarity with the people and protest against the situation in the area concerned.

Although it is quite possible that such a *conjunto* could perform *campesino* dances from its own area, its music is in the first place considered as an interpretation of 'traditional' music generally, in which the various local parts are arranged, that is as a form of 'música popular'.

In principle a melody of whatever origin can be played as part of the repertoire of different genres (including 'música culta' and, occasionally, 'música indígena'), by adapting it to the appropriate instrumentarium for a specific idiom and public. Thus it can rightly be concluded that such melodies are message carriers that become understandable for a specific public when the melody is translated into their own musical language. This means that the 'música típica' repertoire comprises traditional as well as popular numbers, the latter including music from Ecuador. On the other hand there are recordings of 'Lindo Folclor' – beautiful folklore – which indicate that traditional music is interpreted as 'música popular'.

The disappearance of traditional folk music types only becomes a reality when 'instrumentos típicos' are no longer used, so that specific timbres can no longer be produced and the arranged performance takes the place of the role patterns of the traditional performance.

In this respect some 'folclorísta' groups reinforce the feelings and values of group identities which otherwise might totally disappear as the result of depreciation by more dominating groups. To achieve this, these folkloristic groups study traditional music and learn to play traditional musical instruments at the place of the source.

In some cases the *text* can also be adapted for a different milieu by changing the words or the dialect, while retaining the essential meaning. Two recordings of 'Chambú' made by América Libre for wide distribution have alterations to the original text and in the pronounciation of the dialect; for example, the group sings: '*El* Chambú de mi vida' and 'Tierra *bella* y morena Donde vive el *Nariñense*'.

The version of 'Chambú' performed by the salsa group Rumba Brava is different from all other versions, because it is played alternating with 'La Guanena', so that it becomes a hymn to 'my country' ('mi tierra'), while the instrumental part is accompanied by spoken and sung comments emphasising the beauty of Nariño. The Ñapanguita – a traditional Pastusa costume and the subject of a *bambuco* by Nieto – is referred to, as well as the volcano Galeras and the island Boca Grande 'beneath the moon'. As for the musical performance, the rhythm used is that of the *cumbia*, while two flutes in the arrangement can be considered to indicate Nariño's 'música típica' as well as the pre-salsa *charanga*, in which flutes as well as stringed instruments (violins), other wind instruments and various forms of percussion (*cencerro* – bell, timbales) can be used.

In the second version of 'Chambú' by América Libre the instrumentarium was increased by the addition of a session musician playing Fender bass, who introduced the *bambuco* rhythm. Furthermore, to record in a studio, the members of the ensemble had to make music in a totally different way from that to which they were accustomed. Instead of a performance in which the public is present and in which there is moderate use of a PA system, in the studio musicians play without their public and the sound technicians make the acoustic decisions, taping each musician individually as they listen on earphones to the tracks made by the rest of the group. The sound technician thus determines the sound of the recorded group, and his choice (and the addition of the Fender bass) gives América Libre a so-called 'better' sound, suitable for record distribution. América Libre and their interpretation of 'Chambú' could then take a place in the category 'Colombiana'; in other words, popular music from Colombia, subheading: 'música sureña' (music from the South), and even in 1979 reach the Colombian hit parade! In fact in 1977/78 Philips Colombia brought out a double LP *Paz y Alegría* (Peace and Joy) including the following forms of popular music: 'música romantica'; 'música colombiana'; 'música internacional' (including 'Don't cry for me, Argentina'), and 'música de discoteca' (including non-Colombian salsa and North American disco music).

Conclusion

Carlos Vega has made an important contribution to the border areas of musicological research, especially with regard to Latin-America, because he attempted to come to an understanding of what he termed 'mesomusic', and to define the complex and heterogeneous repertoire of popular music. Even if the classification of the various music genres in Latin-America and the participants' evaluation in Nariño are the result of different criteria, they do not so much contradict as complement each other. On the one hand, Vega and other specialists take as a starting point musicological criteria such as form, structure, melody and rhythm, and include the original European versions; on the other, the local people, along with the writer Guillermo Edmundo Chavès, take as their starting point their own local situation of *criollismo*. In this respect the performance process, as it is perceived, is fundamental: 'Se oye, se puede ver' – 'you listen, you can see!' Additional criteria thus include timbre, text, performers, and location of performance, in the sense of the circumstances in which it takes place. The melody, and in some cases the rhythm, are parameters which can be adapted.

It is striking that regional popular music is differentiated from folk music even if it uses the same melody, so that it becomes a metaphor: the local aspect is heard as part of a larger whole which represents regional identity. In such cases 'música típica' is traditional music from part of Nariño, while 'música popular' turns it into Nariñense music, and becomes a general expression of Nariño's music culture. When a normal live performance is recorded, this has only a marginal significance for the musical performance as a whole. It is a totally different case, as we have seen, if it is performed *for* the mass media. Then the music changes from being regional popular music to a form of international popular music. The original context and the interaction between musicians and a live public is eliminated, and replaced by technicians and equipment and an invisible public, potentially global. In such instances gramophone companies in Latin-America are entirely correct in stating on their record sleeves: 'El disco es cultura' – 'records are culture'.

Notes

1 *Criollo*: literally – a Spaniard born in South America. *Criollismo* therefore means: the mixing of European cultural elements with cultural elements originating from indigenous (Indian) and imported (African) cultures.
2 The *bambuco* is considerd to be Colombia's national dance. It is found in the highlands as well as on the Pacific Coast. In the latter case it is one of the rhythms used in the *currulao*, the marimba dance, also performed in Ecuador. A good example of a Nariñense *bambuco* is 'Santa Roseña'.
3 The *bambuco sureno* 'La Guanena' – of anonymous origin and played during the decisive battle against the Spaniards at Ayacucho (Peru) – is possibly Colombia's oldest known *bambuco*.

References

Abadía Morales, G. (1973), *La Música Folklórica Colombiana*, Universidad Nacional de Colombia, Bogotá.
——— (1977) *Compendio General de Folklore Colombiano*, Instituto Colombiano de Cultura, Bogotá.
Aretz, I. (1977), 'La música como tradición' in *América Latina en su Música*, ed. Isabel Aretz, UNESCO, Paris.
Bastidas Urresty, E. (1975), 'Chambú: una expresión Americana', *Cultura Nariñense*, LXXXV, pp. 86–90.
Castro, J. F. (1978), *Luis E. Nieto, Maximo Compositor Nariñense*, Pasto.
Chavès, G. E. (1974), *Chambú*, Editorial Bedout, Medellin.
Hornbostel, E. M. von (1972), 'Ethnologisches zu Jazz', *Melos*, VI, 12, pp. 510–12.
——— (1975), 'The problems of comparative musicology', in *Hornbostel Opera Omnia* Vol. I, Nijhoff, The Hague, pp. 248–70.
Karpeles, M. (1956), 'The International Folk Music Council. Its aims and activities', *Ethnomusicology Newsletter* 8, pp. 15–19.
Kunst, J. (1959), *Ethnomusicology*, Nijhoff, The Hague.
Martí, S. (n.d.), 'Ethnomusicología en Colombia', *Revista Colombiana de Folclor* II, 6, pp. 133–42.
Mora Benavides, R. (1974), *El Folclor de Nariño*, Pasto.
Ocampo Lopez, J. (1980). *Música y Folklore de Colombia*, Plaza y Janes, Bogotá.

Rhodes, W. (1956), 'On the subject of Ethnomusicology', *Ethnomusicology Newsletter* 7, pp. 1–9.
Vega, C. (1944), *Panorama de la Música Popular en Argentina*, Editorial Losada, S.A., Buenos Aires.
Vega, C. (1966), 'Mesomusic: an essay on the music of the masses', *Journal of the Society for Ethnomusicology*, X, 1, pp. 1–17 (Latin-American Issue)

Discography

A *Commercial recordings*
América Libre, Conjunto América Libre (Philips (Colombia) 634 6134. 1979)
El Chambú, Conjunto Rumba Brava, Canta Manuél Agustín (CBS 43 449, 1978, 45 rpm)
Mi Nariño, Ronda Lírica, Canta Bolívar Mesa (Sonolux LP 12-588)
Paz y Alegría, (Philips (Colombia) 10380-1, 2 records, 1977-8)

B *Original recordings*
Chambú – Conjunto América Libre (rec. Broere/Moore, Pasto, 14 March 1979)
Emoción (Pasillo, D. R. de A.) – Trío Santa Barbara (rec. Broere/Moore, Pasto, 3 January 1979)
Jota – Conjunto Chirimía 'Pascual de Andagoya' (rec. Broere/Moore, Buenaventura, July 1978)
Cumbria – Conjunto Chirimía 'Colombia Negra' (rec. van Amstel, Amsterdam, June 1982)

The system of *canzone* in Italy today

A *canzone* is a musical event of short duration (an average of three or four minutes) with lyrics. The system of *canzone* accepts sound selection, notational and structural conventions of the system of European written tradition, including those variations which are derived from contamination with Afro-American, Latin-American and European folk music. Within this system, the principal characteristics of which we will take as read, the *canzone* can be considered a short strophical composition (intending this term in the wider sense of a repetition of similar parts) consisting of a melody which is highly influenced by the rhythmic scansion of the spoken language, usually accompanied. The melodic, harmonic, rhythmic and timbric character of the *canzone* can vary freely within the described system (with differences from genre to genre) but with the exclusion of polyphony and of the techniques of the so-called New Music of the post-war period. Formal and technical rules alone are not sufficient to isolate the sub-system of *canzone*. It is obvious that what has been said up to now can also be applied to some forms and genres of cultivated music – within the considered musical system – which no-one would dream of listing as *canzoni*, whilst at the same time recognising the historical and cultural relationship that exists, for example, between *canzone* and aria, *romanza* and *Lied*. The purpose of this study is not that of listing all the rules on the basis of which a cultivated musical system may be distinguished from that of popular, light or mass music (a distinction which can be taken as read, here, or as the object of specific research). I believe we can accept a definition which limits the set of formal and technical rules mentioned to the sphere of popular music. This is the important point here: it is not necessary to give a

complete list of the *canzone* sub-system rules, but to show 1) that a
definition of *canzone* using these theoretical terms is possible and
2) that some caution is necessary. Proof of this last point can be seen
in the fact that whilst in Italian the term *canzone*, apart from vocal or
instrumental forms of the Renaissance period, is without doubt
limited to the area of popular music, the same cannot be said of its
equivalent in other languages. The fact that *Lied* is not ꞏ .ᴄislatable
as *canzone* without a series of explanations, proves that Italians and
Germans wishing to discuss 'songs' must work from a reasonably
pedantic definition such as the one given. However, I think that the
English word *song* can be used from now on whenever it is intended
in a formal sense, using the Italian *canzone* when referring to the
system or to the genre *canzone d'autore* only.

The genres of *canzone*

The following principal genres based on the form *canzone* (song) are
present in the Italian musical system today: the traditional song, the
pop song, the 'sophisticated' song, the *canzone d'autore*, the political
song, the rock song, and the children's song.

This does not exclude the existence of other genres, which are
however considered sub-genres of those listed. The case of musical
events which are attributed to more than one genre at the same time
is also frequent: *canzone d'autore* and rock song, *canzone d'autore*
and political song, and so on.

The differences between one genre and another will be analysed
here with reference to the types of generic rules I have discussed
elsewhere.[1]

Formal and technical rules

From the point of view of the overall formal structure, only
traditional song obeys a rule which governs the use of a particular
form derived from the *romanza*. The other genres have no specific
forms. However, form is influenced by technical rules which touch
on other structural rules, and which are linked to semiotic rules:
these are rules pertaining to the level of structural complexity of the
single genres. They range from maximum simplicity – recognisable
from the number and regularity with which the single elements are
repeated – for the pop song or children's song, to maximum

complexity for the sophisticated song. One must bear in mind, however, that the same criteria are not always valid for the lyrics: in this case the *canzone d'autore* is at the highest level of complexity, with regard to richness of vocabulary, rhetoric and syntax. Both in the music and in the lyrics the different levels of complexity are expressed in the syntax, intended in the wider sense of relationship between parts. Pop, rock and children's songs are paratactic, traditional and sophisticated songs are syntactic, whilst the political song and the *canzone d'autore* are syntactic with regard to the lyrics but not necessarily to the music.

From the melodic and harmonic point of view, the model for traditional song is Puccini, whilst all the stylistic variations which emerged after the fifties can be excluded. In this sense the traditional song, if only from a musical point of view, is conservative and nationalistic. On the other hand the sophisticated song is cosmopolitan and adopts as its own the most fashionable musical styles even if they belong to other genres, as does the pop song. Compared to the pop song, however, the sophisticated song is decidedly richer, especially from a harmonic point of view. The children's song and the rock song in their choice of musical materials respect their international rules of genre: in the first case using the elementary tonal functions with melodies based on arpeggios and fragments of the major scale, and in the second using blocks of chords together with model melodies with a clear blues influence. It must be said that these formal rules referring to the rock song, vague in themselves, are also weak when compared to the fairly rigid rules of the traditional song. In other words the rock genre can use songs which respect the formal pattern of traditional song but not vice versa. The same formal tolerance under the melodic–harmonic profile applies to the *canzone d'autore* and to the political song. In both these cases we can speak today of a preference for chord blocks and melodies derived from various European folk traditions as well as from American country blues.

From a rhythmic point of view the widest variety of tempos and meters is found in the sophisticated song and in the traditional song: this last saves itself from the abundant syncopation to be found in the sophisticated song, which is influenced more than any other by jazz. The tendency to respect the strong accents in a bar is at its highest in the children's song, whilst the pop song and the rock song are those where the rhythmic pulse must always be in evidence. The *canzone d'autore* is fairly open on this point, whilst the political song usually has a clear and definite rhythm.

Strictly connected with these rhythmic conventions, but moving on to orchestration, we can see that pop, rock and children's song base their rhythmic scansion on drums (and so does sophisticated song but with a more varied distribution of accents). Political song tends to do without, accepting folk percussion instruments instead (exceptions to this rule are very recent). The *canzone d'autore* oscillates between the rules of other genres, whilst the traditional song tends to accept drums only when drowned by violins.

It is almost impossible to think of the traditional song without a kind of symphony orchestra. Up to the moment of its transformation into an exhibition of songs of various genres promoted by the record industry, the Festival of San Remo was a cult centre for traditional song, and it had an orchestra containing string quintet, woodwind, brass and a modern rhythm section. Songs were also repeated by a small night-club group in order to demonstrate their adaptability to small groups, but on the record released the big orchestra was always present. The sophisticated song also has a rich instrumental section, even a luxurious one. The 'musical' concept it tries to put across is that no expense has been spared in the arrangement. Pop song has no specific rules, if not that it refuses both an excessive poverty and an excessive virtuosity, which would be acceptable in rock song. Rock song has a characteristic, 'international' timbre, as does the children's song. The *canzone d'autore* today basically accepts the instrumental set up of rock (drums, bass, electric guitar, keyboards) plus acoustic guitar, which is the favourite instrument of most of today's *cantautori*. In political song acoustic guitar is still dominant, occasionally accompanied by folk instruments. Electrification is still considered a violation (no less than for Dylan at Newport).

The technical capacity of instrumentalists is connected to instrumental groups: for string, woodwind and French horn sections, both for traditional and sophisticated songs, elements, both current and obsolete, from symphonic orchestras are used. The other brass players, saxes and rhythm sections use jazz origins or draw on the idiom of dance orchestras. In pop, children's, rock songs and *canzone d'autore*, autodidacts predominate. In common with most countries where the musical industry is highly developed, the recording of discs which themselves influence live performance is in the hands of a restricted group of session men, who are proud of their ability to perform in various genres. Technical competence is therefore standardised. It is obvious that, when left to play what they like, these musicians tend towards that which is almost everywhere known as 'fusion' music. For the many unwritten parts the producer, whose job is to organise the respect or violation of the rules of genre, communicates with session men using examples of genre, such as: 'This is a pop song: don't play that kind of Jaco Pastorius bass'.

The amateur status of the political song separates the technical skills of its players from those of session men, and also from the session men's fetishism for big name instruments; a *cantautore* (not his accompaniers) can be a fairly poor player of his instrument.

Composers of traditional or sophisticated songs generally work using a piano, the others more often a guitar; for other genres piano is not excluded, except in the political song – where the composer is often the performer as well – for obvious historical problems of availability. In each of these cases the instruments connote the degree of knowledge of the techniques of classical composition.

Noticeable differences can be seen from a vocal point of view. In traditional song the requirements of intonation, extension and voice power are close to those for operetta, especially for male voices; whilst sophisticated song adds the need for competence in the techniques of emission deriving from jazz and of a typically feminine nature. The good male singer is a tenor and sings traditional songs, the good female singer is a star of musicals (a genre that, however, does not exist in Italy) and sings sophisticated songs.

Children's songs are sung by children, or by singers of various genres who imitate the voice most adults consider should be used when speaking to children.

Pop song does not require particular vocal gifts, whilst rock song requires a notable extension towards high notes, and phonetically a highly accentuated vocal mask. In political song ideological attention is given to the modes of traditional folk singing, but practice tends towards an operatic model, whilst accepting a popular type of deformation of the model.

In the *canzone d'autore*, things that might be considered mistakes of intonation and emission or bad pronunciation in other genres are accepted as characteristics of individual personality, which is of primary importance in this genre.

Finally, we come to the rules governing lyrics. The tendency of the *canzone d'autore* towards individual characterisation can be seen above all in its lyrical vocabulary, which is richer and more open to literary suggestions. Among other genres, a rich lexicon can also be found in sophisticated and political song, where the influence of the written language is also evident, but, obviously, pertaining to other types of literature. Certain expedients connoting a lower, old fashioned form of poetry, like putting the adjective before the noun (which is admitted in Italian, but not frequent), or apocope to obtain words accented on the last syllable (*amor* instead of *amore*), are typical of the traditional song, and in the *canzone d'autore* constitute only individual variants. The poetical character of the *canzone d'autore* is more commonly based on preference for metaphors. A big problem for all genres of Italian *canzone* is that of words accented on the last syllable, especially where the English and American musical influence is strongly felt. The ideology of the rock song genre, for example, is that the Italian language is not suitable for this music, and that it is sung in Italian only for questionable commercial reasons. Italian rock singers are all trying to persuade their record producers to let them conquer the world market by singing in English. Many rock and pop song composers and also perhaps a few *cantautori* compose their melodies singing in a false English which they then translate into Italian. This results in a vast amount of words accented on the last syllable, and since these are very limited in number in Italian, repetition and impoverishment of vocabulary are automatic.

Semiotic rules

Textual strategies vary from genre to genre. Political songs must show without doubt that the world they speak of is the real world, as it is today or as it was during a particular moment in history. Traditional, pop, rock and sophisticated songs show a possible world which is an elementary variant of the real one, a scene in which the listener can take the place of the song's protagonist. Generational and sociological connotations can vary in these genres, but not the identification mechanism. This is also valid for children's song, where the possible world coincides more obviously with the infantile imagination, which cannot be denied to contain a reality comparable to the real world of an adult.

The case of the *canzone d'autore* is different: the listener must always remember that the song's protagonist is another person and, if there is identification, it is directly with the singer, not with the protagonist of each song. The *cantautore* is a poet to whom the listener relates: this will be shown later to be a fairly recent rule.

To this we can connect the aesthetic and metalinguistic functions which predominate in the *canzone d'autore*. Traditional and sophisticated songs are also objects of aesthetic attention, but the principal communicative function is the emotional one, as in pop, children's and rock songs. In rock there is a big imperative component, whilst political song often has a referential and emotional function and is exempt by rule from aesthetic judgement.

Since a song is a complex system of signs, the various communicative functions are sustained in various degrees by the component signs. In the musical event consisting of one song only, aesthetic attention is concentrated mainly on lyrics in the case of *canzone d'autore*, on the vocal interpretation of a traditional song and on music in a sophisticated song (with other contributing elements of course). Obviously one can say that any one song is 'beautiful', but what I have been trying to underline is that in some genres a particular self-reflexivity is essential before a certain song can become a part of that genre. The iconographic codes of record sleeves and photos of singers are also adapted to the aforementioned communicative functions.

Prosemic codes are closely bound to the spatial structure of the places in which musical events of various genres are performed. That these are codes of space and not simple derivations of the economy of a genre can be seen by noting that certain typical distances are observed even in places not usually associated with that genre. So a typical theatrical set up with audience in seats will be seen in a traditional or sophisticated song concert even when held in the open air, whilst the fact that the audience stands or sits on the ground marks a conventional line between performances of political songs and *canzone d'autore*, thus demonstrating that these codes are not only linked to the average age of the audience.

Children's songs exist exclusively on records or in television, whilst a rock concert tends to offer a spatial relationship between musicians and audience of a dictatorial nature. An interesting aspect of prosemic rules in Italian *canzone* is the fact that there are very few places suitable for holding musical shows in Italy, so that the various genres are often performed in the same places. This does not stop violation of the rules from being noticed: this shows that a rule of genre is not established as a statistical fact but through the opposition to other rules and the relationship with the whole system. For example, the opinion shared by the *canzone d'autore* community is that the best place to hold a recital is in a theatre with low acoustic resonance, in which the audience can be near the stage dominating it from above rather than being dominated, and without the audience being too spread out. Such a theatre probably does not exist in Italy.

One of the reasons why some *cantautori* have started using a form of concert similar to a rock concert in recent years can be traced to the lack of suitable facilities. You cannot entertain your audience between one song and the next or count on the fact that everyone will see your expression of suffering when you are reduced to the size of a pin in the middle of a stadium. It can be seen from this how the spatial codes are connected to gestural, mimical and facial codes. Due to the lack of detailed study on this subject, for which the numerous photographs existing would provide abundant material, this subject will be dealt with in the next section, dedicated to codes of behaviour.

Behaviour rules

The instrument that reveals these codes in detail is the television camera, thanks to its capacity for entering the 'private distance' of a singer. Traditional and sophisticated singers are in their element on television; their gestures are no different to those of the presenters (whom they often replace). The pop singer is in his element too, but tends to overdo the smiles and raised eyebrows which reveal his underlying anxiety to please.

The rock singer and the *cantautore* are uncomfortable on television: the former because television is too bourgeois, and is too small for his exaggerated gestures, and the latter because it is too stupid; anyway the *cantautore* must always give the impression of being uncomfortable in front of his audience, because privacy is his 'true' dimension. In either case nervous tics are acceptable. The singer for children has no specific image: in some cases he is a *cantautore* who decides to write children's songs, but in most cases he is an anonymous singer who records the theme song of an afternoon television programme, but who does not appear in public, not even on television. The political singer hardly ever appears on television, and the gestures associated with him are those of the participant in a political meeting, though he is also permitted a degree of the 'privacy' of the *cantautore*.

Rules of conversation and codified etiquette exist for every song genre. For example, there are those regulating the behaviour of interviewer and interviewee, those which say what should happen to a singer after a concert, those referring to the behaviour of the audience and those referring to the relationships between critics and organisers when they meet.

Coverage of all these would take more space than the whole of this study put together: therefore I shall limit myself to the more obvious cases of violation. The semiologist Umberto Eco has said that the difference between comedy and tragedy is that whilst both are cases of violation of rules of behaviour, in a tragedy the broken rule is mentioned frequently, while in a comedy it is never mentioned, thus taking it for granted that everybody knows (except of course the one at whom the laughter is aimed). This, according to Eco, is the reason why Greek tragedies still have an effect on us, whilst for the most part the comicality of comedies is lost. If this theory is valid, then laughter is a sign of transgression of a rule known at least by the people laughing.

In Italy, for example, people laugh if, during a *cantautore*'s press conference, someone asks him if he is going to get married, a perfectly normal question for traditional or sophisticated singers (even if with different meaning from one to the other), and absolutely prohibited for a rock singer (even if the Italian rock singer is not as aggressive as his Anglo-American models, and behaves like a 'good boy' in front of the journalists, just like a pop singer, or is accessible, ironic and moderately intellectual, like a *cantautore*).

An example of how rules of behaviour are linked with the ideology of a genre, and with other rules, comes from the *canzone d'autore*. In reaction to a period during which the *canzone d'autore* was the object of attention by critics in a very pedantic, ideologised way, and in which the *cantautore* had to learn to act like a politician or a philosopher, the opinion spread that in fact these were only songs after all. A *cantautore*'s sentence, 'It's a matter of *canzonette* (light songs)', echoed in songs, interviews, articles and even in the title of a record, sanctioned the implicit rule that a *cantautore* should not make serious declarations longer than one phrase (and then should make fun of that phrase too). Thus an interviewer who quotes Adorno will be laughed at in exactly the same way as the one who speaks of marriage. But the ideological character of this rule can be seen from the fact that no *cantautore* would dream of not following all the other rules that distinguish him from the true producers and singers of *canzonette*, those who work in the fields of traditional or pop songs. First and foremost, no *cantautore* would decline from affirming his sincerity. In traditional or pop song, sincerity is not a problem: no one cares if the singer suffers or is happy in the same way as the song's protagonist, as long as the imitation is plausible and does not disturb the listener's identification with the standard situation described. But no one would stand for a *cantautore* or a political singer who shows false sentiments or ideas. The cases of rock and sophisticated song are slightly different: in these two genres the sociological character of identification is more marked, and therefore we ask for, if not a soul-baring sincerity, at least a higher grade of generational or social credibility.

Social and ideological rules

These rules, at a macro-social level, have nothing to do with statistical consumer data. The working class for example buy mostly pop songs, but in a strict connotative sense the term 'working-class song' generally meant, until a few years ago, political song and today it probably means, if anything, traditional song. Consumption of rock music connotes the social sphere of unemployed and marginalised young people, even if the major part of those attending rock concerts are students from the lower middle and bourgeois classes (since young people in Italy are much more and longer dependent on their families, rock has never had an audience comparable to those of its original countries). Sophisticated song is also ideological in this sense, as it always tries, through its lyrics, arrangements, record sleeves, etc. to connote a social position superior to that of its consumers.

Less easy to locate is children's song: it is legitimate to assume that a large proportion of children's records which enter the charts are bought by adults for them, but their success is so great, constituting a considerable slice of the singles market, that one must believe that children themselves form a consistent part of it.

The *canzone d'autore* (perhaps this is an aspect of its 'sincerity') appears to have a social image which corresponds to its actual area of consumption: that is, lower middle and middle-class intellectuals, students, the Italy of mass scholarisation, the university open to everyone, intellectual unemployment.

At the musical community level, the *canzone d'autore* can be distinguished from the others by the identification between singer and author, in terms of both lyrics and music. This – it must be said – is in spite of the numerous attempts in its history to qualify it simply as art song, or quality song. Probably this rule, to which very few exceptions are tolerated, is due to the particular stress on sincerity: singers cannot be considered sincere if they are singing music, or worse still, lyrics not written by them. To give an example, a song like 'You've got to hide your love away', which according to a famous John Lennon interview is the dividing line of his transformation from pop to that which in Italy is called *canzone d'autore*, could not have been considered a *canzone d'autore* if it had not been ascertained that Paul McCartney had nothing to do with it. But of course Lennon should have sung it alone or with an accompanying group, and not with the Beatles: all the Beatles became, in a way, *cantautori* only when the group split.

Two or three Italian musical groups who could be included in the genre of *canzone d'autore* are barely accepted as such because of this, and when they are it is usual that one member of the group is described as a *cantautore*, and the others his backing group, even if this is clearly not true.

In other aspects, the musical communities of various genres of *canzone* are fairly homogeneous, if we exclude the case of the political song, where the singer is usually also his own manager producer and discographer. This synthesis of roles, but with a more marked division of labour, can be found in other genres as well, but not as a rule.

Economic and juridical rules

With the exception of the political singer, all singers belong to the same economic system, characterised by the presence of the larger record companies and management agencies. But there are differences between one genre and another. The *cantautore*, thanks to his copyrights, can almost double the sum other singers receive from the sale of their records, and since in Italy performance rights are not recognised, he is the only one to earn anything, or a lot, from diffusion by radio or television.

This has created a situation whereby the *cantautore* is less economically dependent on live performances; moreover, until a few years ago it was the rule for *cantautori* to perform alone. Their concerts therefore had only the overheads of advertising, theatre and PA hire, and copyright taxes (of which almost a half are returned to the *cantautore* himself). Today a *cantautore*'s tour is more costly and has assumed a more promotional character. The same applies to rock singers and groups, though these have much higher overheads, must divide royalties and copyrights with far more people, and can count on a proportionally smaller record market compared to the expense. When you know that the average price of a ticket to a *cantautore* or rock concert in Italy is less than half that of other European countries, you can understand why the rock group phenomenon cannot reach really professional levels in Italy: even the most famous groups on the scene, frequently present in record charts, do other jobs, principally as session men, in order to earn their living. The only rock singers able to achieve a certain degree of prosperity though their work are, in fact, *cantautori*.

Pop, traditional and sophisticated singers rely above all on performances in dance halls, which can pay pretty high fees all year, thanks to the fact that there are no particular limits to the price of tickets. For these singers the record is their main promotional vehicle. Children's song, as has been said, is exclusively a recorded product: its economic rule consists in convincing, in various ways I leave to your imagination, TV programmers to choose this or that number as the title song for some Japanese cartoon.

Up until a few years ago political song concerts were offered free by the various political parties and other mass organisations, and frequently groups or singers were commissioned for a series of performances, sometimes with a fixed salary. Then political song was equated with the *canzone d'autore*, which brought about an economic crisis even before an artistic–ideological one, since all the other singers' economic conditions are far inferior to those of the *canzone d'autore*. In this case another factor which characterises the Italian situation is the rigidity with which concert ticket prices are established. The variation between minimum and maximum is the same, 500 lire, within the same group of genres: *canzone d'autore*, rock, political song on one side, traditional, pop and sophisticated on the other. If an increase or decrease on this amount is tried, it can mean a risk of disturbances or desertion (if it costs too little, it is probably worth little); even a minimum increase is a risk. There is a precise idea within the musical community of what a concert should cost: frequently the same person may be willing to spend 7,000 lire in a discotheque and then protest if a rock concert ticket costs 4,000 lire. Inherited from some components of the political movement between 1968 and 1977, this economical, ideological rule afflicts first and foremost those musical genres (such as political song) which identified to the greatest extent with this movement.

And now that history has made its entrance into this study, we should take a closer look at it.

Development of the *canzone d'autore*

The *canzone d'autore* made its appearance at the end of the fifties, in a system of *canzone* radically different from that in existence today. The principal genres in Italian *canzone* at that time were: the Neapolitan or dialect song, the traditional song, the variety show song (a genre which is no longer present) and the night-club song (a genre which has divided and been transformed). Research in the field of folk music began in these years, and there was no political song as a genre (the rebirth of this genre in Italy is connected to the rediscovery of resistance songs within the studies on folklore). At this time there was no children's song genre, American rock songs were consumed in no specific context, and the production of records for simultaneous mass consumption could not yet be said to exist. The *canzone d'autore* was born into this system, from an accumulation of transgressions of the rules of the genres which formed it.

Since the strongest rule of genre in the definition of the *canzone d'autore* is, as we have seen, the joining of the roles of author and singer, it may be useful to look at a few examples of *cantautori ante litteram*, singers and songwriters who had done similar work in the years immediately preceding the birth of the new genre.

Of these, the most famous, outside Italy too, was Domenico Modugno. Modugno's career was marked from the beginning by the search for a characteristic which would become a rule of genre for the *canzone d'autore*: being a 'personality' identifiable with the song's protagonist. Modugno carried on this search first as a dialect singer (born in Puglia, his first song was Sicilian, his next Neapolitan), with a strong vocal characterisation and very particular emission of vowels like 'o' and 'e', which accentuates the popular character of lyrics and music. After a spell in cabaret in Rome, he then entered the musical world of the traditional song, playing the role of an extrovert innovator. The text of his 1955 song, 'Vecchio frac', seems today to be a barely disguised metaphor for his farewell to the old ways of considering show-business and song. Paradoxically, however, the world-wide triumph of 'Volare (Nel blu dipinto di blu)' elevated Modugno's 'traditional' characteristics at the expense of his personality as an autonomous creator: 'Volare', instead of becoming the first song of a new genre, was the last great celebration of the traditional song, a modern version of 'O sole mio'. Modugno's personality, from then on, was more useful to television, cinema and theatre (*Mackie Messer* with Strehler) than to the *canzone d'autore*.

Of different origins were Renato Carosone and Fred Buscaglione. In fact, neither of them wrote their own songs (this was also true for many of Modugno's songs), neither were they soloists (they were both leaders of small night-club groups), and their personalities were more those of variety entertainers than *cantautori*.

What brought them closer to the dawning *canzone d'autore* was the fact that they realised the deterioration of existing genres, and showed the will to renovate the tired framework of Italian *canzone*: Carosone and Buscaglione did this by using satire or parody, both in the lyrics and in the music. There are notable differences between the two: Carosone mixed Neapolitan and American elements in a sometimes moralistic satire of the Italians' dependence on foreign cultural models, or in the parody of tear-jerking traditional songs. Buscaglione played the role of a provincial Humphrey Bogart, distorting the American cliché in the way he Italianized it for himself.

But in spite of their great success, in spite of the modernity and realism of their songs, no new genre was born after Carosone and Buscaglione. However innovative, their ideas were tied to mechanisms of consumption which were becoming decadent (night-clubs), whilst the time in which more could have been made of their visual impact was still far off. It is significant that today Carosone and Buscaglione records have become a cult with certain audiences, who consider them the unconscious anticipators not of the *canzone d'autore* but of Frank Zappa and cabaret-rock.

The *canzone d'autore* was born at a time when the visual image of a singer was given mainly through magazines, partly through record sleeves (many singles were still sold in a standard sleeve with no photo), whilst the only television channel broadcasting popular music was occupied with review shows or with already famous guests, traditional or foreign. The media through which the industry could reach the audience promotionally were mainly two: radio and jukeboxes. The radio, firmly under the control of the Christian Democrats, had a 'listener's commission' which exercised (and would continue to do so for many years) censorship, principally of lyrics but also of music (using technical pretexts). This meant that the only means for bringing new ideas to the public's attention, to the young audience in particular, was through the jukebox or record shops, whose proprietors were still in the habit of letting customers listen to a wide selection of new records without any obligation to buy.

This being the situation, it was easier to get mass diffusion for a product which was not too far removed from existent standards, not too attached to a definite way of consumption, and whose elements of difference, if any, were easily identifiable through the most important media of the moment.

The first song by a *cantautore* to have success was 'Arrivederci' by Umberto Bindi, not in the composer's version but that of Marino Barreto Jr., a night-club singer of Brazilian origins. Apart from the good musical construction and the high level of production compared to that of light songs of the day, there were two elements which contributed to the song's success and helped create two rules for the new genre: the lyrics which did not overdramatise the classical situation of two lovers parting, substituting the emblematic *addio* (goodbye) with a more day-to-day greeting; the voice, which even if not that of the songwriter, thanks to a certain hardness in the pronunciation and the aphonia of Barreto, broke with the tradition of 'belcanto' tenors, emphasising sincerity such that 'correct' vocal performance became a thing of secondary importance. Whilst Carosone's parodies of Italian drama (in songs like 'E la barca torno sola') only defined what could be done in a negative way, and whilst Modugno had only brought up to date classically beautiful Italian singing, the success of 'Arrivederci' demonstrated positive variants of the song model within its most popular theme, that of love.

'Arrivederci' was followed by 'Il nostro concerto', sung by Bindi himself, which accentuated another characteristic of the *canzone d'autore* in this early period, the search for good musical quality, and there was in the ideology of the dawning genre, a suggestion that the task was to save the Italian *canzone* from the stupidity and standardisation to which the record publishers' routine had brought it. Not by chance were men of letters involved in this ferment – Italo Calvino wrote lyrics for the group Cantacronache – and songwriters willing to sing their own songs to prove to uncourageous publishers that they could be a success.

The birth of the *canzone d'autore* took place at a moment of great transformation for the music industry: the music publishers, who, until a few years before had wanted their songs sung by as many singers as possible (success was measured by the number of versions made), were beginning to integrate with the record industry, and the success of a song depended increasingly on one performer and one version. A single radio play could reach far more people than any number of live performances. Within a few years publishers had assumed the role we know today: the means through which the record industry is indemnified, if possible with a profit, for the promotional costs of radio and television.

The fact that with the *canzone d'autore* songwriter and singer become one (and the same thing would happen with the Beatles a few years later) cannot be considered simply a coincidence. The *cantautore*, who maybe sings out of tune, but who has a good song and arrangement, was worth more to the record industry than a musical score which could sell only to a few hundred small dance orchestras.

The failure of the hypothesis of radical innovation (put forward by early performers like Cantacronache) is understandable – it was still attached to the old conception of song as a text, independent of its musical performance, and therefore adequately documented on cheaply produced records (it is also understandable that the main result of the Cantacronache's success was the re-establishment of political song). However, the capitalist industry was no more far-sighted. In the beginning the recording company Ricord, who signed the first *cantautori* from Genoa (Bindi, Paoli, Tenco) and from Milan (Jannacci, Gaber), did not have too much faith in the phenomenon, considering it limited to a bourgeois intellectual audience, for the most part cabaret fans. It is true that the cultural

horizon of the individual *cantautore* was literary, with influences
from French existentialism – gained from the *chansonniers* – or jazz
and rock (both were of interest in Italy only to a few connoisseurs,
both were therefore intellectualised), but it is also true that there
already existed a vast student audience ready to recognise in these
imported values an alternative to the then current Italian productions. This audience did not live in garrets, did not fall in love
because they had nothing better to do, did not go to dubious bars (all
situations described in *cantautore*'s songs of that period) but they
were nevertheless more willing to relate to this type of life, in reality
lived by few, than to the mammas or broken hearts of traditional
songs.

The important thing was not a particular conception of life, but a
general non-conformism, connected with a certain musical renovation. A new generation of consumers, young consumers, was being
born in Italy, and their main characteristic was that they opposed
the musical consumption of older generations.

It was not just by chance, therefore, that the real push towards the
diffusion of the *canzone d'autore*, along with the invention of the
name *cantautore* (in 1960), came for the multinational company
RCA. The first *cantautori* of Italian RCA (Mecci, Vianello,
Fidenco, all from Rome) were much more juvenile than their
colleagues from Genoa or Milan, and their anti-conformism was
much less literary (one song was titled 'I Hate All Old Women').
The music too was new, thanks more to the use of special
arrangements and recording techniques than for reasons of compositional structure; and it was far closer to American styles than the
Genoese or Milanese were. If Neil Sedaka did not have such
atrocious pronunciation his Italian records which were very
successful, could easily be confused with those of the first Roman
cantautori. In fact, after a short time those for whom this name was
coined stopped being true *cantautori*, contributing, rather, to the
birth of the modern Italian pop song: fashionable, easy to listen to
and realistic. But the genre *canzone d'autore* was already established,
and RCA covered the situation by signing some of the best Genoese
cantautori, using the best arrangers and launching them on a vast
scale, during a period when this American company had the
monopoly of the Italian market.

From a tired musical system, in need of renovation, the birth of
two new genres was thus achieved: the pop song, which under

American influence united in the same genre the anomalies created in the preceding years by Adriano Celentano's rock and the so-called *urlatori* (shouters); and the *canzone d'autore* (which at that time was called 'quality song') as the interpreters of what we today call sophisticated song began to emerge from the world of light songs, *canzonette*, by singing songs of the *cantautori*.

However much the musical journalists of the time talked about the 'difficult' nature of the *canzone d'autore* (comparing it with 'escapism' of other genres) the *cantautore* was still regarded as a songwriter rather than a poet. This observation was valid both from the point of view of the ideology of genre and from that of the objective importance of the lyrics compared to the music. But many other new things were happening: the world-wide success of the Beatles moved pop innovation in another direction, whilst the professional songwriters soon understood that a song of quality could be made without using the old models, and using new interpreters. The *cantautori* found that a considerable part of the young audience (and of the bourgeois audience too) was being taken away from them. And they also found themselves with limited autonomy within their genre, having to compete with beat music on the one hand and the more commercial song genres on the other, even in their own territory. The suicide of Luigi Tenco at the 1967 San Remo Festival, when his song failed to reach the final, is symptomatic, whilst the world-wide success of Bob Dylan already indicated a new road: a song form nearer to traditional folk ballad than to the melodramatic model, poorer in melody but metrically freer, richer in syllables, thanks to the possibility of repeating notes and even recitative.

The first to follow this model was Francesco Guccini. His first record was released in 1967, but some of his songs had already been successful in the preceding years when sung by rock groups. Guccini translated the tones of Dylan's protest and apocalypse as well as those of the beat poets into Italian; the anarchical, visionary nature of his early lyrics brought him to the fore in the climate of the rigorous protest of the reborn political song (and the domesticated protest of other genres – all Italian songs at that time were protesting against or for something).

The *canzone d'autore*'s student audience had their attention fixed on social and political motives, and this made them concentrate more and more on lyrics, considering them the only measure of a song's quality. Whereas in rock – which was based on English 'progressive' models – lyrics were an excuse to have a voice participating, or, at the most, an illustration of the music, in the *canzone d'autore* and in political song the music became a background only occasionally illustrating the lyrics.

During the early seventies, when political song appeared to have covered the whole area of the *canzone d'autore*, one of the first generation *cantautori*, Giorgio Gaber, made his debut in the theatre with a show consisting of songs and monologues, indicating his desire to maintain the autonomy of his genre, and proving the importance now assumed by the verbal text. It was by putting the accent decidedly on lyrics and on their poetic function (rather than on the mainly referential one of the political song) that the *canzone d'autore* achieved its final comeback. For a brief period the new *cantautori* (such as Francesco De Gregori and Antonello Venditti) were presented as representatives of 'new song' (by an association with the 'nueva cancion chilena' of the Unidad Popular period), but this political connotation was soon overcome, and, especially with regard to De Gregori, the new singers/songwriters were spoken of as 'poets'.

In 1974 the genre received its first official constitution, with the initial meeting of the *canzone d'autore* ('Rassegna della canzone d'autore') organised by the Tenco Club at San Remo.

The reborn autonomy of the genre met with some difficulty: a big impression was made by the 'political trial' conducted by the audience against Francesco De Gregori during a concert at the Palalido in Milan, a trial which ended with some people inviting De Gregori 'to commit suicide like Mayakovsky'. The real accusation was that a singer who had been considered a political singer was not following the rules of that genre, *not* that he was a non-political *cantautore*. But the equation *cantautore* = poet was quickly established (the formula of the condemnation implied it), showing itself in various ways, from the poetic content claimed by amateur imitators, to the collaboration between a *cantautore*, Lucio Dalla, and a 'real' poet, Roversi; naturally this affirmation was not unrelated to the falling tide of political experiences in the early seventies – the average Italian's culture locates poetry in a purely private, subjective life.

In this concentration of aesthetic attention, the impoverishment of the musical content was soon noticed: the answer – an answer also to foreign competition – was richer arrangements. It was the period of the triumph of disco-music, and many rock groups were in difficulty as a result. Fabrizio De André, one of the *cantautori* of the sixties, went on tour with PFM, one of the best known rock groups, and had great success.

'At last,' everyone said, 'the *canzone d'autore* has its own musical dimension.' But this tour demonstrated something else besides: that, in spite of the fact that big rock concerts in Italy had been the scene of disturbances for years, to the point where foreign singers and groups avoided the country until 1979, the *cantautori* could fill a gap, maintaining something of the political meeting and integrating it with the rituals of a rock concert. The height of the *cantautori* success was reached in 1970 with the colossal Dalla–De Gregori tour, when these two appeared in stadiums like rock stars do, and like rock stars were greeted by the lighting of thousands of matches. The first foreign rock star to return to Italy was Patti Smith, who was presented as a *cantautrice*, 'poetess of rock', but the following year, in spite of the successful tours of Edoardo Bennato and Angelo Branduardi, was a year of crisis for the *canzone d'autore*, at least according to the Club Tenco members, who entitled the discussion at their congress: 'Rock Versus Canzone'. The *canzone d'autore* had been pushed so close to rock (as it was years before to political song) that it was beginning to feel the consequences of the competition financially (this was the year of a world comeback of rock) and in technical terms had to redefine its own confines and ideology. This was a task which involved not only the critics but the whole *canzone d'autore* community, so that, whilst the specialists in the field were discussing a musical revaluation which excluded the rock aspects and easy solutions in terms of arrangement, the audience acclaimed the success of Enzo Jannacci and Paolo Conte. The former was among the *cantautori* of the first generation, the one decidedly the least literary, tending more towards comedy (thanks also to his collaboration with Dario Fo) whilst the latter, after writing successful pop songs, started recording by himself only in 1975.

Jannacci is a doctor, Conte a lawyer; both are over forty, both sing in an untidy way with a certain gestural embarrassment, both have a solid musical preparation even if they are self-taught. Both use a particularly rich vocabulary, which is characterised by social extraction or geographical location (Jannacci lives in Milan, Conte in Asti, a small town in Piedmont); both knowledgeably mix poetic and prosaic tones, both use metrics without recourse to banal words accented on the last syllable. If their songs are musically fairly well characterised (with frequent stylistic quotations from various genres or periods), arrangements appear deliberately anonymous and out of fashion.

In other words these two accumulate a series of violations of the current rules of the *canzone d'autore*, partly by returning to the character of the origins, and partly by showing that they share the hope for renewal, whilst respecting many of the fundamental rules. It is possible that a future study of the *canzone d'autore* will show as rules of a future period features which today appear as individual characteristics of these two *cantautori*.

Note

1 This is the second half of a long article. The first (theoretical) half was published in *Popular Music Perspectives*, IASPM, Exeter and Gothenberg, 1982 and is reprinted in Simon Frith and Andrew Goodwin (eds), *On Record*, Pantheon, New York, 1989.

The field of popular music in Israel

Introduction

Being an immigrant country of people from various cultures, and lacking a clear and given cultural code for the immigrants to learn, Israel is a unique arena for stresses and conflicts between different cultural patterns, on the one hand, and for processes of merging and mutual influence between such patterns, on the other hand.

The field of popular music in Israel is a clear illustration of this. The aim of this paper is to review this field as a framework for the action of different social forces negotiating the nature and meaning of popular music in Israel. It should be obvious that some of these forces are active in preserving an existing situation while others are active in an attempt to change it. The paper will present, therefore, a synchronic sociological picture of the field at the present time, while pointing at both kinds of forces.

The understanding of popular music as a field in which different social forces are active in the production of cultural goods (Bourdieu, 1983) involves a discussion of several central topics: the different musical genres in the field and their social context; the hierarchy between those genres; the social and cultural factors involved in producing and preserving the hierarchy; the social forces and musical genres in conflict with the existing situation, and the dynamics of change resulting from this conflict.

The genres composing the field

1 The songs of eretz Israel (EI songs)

The word *eretz* means 'land' in Hebrew. This genre is often identified as the Israeli folk music, the kind of music taken-for-granted as 'typical' Israeli. The origins of the style are Russian

ballads and East-European rhythms, brought to Israel by the
founders of Israeli society in the first half of this century. Over
the years, however, French and American folk influences have
penetrated the genre. The song lyrics generally deal with national
themes (wars, history, the Bible), with agricultural topics, the
scenery of the land and with specific Israeli phenomena (the
Kibbutz, for example). The creators – composers and lyricists – are
not, for the most part, anonymous. The arrangements tend to be
acoustic, based on accordion, guitar and piano. EI songs are played
and performed at ceremonial occasions and are strongly connected
to another unique Israeli phenomenon: *shirah batzibur* (singing in
public).[1] EI songs symbolise national consensus and patriotism.

2 Oriental music

The term 'oriental music' has in Israel a very specific meaning. It
relates to the genre which is the result of changes to the ethnic music
of Oriental Jews in the country (Shiloah and Cohen, 1983, 1985).
This music is currently a mixture of influences from Mediterranean
and Middle-Eastern cultures, played with rock instrumentation:
electric guitars, synthesisers, drum-machines. The most remarkable style here is a fusion of Greek and Yemenite music, although
under the same headline fall also Italian ballads in the San Remo
festival style and Spanish traditional music. 'Oriental music' should
be understood, therefore, as a musical genre in the sense of a
'cultural unit' (Fabbri, 1982) and not as a musical style. The genre is
widespread mainly on cassettes, of which a large proportion are
pirated. The phenomenon resembles the cassette market of local
music in other small countries such as Tunisia and Sri-Lanka
(Wallis and Malm, 1984). Performers of 'oriental' music reach their
audience mainly through family festivities or specific night-clubs.
This musical genre is usually identified as 'belonging' to the lower
social strata, composed mainly of Jews of oriental origin.

3 Israeli pop

Israeli pop is the result of the meeting between the tradition of EI
songs and the western popular music industry. It is hard to
generalise here in regard to musical style, but it is possible to delimit
Israeli pop between two extremes. At one end we find the influence
of both EI songs and contemporary rock and jazz, the result being
the individual music of specific musicians: sophisticated in its

compositions and arrangements, played on a wide range of instruments, highly conscious of technological aspects of production and reproduction, and very 'personal' in its lyrics. At the other end we find Israeli versions of typical western pop and rock phenomena. Whilst on the one hand there are standard products, catchy and simple, made to the measure of the Eurovision song contest (Israel has won this contest twice), on the other hand, there are *avant-garde* rock and jazz musicians, some of them performing their songs in English.

Between these two extremes, Israeli pop exists as a mixture of a variety of musical styles. Next to the music we find here the typical patterns of the popular music industry: 'stars', 'hit-parades', the short life-span of songs, etc. Israeli pop makes up most of the Hebrew music played on the radio and most local record companies' investments are concentrated on it. Pop performers reach their audience through the conventional pattern of concerts in halls or small clubs. Israeli pop is mainly youth-music, but it is hard to relate it to a specific class group. Its 'personal', 'artistic' extreme, however, is usually identified with higher status groups in Israeli society. More than anything else, Israeli pop symbolises the westernization of Israeli popular culture in the last fifteen years.

4 Non-Hebrew popular music

An additional and central component of the field of popular music in Israel is foreign popular music. The Israeli market, despite being small in size, consumes a large quantity of foreign popular music, both on records and in radio broadcasting. Israelis hear and listen to almost every style of western pop from Johnny Mathis to Robert Fripp, from Julio Iglesias to the Residents. British and American contemporary hits – Top Twenty music – constitute most of the music consumed in this genre, but in addition, French and Italian hits are occasionally successful, and in recent years Israelis have been heavily exposed to Brazilian popular music. Foreign pop constitutes half the radio broadcasting of popular music. It arrives in Israel mainly through the local pressing of records by local record companies functioning as the formal representatives or branches of international companies. In addition to records, foreign performers arrive once in a while to give concerts. For example, in recent years, Israelis have been able to see such stars as Julio Iglesias, Gal Costa, Rod Stewart, Dire Straits, Siouxsie and the Banshees, and Peter

Hamill. Again, it is hard to relate foreign sounds to particular groups in Israeli society, since the public is equally exposed to the whole variety of mainstream pop. Some elite groups, however, do tend to prefer specific styles such as art rock or *avant-garde* rock and jazz.

The hierarchy between the genres

Since this is not the place for presenting a structural analysis of Israeli society, it should suffice to state that the stronger groups in Israeli society are, traditionally, those linked to western culture – whether by owning cultural capital, by holding a proclaimed ideology, or by ethnic origin. It follows that the criteria by which the hierarchy between the genres in popular music is established are the criteria that stem from the cultural assumptions of the dominant groups – the point of departure for the evaluation of popular music is that the best sounds will be, musicologically, what in western culture counts in a taken-for-granted manner as 'music'. There are two additional measures of excellence. One is the common view that sees an opposition between standardisation, mass production and economic interests, on the one hand, and musical art as a personal statement (emotional or intellectual) about different aspects of social reality, on the other. The second is the specific aesthetic of popular music in which its technological elements of production as well as reproduction determine its quality – sound production and technology have also become an 'art' (Kealy, 1979).

Consequently, the musical genre that is the least appreciated is oriental music. Since the roots of this music lie in non-western cultures and traditions, even the basic assumption of (western) musicality is not always applicable to it, while the creative consciousness of the creators and performers of oriental music is not clearly moulded. Thus the music is no longer really traditional 'ethnic' music about which it might be said that its aesthetic qualities are different from those of the west and should be understood accordingly, but, at the same time, although oriental music is played on electric and electronic instruments and is recorded in well-equipped studios, the careful attention usually given in pop music to the technical qualities of sound is lacking. The result is that in relation to pure ethnic music the genre is considered as a vulgarisation, while in relation to pop it comes across as inferior and deviant.

In contrast, the musical genre that combines both a highly 'artistic' consciousness and a high level of technological knowhow, is the most highly valued, the most prestigious in the field – this is the genre which merges EI songs with the aesthetics and sophistication of contemporary rock and jazz.

EI songs are highly ranked as far as the older songs – those written twenty or thirty years ago – are concerned. When it comes to newly written songs in this genre, the appreciation is low-key – they are considered as a 'cheap' kind of nostalgia.

Most pop, be it local or foreign, is treated the same as everywhere else in the west. No deep meanings are attributed to it, and a song is judged by its ability to make people dance, to be hummed and to be catchy. Pop is a musical 'taken-for-granted' in the sense of being a normal part of the musical soundscape in both the private and public sphere. Some rock and jazz styles are, however, of a different nature. Most of the public, being unacquainted with them, regard them as another variation of mainstream pop, while certain groups rank them highly.

Another dimension of the hierarchy between the genres, besides prestige and 'quality', is popularity. The most popular genres in Israel are oriental music and mainstream pop. Popularity is measured not only by sales of records and cassettes but also by the success of performers (their ability to fill up halls or to be engaged constantly) and to some extent by radio air-play.

The only genre for which some convergence exists between prestige and popularity is 'artistic' pop. The popularity of EI songs is harder to estimate. The genre does not sell many records, but a substantial part of its repertoire is known to almost all Israelis.

The sharpest contrast exists between the popularity and prestige of 'oriental' music. In terms of sales of its cassettes and busyness of its performers the genre is very popular, but, as mentioned above, it is the least valued of all Israeli pop genres.

This situation, in which a discrepancy exists between the value attributed to a genre and its popularity, can last only if most of the forces active in the popular music field give it a certain degree of legitimacy. In Israel they do not and established pop values have been subject, in recent years, to a frontal attack from performers of oriental music. But before being able to understand the resulting cultural negotiations we need to examine the mechanisms for the reproduction and maintenance of the prestige hierarchy.

The 'gatekeeping' system

A number of factors join together in the preservation of prestige. Since the cultural and social circumstances which led to its formation are not our concern here, it should be stated that the prestige hierarchy has an ideological significance. The placement of 'artistic' pop and EI songs at the top of the hierarchy and of oriental music at its bottom is in accordance with one of the basic social stresses in Israeli society – the one between Jews of Eastern-European origin and Jews from North Africa and the Middle East (Smooha, 1978; Ben-Rafael, 1982).

The central factors in the ideological presentation of different social worlds and social realities are the mass media (Hall, 1977). In the specific case of popular music, the most important ones are radio and the music press, which function as a system for the 'production of meaning' of musical genres (Frith, 1976) and for the 'production of belief' about the relationship between them (Bourdieu, 1980).

1 Radio

Hebrew broadcasting can be found at five points of the radio scale. Four of them are part of a governmental body (Israel Broadcasting Authority) and the fifth one is a military station (*Galei Zahal*). Two of them are responsible for most of the popular music broadcasting: *Reshet Giomel*, the IBA pop-station, and *Galei Zahal*. The general policy of both stations is to play at least 50 per cent Hebrew music.

The prestige hierarchy, as a cultural reality, is materialised through several radio practices. First, there are variations in the amount of airtime allocated to different types of music. It has already been mentioned that most of the music played on the radio is Top Twenty music, both from the Hebrew and foreign charts. 'Artistic' pop songs also take up a significant amount of the Hebrew play lists so that the musical soundscape produced by these two radio stations contains mostly pop music. 'Oriental' music gets a very small hearing. Secondly, variations exist in the pattern of playing of the several types of music played on the radio. One of them is 'mere' playing on talk programmes. Music here fills the gaps between different parts of a programme or simply signals a shift from one subject to another. Tracks are chosen for their general appeal, because they will not cause any 'disturbance' to potential listeners. Some music is culturally 'natural', in these terms, other music is therefore 'unnatural'. Again, there are music programmes which have no specific title, programmes that simply supply a musical soundscape for its own sake. Here too, the music played is the music taken to be 'undisturbing', 'light', familiar and liked. Practically all of the music played in these two kinds of programmes is mainstream pop (Hebrew and foreign), 'artistic' pop or EI songs; the playing of oriental music is very rare. Mainstream broadcasting thus provides a public musical world in which pop and EI songs are taken for granted while oriental music is unfamiliar. In addition there are programmes dedicated to a specific genre or style. Two genres have featured steadily and continuously in such programmes in recent years: oriental music and *avant-garde* or 'pure' rock and jazz. However, while special playing frames for rock and jazz contribute to the meaning of these musics as genres which require careful listening, the special framing of 'oriental music' comes across as a form of 'ghetto' – the implication is that there are special programmes for oriental music because it is unsuitable for playing otherwise.

The different interpretations of these genres stem from the varying manner in which music is discussed and referred to by radio presenters. In progammes where the music is played under no specific label, songs are treated in terms of amusement, non-seriousness, in an informal manner and with superlatives. When it comes to the more 'artistic' side of pop, however, presenters tend to refine and modify their formulations. They become slightly formal, shifting to phrases which treat the music 'seriously', referring to the lyrics and production qualities and commenting on songs' musical sophistication.

This tendency becomes extreme in programmes devoted to rock and jazz. Here the music is treated according to patterns taken from high culture art criticism. In contrast, in oriental music progammes, the music is played successively without any verbal interference or, alternatively, presenters adopt a kind of sub-standard, simple folk language (Hebrew slang tends to be oriental in its syntax and in the use of Arabic words).

A last point regarding radio's maintenance of the hierarchy between the genres is that popular music editors and presenters are individuals belonging to the dominant groups in Israeli society – those with a western orientation. It follows that the decisions as to what kind of music will be played, and how it should be treated verbally, are taken from within the cultural and musical world view of these individuals. This world-view adopts the evaluating criteria described above and oriental music (as well as some *avant-garde* rock) has a marginal place in it. Thus these individuals serve, not necessarily in an intentional manner, as 'gatekeepers' of the cultural hierarchy.

2 *The music press*

There is no popular music press in Israel. Most newspapers and magazines do contain, however, sections devoted to reviews of and reports on popular music. Some of the reports or interviews are translated from the western press, mainly those concerning foreign music, but the large proportion of writing in recent years has been local. Here, as on the radio, music journalists are individuals belonging to the culturally dominant groups in Israeli society. It follows that the language used and the terms applied for presenting questions, for reporting on musical events, and for evaluating music are, *a priori*, terms taken from western pop frames of reference. This is most obvious in the record review columns, where young critics apply review standards taken directly from the pages of the British and American rock press. Consequently, both EI songs and oriental music records are seldom reviewed, and when they are, receive negative reviews, simply because the standards applied are strange to these genres.

EI songs' lack of positive record reviews is compensated, in a sense, by reports on the genre and by interviews. These tend to be phrased in a way that flatters the musicians and the performers, creating a feeling of nostalgia. Thus EI songs are placed by the media outside the realm of pop, but in a prestigious status.

In the case of oriental music, the journalistic cover of the genre is concerned with almost everything around the music – from the private and social life of performers to gossip about the amount of cassettes sold – but not with the music itself. The genre is covered and presented as an independent cultural phenomenon existing in its own terms, with its own aesthetics – as a kind of an artistic 'cultural system', to borrow an anthropological concept (Geertz, 1976).

3 *Organisational factors*

In addition to the media, several organisational features of the pop field work to preserve a musical hierarchy. Record companies in

Israel act both as producers of local performers and as representatives of international companies. They print a large variety of foreign pop records, mainly because of reasonable chances to make profit (most of the records cover the costs after selling around 1,000 copies, so it only takes two or three 'gold records' – which in Israel is 20,000 copies – to balance poor sales of many other titles). In the case of Israeli pop, chances for profit are lower, since in order to cover the costs of production a record has to sell around 8,000 copies, which is a high figure for the Israeli record market. Record companies are, therefore, careful in their involvement with local performers, especially with new ones. This leads to a situation where many performers finance their records independently, with the record companies serving as distributors.

Record companies assume anyway that a record's sales potential depends on its radio play and general exposure in the media. As a result, most records manufactured and distributed by established record companies are of performers working in the pop and EI songs genres. (EI song records are either 'evergreens' whose success in the market is guaranteed, or projects financed by public bodies for ideological and educational reasons.)

Oriental music exists mainly on cassettes and hardly at all on records. The reason for this, it appears, is its small share of radio exposure. The cassette player, being portable and easy to carry anywhere led oriental music to find in the audio cassette an efficient means of wide circulation as an alternative to radio broadcasting. The cassettes on which oriental music is produced and distributed are manufactured by small independent entrepreneurs. While some of these entrepreneurs do serve as mediators between the creative side of music – musicians and performers – and the organisational and economic side, many others are engaged in unauthorised reproduction of recorded cassettes, so that a large proportion of the cassette market has the nature of piracy.

In addition, as has already been mentioned, oriental music, musicians and performers are not imbued by the technology which is an inseparable part of pop aesthetics. The production quality of oriental music is, therefore, generally considered 'below standard' in relation to pop products. This, together with the bad quality of printed cassettes, creates a situation in which oriental music is identified with lower qualities of production and products.

Therefore, while all pop styles and EI songs are produced and distributed by large and established record companies, oriental music exists in cassettes of inferior technical quality, produced and distributed through piracy.

Patterns of live performance vary between the genres. It has already been mentioned that EI songs are usually performed at public events and national ceremonies (or as 'singing in public'); it is a rare occasion that an old singer in this genre gives a concert. When, occasionally, pop performers include some EI songs in their programme, it is done as audience-participation in the 'singing in public' pattern. Performing EI songs in this way strengthens the genre's role as a 'national' folk music.

Oriental music, by contrast, grew as a genre out of the traditional music of Oriental Jews. The central occasions for performing this kind of music were religious rituals and family celebrations. The main settings, therefore, for live performances of oriental music were, from the beginning, such festivities as weddings, bar-mitzvas and the like – and this continues to be the dominant pattern. Performances that are not part of family celebrations take place in a similar context – accompanying a meal and making people dance – in specially designated clubs.

A central point here is that the careers of oriental music performers bring only a few of them to concert halls, while most of them continue performing at weddings and family festivities even at the peak of their career. Since the music at this kind of performance is generally 'made to measure', according to requests of the celebrators, careers that are focused around this pattern of performing are considered inferior when measured against a pattern in which the audience arrives at a concert in order to hear and listen to music and only that. The difference between a performing pattern in which music as entertainment is accentuated and a performing pattern in which 'music for music's sake' is the underlying value, is yet another factor working in the maintenance of the hierarchy between the genres.

Change, negotiation and incorporation

The order of things described sociologically above is by no means static; but different forces attempt to bring about changes for different reasons. For example, some EI song musicians would like to protect the genre from its western pop influences and keep it as a unique Israeli style, while a steady nucleus of *avant-garde* and basic rock musicians, as well as some radio editors and journalists, continually try to make Israeli rock more 'artistic' (and more popular) than mainstream pop. The main conflict in recent years, however, has been between oriental music and the rest of popular song. It is too early to be certain yet how this conflict will be resolved but several points are clear by now, and together they shed a certain light on the sociological process.

First, the dispute over musical resources has to be understood in light of the wider conflict in which groups of Jews of oriental origin are demanding a new, or at least different, distribution of economic resources, political power and cultural capital. This is the context in which oriental musicians demand more radio play for their music outside the 'ghetto' programmes, and a different verbal attitude towards their music in general. One aspect of this argument is the claim that oriental music, being widely popular (and Israel is in the orient, geographically), is the 'real' Israeli popular music, as opposed to what is usually identified as 'Israeli music' – EI songs and 'artistic' pop.

Second, the media in general, and particularly the radio, have tried, under pressure, to meet some of these demands – hence the creation of the special oriental shows and more airtime for oriental music in other kinds of programme. The basic criteria that make a record 'suitable' for radio-playing, however, have not changed (quality of technical production, standard Hebrew, and the like). As a result, it is usually only those performers who have made their music sound more like pop who are played on the general pop programmes.

Third, a growing number of musicians and performers of oriental music have adopted the common pop standards of production and musical arrangement. In addition, some of them, usually the more successful, have widened their repertoire by performing music that is not typically oriental.

As a result of these last two developments, oriental music has undergone a modification of its uniqueness as a musical genre with its own aesthetic. The music has become another style or trend in the pluralism of contemporary pop. The fact that the most successful oriental music performers shift to a more ordered production of records and to performing in concert halls (to the point of abandoning their work at family celebrations) contribute to this process.

Finally, a growing number of pop performers and musicians are composing and recording songs influenced by oriental music, which are both highly valued (by the system's 'gatekeepers') *and* widely popular. These songs, despite being 'poppish' in the sophistication of their studio production, meet up musically with pop influenced oriental music and have therefore contributed to the reordering of the genre hierarchy.

The process of change described here is the result, on the one hand, of oriental musicians' demands for a democratisation of Israel's popular music institutions and, on the other hand, of modification of the attitudes of the 'gatekeepers' towards oriental music. This might be understood sociologically in terms of a cultural negotiation over the nature and meaning of Israeli popular music, but as oriental music is, in fact, going 'pop' in its economic organisation, its patterns of performance, its standards of production and its aesthetics, the process of change might equally well be understood as the incorporation of an alternative genre of popular music into the popular music mainstream.

Note

1 'Singing in public' is a pattern of performing music in which a group of people (a small one or a large audience) sit and sing together songs known to everyone. It varies from spontaneous singing of school children on a trip to specially organised events. Sometimes the lyrics are circulated to the audience on a stencil or they are projected in slide form on a screen. An individual playing the accordion or the piano accompanies the singing and 'directs' it. The patterns reflect, in a sense, the ethos of collectivism in Israeli society.

References

Ben-Rafael, E. (1982), *The Emergence of Ethnicity: Cultural Groups and Social Conflict*, Greenwood Press, London.
Bourdieu, P. (1980), 'The production of belief: a contribution to an economy of symbolic goods', *Media, Culture and Society*, II.
Bourdieu, P. (1983), 'The field of cultural production: the economic world reversed', *Poetics*, XII.
Fabbri, F. (1982), 'What kind of music?', *Popular Music*, II.
Frith, S. (1976), *The Sociology of Rock*, Constable, London.

Geertz, C. (1976), 'Art as a cultural system', *Modern Language Notes*, XCI (6).

Hall, S. (1977), 'Culture, the media and the "Ideological Effect" in Curran, J. *et al.*, *Mass Communication and Society*, Edward Arnold, London.

Kealy, E. R. (1979), 'From craft to art: the case of sound mixers and popular music', *Sociology of Work and Occupation*, VI (1).

Shiloah, A. and Cohen, E. (1983), 'The dynamics of change in Jewish oriental ethnic music in Israel', *Ethnomusicology*, XXVII (2).

Shiloah, A. and Cohen, E. (1985) 'Major trends of change in Jewish oriental ethnic music in Israel', *Popular Music*, IV.

Smooha, S. (1978), *Israel, Pluralism and Conflict*, Routledge and Kegan Paul, London.

Wallis, R. and Malm, K. (1984), *Big Sounds from Small People: The Music Industry in Small Countries*, Pendragon Press, New York.

Part 4
Rock and politics

Editor's note

The last section of this book continues Regev's discussion of power and privilege in a more explicit examination of the politics of rock. The papers here address *state* music policies, on the one hand, *nationalist* music ideas and identities on the other. There is, finally, a discussion of the 'world politics' of rock, as articulated by Band-Aid, Live Aid and USA for Africa.

In looking at how governments attempt to manage rock (as in Hungary and Cuba) or promote it (as in Norway and the Netherlands), at rock's own recent pursuit of charitable ends (as with Live Aid), the authors here are all trying to understand how sounds are heard to carry political messages, to shape political beliefs. Two questions in particular stand out. First, under what circumstances does popular music threaten a dominant ideology (whether in communist or capitalist societies)? Second, how is such musical 'rebellion' routinised?

Peter Manuel approaches the debates about rock in Cuba as a political scientist. His interest is in how the Cuban state interprets rock and how its judgements are expressed in state policy and rhetoric. His essay is unusual in focusing almost entirely on the consumption of rock records (rather than on musicians' use of rock sounds), and he shows how Cuba's Marxist regime acts on the assumption that the meaning of music is *not* determined by its mode of production. The aesthetic value of rock (in Cuba) can thus be detached from its commercial origins (in the USA).

Geir Johnson writes about recent Norwegian pop in the contrasting style of rock journalism, with an insider's knowledge of performers' intentions and audience reaction. His argument is that the unusual 'Norwegianness' of Norwegian popular music in the late 1970s and early 1980s depended on a particular confluence of social, political and musical circumstances – and as these changed, so did the meaning of the sounds. Johnson stresses that the humour of Norwegian pop, its self-conscious commentary on its own marginal status, was an ironic humour and needed an audience which could read (or hear) behind the lines.

In Anna Szemere's musicological account of Hungarian new wave music the same sort of humour comes across more blackly, as something decadent – in the East European context popularity itself is a threat, not only to the political authorities but also to the state controlled record industry. Szemere's detailed analyses of how musical (and lyrical) signs worked to construct Hungarian new wave ideology also show that the music created (rather than simply reflected) a political position and that when the sounds became, in turn, familiar, so they lost their implications of dissent.

The Dutch sociologist P. L. van Elderen discusses the contrasting experience of bureaucratic rock management in the Netherlands (one of the few places, along with Denmark, to have state rock support). Van Elderen suggests that Dutch policy actually confuses issues of culture (and cultural nationalism – the promotion of Dutch music) with issues of welfare (keeping youth and/or musicians off the streets), and has had the effect of making rock performers and fans just another state problem, like 'young Mediterranean immigrants and the old ladies' book club'. But van Elderen's general concern is the ideological consequences of official support, given the usual belief (apparent in this book) that the politics of rock depends on its 'unofficial' status.

This question is taken up, finally, in the discussion of 'Rock for Ethiopia' between Stan Rijven and Will Straw, which is extracted from a long and noisy session which took place the day before Live Aid at IASPM's third conference. Their arguments return us to our starting point – to the meaning of cultural imperialism and the impact of western pop on Africa – but they also describe a problem that faces IASPM itself: what effects do *our* attempts to make popular music respectable have on the music's meaning? Is the appropriation of other countries' musics by western scholars just another aspect of their appropriation by western record companies and western consumers? Is IASPM's determined cultural relativism – all popular musical genres given equal attention – just another sign of the pluralism of the market place? As both Straw and Rijven argue, whatever one's views of Live Aid, it certainly made IASPM members think!

Rock music and cultural ideology in revolutionary Cuba

Studies of popular music in Cuba have tended to focus – not without justification – on Cuban musical forms, especially dance music and, more recently, *neuva trova*. In this paper I would like to focus on another aspect of the Cuban musical scene, namely, the status of rock music, which merits some attention not only because of the absence of relevant studies, but, more importantly, for the ideological problems posed by the popularity of this music in Cuba, and the way in which Cuban reactions to this situation reflect broader aspects of Cuban socialist ideology and cultural policy.

Modern Cuban writers on music, while acknowledging the vitality of Cuban popular music in the pre-revolutionary period, tend to denounce what they see as the excessive influence of commercial North American culture at that time. The inundation of the island with 'cheap North American music' (Thomas, 1971, p. 1164) is seen as a manifestation of 'cultural colonialism', reflecting and accompanying Cuba's abject and humiliating economic domination by the United States (see Villar, 1981). The Revolution of 1959 meant liberating the island from the worst aspects of foreign commercial musical influences, both by putting an end to North American economic exploitation, and by replacing the capitalist socio-economic substructure with a socialist one – a process which, in orthodox Marxist theory, should have lead to a natural decline of bourgeois art forms in the superstructure.

While Cuban popular music has thrived since 1959, foreign pop music, and especially rock, have continued to enjoy prodigious popularity among Cuban youth, in apparent contradiction to the aforementioned attitudes and expectations. The true popularity of rock is difficult to estimate; it is said to have been the favoured idiom of Cuban youth in 1962 (Díaz Ayala, 1981, p. 278), and a preliminary survey of the dance music tastes of 100 students in Havana in 1982 revealed that among this group, rock was roughly equal in popularity to salsa and Cuban dance music. Several youths interviewed by me in 1984 expressed their preference for rock; these young people included teenagers for whom nightclubs featuring Cuban dance music were too rough, and alienated black-marketeers loitering around hotels. Rock's popularity cannot be gauged from live performances, since, aside from some incorporation of rock elements into *nueva trova* and Cuban dance music (e.g. the *sougo*), rock is consumed but not produced in Cuba; nor can its appeal be estimated from record sales, since these are limited to a few (uncopyrighted) state releases of selected foreign hits. Instead, public access to rock occurs largely through the mass media, including Miami-based radio stations.

Media facilities are extremely well developed in Cuba, the state having invested heavily in these to the extent that practically all households have radios, and most have televisions. The 1971 Congress on Education and Culture declared that the mass media 'are powerful instruments of ideological education whose utilization and development should not be left to spontaneity and improvisation', and the state's reliance on the media has often been referred to as 'government by television' (Nichols, 1982, p. 71).

Given the state's deliberate use of the media and its hostility to cultural imperialism, one may be surprised by the amount of air play given to rock on radio and television. The only break in rock air time occurred in early 1973, when the Cuban government did prohibit stations from transmitting any North American or British pop and folk, alleging that they promoted alienation. Not even protest songs were tolerated; Cuban officialdom regarded North American pop culture, and especially hippie culture, as self-indulgent, drug-induced escapism, an aberrant degeneration of bourgeois culture (Thomas, 1971, p. 1435). The ban appears to have been part of a general defensive crackdown in culture and ideology, encompassing a tightening of censorship, curbs on travel permits to foreigners, opposition to 'imperialist' cinema, television and art, and condemnation of writers like Sartre and Carlos Fuentes who had protested Cuba's persecution of the poet Padilla.

Foreign pop music was reintroduced in 1974, in a general relaxation of tensions which Mesa-Lago (1978, p. 111) relates to the atmosphere of detente following the Vietnam withdrawal and Nixon's fall from power. (A Cuban friend insisted to me, however, if with some exaggeration, that another factor in the reinstatement of rock was a 'near rebellion' on the part of Cuban youth.)

Undoubtedly, a primary reason why the Cuban media devote so much air time to rock is the competitive lure of Miami-based stations. Commercial medium-wave stations, the Voice of America (short-wave), and, more recently, Radio Martí can all be picked up throughout much of Cuba except during inclement weather, and the attraction of these stations for some young Cubans has been a cause of concern to the state; Fidel Castro, among others, has argued that the appeal of Miami radio was a major cause of the Mariel exodus of 1980 (Nichols, 1982, p. 94). Meanwhile, the Reagan Administration's Radio Martí devotes much of its air time to rock – especially Cuban favourite Michael Jackson – and the station's slick popular music programming is perhaps its strongest attraction to Cubans (Wald, 1985).

Rock is primarily a product of the capitalist West and is intimately associated with the commercial music industry, bourgeois life-styles, and a generally individualistic worldview. As such, its popularity in socialist Cuba presents a contradiction that Cuban commentators have felt obliged to confront. Media rock pro-gramming, and the appeal of rock in general are currently criticised on two grounds. First, musicians and commentators lament from a nationalistic viewpoint that rock is usurping Cuban music; composer and bandleader Enrique Jorrín, for example, complains of his chachachá radio show being replaced by a rock progamme (Martinez, 1979, p. 74). Even right-wing Cuban exiles have criticised the Cuban media's rock airplay as a reflection of the supposed stagnation of Cuban music on the island (see, e.g., Díaz Ayala, 1981, pp. 315–16), and as an expression of the alleged alienation of Cuban youth.

A justification for rock progamming was offered to me by Argeliers León, one of Cuba's leading composers and musico-logists. León asserted:

First of all, in American popular music, there are many very good things . . . Such music has been coming to us since the previous century, and one can say that there has always been some incorporation of American popular music into Cuban music . . . In this century there has always been a

tremendous interchange of Cuban and North American music and
musicians, and if it is restricted now, that is not because of us but rather
because of the limitations imposed by the US government.

Indeed, a healthy interest in and borrowing from foreign popular
music hardly seems ground for criticism in itself, and as such, most
of the concern over the question of rock in Cuba centres, on a second
objection, concerning the degree or significance of ideological
incompatibility between rock and Cuban socialism. We have
mentioned that Cuban officialdom has denounced North American
youth subculture as decadent and alienated, and while state cultural
policy has been generally inclusive, it has made efforts to guard
against 'cultural imperialism', that is, the use of media symbols
(especially in cinema and literature) as 'a Trojan horse of capitalist
North American values' (Weiss, 1985, p. 117). Evidence suggests
that while most Cuban youths take an active interest in North
American pop culture, they tend not to identify with it, regarding,
for example, the hippie movement as a bourgeois perversion of the
Guevarist 'new man' (see, e.g., Hochschild, 1972, p. 228). León
insists that the imported rock in Cuba brings no disruptive
ideological ethos with it:

The phenomenon of commercialism is independent from aesthetic values;
commercialism concerns the use to which music is put . . . Here we receive
only the music, not the commercialism . . . Here we don't use the music to
sell a product, or to promote the curls of such-and-such a singer; rather,
we're interested in the singer's voice, and it is that which reaches us. We
aren't interested in the singer's sex appeal, only in his or her value as a
singer. So in ideological terms, this music doesn't bother us at all, because
what it has is only aesthetic meaning and value for us . . . If we can take from
North American music when it serves us, it's a form of winning against
imperialism – taking the good of the North American people without their
system.

It is interesting to hear from León the argument that a music can
shed the ideology of the class that sired it, since this viewpoint might
be questioned by other Marxists, Cubans, and ethnomusicologists.
The 1971 Cuban Congress of Education and Culture, for example,
declared that 'Culture, like education, is not nor can ever be
apolitical or impartial, insofar as it is a social and historical
phenomenon conditioned by the necessities of the social classes and
their struggles through the course of history.' One might argue

unsympathetically that León's attempt to deny rock's ideological content derives in part from the impossibility of restricting its appeal in Cuba. Yet the heart of the question is the degree to which a music like rock possesses and expresses an inherent ideology, and the levels at which such ideology is manifest. As León eloquently states, the *extra-musical* commercialism of rock does not reach Cubans, and it is likely, for example, that many of Michael Jackson's Cuban listeners have no idea what he looks like. Moreover, since most Cubans do not understand English or, by extension, rock lyrics, the only ideological content which could reach them would be that which is inherent in rock style, instrumentation, timbres, formal structure and the like.

Many scholars would argue that these more abstract parameters do in their own way express ideology, contrary to León's disclaimer. Yet as León and others have argued, more important than these relatively intangible factors are the extra-musical contexts in which music is disseminated and consumed. On this level, León is expressing a faith in the strength of Cuban socialist culture, its capacity to absorb foreign influences while retaining its own integrity. León's views are echoed by Jorrín (in *Bohemia*, 14 October, 1983) and Villar (1981, p. 7), who argue that while some pop music may have a reactionary class ideology, it can be digested with impunity by an educated and politically aware audience in a socialist society, where any implicit commercialism or alienation in an imported art is dissolved in the surrounding atmosphere.

Historians have pointed out that since even a dramatic social revolution does not obliterate all pre-revolutionary ideology, its ideas and values may continue to co-exist alongside the revolutionary ideology for a protracted period. The resulting social order is characterised by a dialectic between two competing cultures (Starr, 1973, p. 11), which, to the extent that they are compatible, may be synthesised. To this picture, as the Cuban example illustrates, there must be added the impact of continuing cultural impulses from outside. These may constitute a continuation of certain pre-revolutionary modes or, alternately, a third cultural factor. As Judith Weiss has observed, North American rock has had sufficient impact over three decades that its values are indeed part of Cuban popular culture, which is itself a hybrid entity dominated by, but not confined to, Cuban Revolutionary culture (1985:131).

Whether rock and socialism are compatible or not, the Cuban media's tolerance and dissemination of rock, in spite of official denunciations of bourgeois influence, illustrates a pragmatism in Cuban socialism that has been noted elsewhere: Nichols observes that Cuban media functions are 'the product of economic and technological constraints and especially social conditions that to a large extent transcend political ideology' (1982, p. 106). Cuba's use of rock also illustrates how one society has attempted to contend with an imported art form from a neighbouring society with which it has strong cultural affinities and equally fundamental socio-political disparities. Yet the implications of rock's popularity and influence in Cuba must remain unclear until we are better able to decode *musical* ideologies and the levels at which they operate.

References

Díaz Ayala, Cristobal (1981), *La música cubana del areyto a la neuva trova*, Editorial Cubanacan, San Juan.

Hochschild, Arlie (1972), 'Student power in action', in *Cuban Communism* (2nd edition), ed. Irving L. Horowitz, Transaction Books, New Brunswick, pp. 212–29.

Martinez, Mayra (1979), 'Música popular: sigue la encuesta', *Revolución y cultura*, LXXXV, pp. 74–6.

Mesa-Lago, Carmelo (1978), *Cuba in the 1970s*, University of New Mexico, Albuquerque.

Nichols, John Spencer (1982), 'The mass media: their function in social conflict', in *Cuba: Internal and International Affairs*, Sage Publications, Beverly Hills, pp. 71–112.

Saenz, Carmen M. and Maria Elena Vinueza (1982), 'Los jovenes prefieren la salsa?', CIDMUC, Havana.

Starr, John Bryan (1973), *Ideology and Culture: An Introduction to the Dialectic of Contemporary Chinese Politics*, University of California, Berkeley.

Thomas, Hugh (1971), *Cuba, or the Pursuit of Freedom*, Eyre and Spottiswoode, London.

Villar, Juan (1981), 'Incidences sociohistoricas y politicas de la canción cubana y latinoamericana en el desarrollo de la cultura popular tradicional', *Música* (Havana), LXXXIX–XC, pp. 5–18

Wald, Karen (1984), 'Radio Martí: popular music, slick soaps, loaded analysis', *The Guardian*, 6 May 1985, p. 14

Weiss, Judith (1985), 'The emergence of popular culture', in *Cuba: Twenty-Five Years of Revolution, 1959–1984*, ed. Sandor Halebsky and John M. Kirk, Praeger, New York, pp. 117–33.

Changes in Norwegian popular music, 1976-81

This paper will deal with the question of how the new popular music was formed in Norway in the late 1970s. The fact that the Norwegian music market expanded enormously in this period, before collapsing in 1982, has not yet been regarded as an interesting topic for musicological research.

I would claim my position to be that of a former new wave musician, one of the many who worked to establish a new basis for Norwegian popular music – a position of critical solidarity with both the music and the audience. It is therefore inevitable that my perspective of the development of Norwegian popular music in these years should catch a certain flavour of my own experiences.

To a non-Norwegian the title of this paper may seem too absurd or narrow to provide a perspective worthy of analysis; however it seems to me that the vast changes that Norwegian society underwent in the fifties and sixties were visible on a cultural level only late in the sixties. This may be the reason why a national popular culture developed as late as ten or fifteen years ago. I would contend that at the start of the seventies Norwegian musical life was without a genuine popular music culture and industry. The first attempts at making a Norwegian popular music after the Second World War had long since been crushed by the international sounds of beat, pop and rock music from overseas. Compared to the quality of songs being launched by British and American groups almost no Norwegian ideas were worth listening to, let alone recording. In general there was only one way of achieving success in pop in the sixties, namely by performing the translations of international hit songs.

On a local level, therefore, the new music cultures developed slowly from behind, in the areas of accompanied song and experimental jazz. Concluding this relatively dark chapter of Norwegian popular music history, we might say that the music market was a field with no need for local artists, and that those artists wanting to communicate to a Norwegian audience were not yet able to establish any contact.

At the beginning of the seventies this situation changed rapidly. Looking back, it seems to me that two important elements in particular paved the way for such a development:

(1)   the rapid growth of a new generation of young people in education in Norway, with substantial amounts of money and in need of a musical culture of their own;

(2)   a change in the political climate, as the question of whether Norway should join the Common Market almost split the country in two.

As far as the first is concerned, the growth of a new youth culture in Norway was closely linked with the growth of the welfare state. The expansion of the welfare state made possible new jobs inside the education system, the social security system and the health and welfare administration; together with the technically and commercially employed, those employed by the state represented some 20 per cent of the working population, according to statistics compiled in 1976. This group of people, sociologically and politically uncommitted either to the bourgeoisie or the working class, can be called the medium stratum. In Norway this new social group claimed to have its own cultural identity. The socio-cultural expression of this was the artist committed to a certain cause, be it of a political or other perspective. Artists who appealed to these social categories provided them with a feeling of freedom, spontaneity and protest against the establishment. The Norwegian trend of experimental jazz was basically a music for this audience.

As for the second change, the split in the population over the EEC campaign made the political climate much tougher. Several artists participated actively in the campaign against membership, whereas the government and the economic elite joined their forces for membership. The political debates and struggles provided the basis for the growth of new music cultures, strongly nationalistic in character, and opposed both to the international sound of rock and to the recording industry. Those musicians who participated in this political struggle playing jazz, traditional folk music, accompanied songs or even rock – discredited as it was – were eager to continue their production of music for the Norwegian market even after the decision to join the EEC had been made.

At the beginning of 1973, therefore, with a new interest in Norwegian music, *Norsktoppen* was launched, in order to provide the radio with a weekly presentation of popular music. At first its charts were looked on with contempt by the non-commercial artists and their audiences, as if the risk of commercialising the local music production were overwhelming and a destructive force for the artists. However the critics soon disappeared as *Norsktoppen* turned out to be a forum for both the commercial pop songs of the international style and the local artists 'doing their own thing'. Today the most relevant critique seems to be the question of how the so-called expert jury selects the songs and whether their criterion is more of a musical–political evaluation than a purely commercial one.

In the ten years that have passed since it began, *Norsktoppen* has established itself as one of the most popular radio programmes, with an audience equivalent to some 30 to 40 per cent of the population. The programme has presented and reflected the development of Norwegian popular music, the main points of which may be summarised as follows:

(1)   a general tendency to write new songs instead of translating international hits;

(2)   a change in attitude towards rock from one which, in 1976, viewed it as the rebellious music of youth, to one which now regards it as family entertainment;

(3)   a renewal of musical style as reggae and new wave ideals fuse with music and texts based on Norwegian dialects and local traditions;

(4)   a remarkable breakthough for the politically committed pop song represented by left-wing bands and singers;

(5)   the development of a bizarre musical humour, linking *Norsktoppen* with TV shows, cabarets and other media happenings.

There has been a considerable ideological shift amongst musicians both as regards their own work as artists and their views on their own function; the latter change has resulted in a large campaign for improvement in the living conditions of artists in all fields, popular as well as serious. As for the more internal problem, the question of how to write songs that communicate with a wide audience, song-writers have had to move a long way since the rise of political song in the sixties. The political song tradition was a vital force, although it was never strong as a movement and never attracted many listeners. Its main perspective was that of 'anti-rock', based on the use of traditional folk instruments and on an acceptance of the notion that the latter are closer to human values than are electric ones. This tradition achieved its most notable success with the group Vömmöl who suddenly entered the pop charts in 1974 and stayed there for almost two years. Vömmöl were in some ways pioneers, although their music had no successful followers. Vömmöl's project was basically a political one, as their strategy was to show the vulgarities of capitalism in a small Norwegian community. The songs were based on folklore with a strong local colour and considerable humour. Most artists were unwilling to risk a commercial position around 1975 as they considered personal contact with the audience to be important and resented the thought of changing the music into a more 'industrialised' sound.

The sudden breakthrough of reggae and punk internationally and the establishment of a Norwegian new wave movement around 1977 were the most important reasons for a new orientation in the musicians' attitude towards the commercial market. Norway with its approximately four million inhabitants, spread out over 300,000 square kilometres, is quite a difficult market for musicians. Playing in bands is extremely expensive because of the small audiences and the big transport costs. The dance bands that were established in the late sixties are the only people in the popular field who steadily make money in such a market, apart from a few professional artists who are actually able to live off the sales of their records. For several years the dance bands had consisted of musicians with mixed feelings about playing songs from the international hit parades. The sudden appearance of a music movement, not at all technically skilled but with a considerable musical imagination, came as something of a shock. For several of these musicians inspiration from the new wave provided the necessary encouragement to trust their own talents as song-writers. One of the leading groups in this field has been Stavangerensemblet who, from a base on the southern coast of Norway in the oil district, achieved a quick, and (hitherto) lasting, success based on the use of their own dialect, local slang which, when sung, is almost impossible for those from outside the district to understand. But people loved it, partly thanks to the singer Froddi, whose performances are always a treat, quite different from other Norwegian artists. His performance at the big Rock Revival Festival in Oslo in 1982, at which all the main rock groups from the last twenty-five years were presented, occasioned the following comments:

Froddi is the exhibitionist whose performance is improvised from the very first moment. He lifts up his T-shirt showing his belly to the audience, beats it in a friendly fashion before kneeling to the audience, gets up and jogs across the stage which is about twenty metres wide. All this happens while the guitarist is playing his solo. As far as the text is concerned (and it is quite hard to get the meaning of it anyway) the song is about a man who wants to enter a woman's room – and of course the text at this point has a double meaning. Froddi expresses this by throwing himself against the loudspeakers, hitting them with his fists or hitting the floor while screaming the woman's name in the mike. Every now and then he walks, jumps and stumbles across the stage. Then, during the next guitar solo, he mimes playing the guitar and proceeds to play with the microphone cable that has been lying like a rope around his neck. One is tempted to ask, 'is the rope the symbolic expression of the short duration of his performance and in a wider perspective the short duration of his career?' Only by giving himself away totally will he be able to survive as a performer. His big body is sweating profusely. The whole concert ends with Froddi on his knees in front of the audience like a Mohammedan praying to Mecca. When the male rock singer mimics the guitarist on the stage a secret male dream becomes evident, one which combines ideas of sexuality and dominance, as the solo guitarist in a rock band traditionally was a front figure, the most competent performer in a live situation.

Stavangerensemblet established itself as the leading local rock group between 1980 and 1983, which must have been a strange experience for musicians who had been on the road for ten or fifteen years. The authenticity of the band was so strong that for the first time in Norwegian music life a commercial trend developed popular enough that three or four groups were able to sell the same basic commodity. The next group from Stavanger, Asfalt, managed to sell the idea of the new 'Stavanger sound' even before they had written their first song. This was only possible for a short time, however. The music industry could not afford to record all the groups that wanted to achieve success by singing in dialect. In short, the specific flavour of the use of dialects which we find in Stavanger-rock, Trönder-rock, pop and accompanied songs from Northern Norway, was not the result of an extension of the market as such, nor of a broad acceptance of musical styles. The rapid boom in the late seventies was followed by a massive closure of companies in 1982. The use of dialect turned out to be a significant feature only for a small number of artists who, for a short period of time, were able to create a position of some importance, thanks to a characteristic trait in the cultural commodity store. But for bands using other dialects than Stavanger (for instance, the bands from Bergen), the result was an economic failure.

This of course gave way to uncertain feelings among the musicians themselves as to how to meet the audience. To some groups the obvious path seemed to be to choose English as their language, in the hope that this might spread the knowlege of their music abroad; in the event, the opposite happened and they were cut off from Norwegian record buyers as well.

Stavangerensemblet are the leading rock group of the last three years. Two other important artists, who were similarly active on the Norwegian scene in the seventies and have achieved great popularity in the eighties, are the two male singers Finn Kalvik and Jahn Teigen. They started from opposite positions, Finn being one of the musicians in the tradition of accompanied song of the early seventies – which we called *Visesang* – songs with a quite extraordinary interest in nature and romance. During the seventies no single one of Finn's records sold more than 6,000 copies but he was steadily giving concerts in all parts of the country and his songs have made their way into the song books of both primary and secondary schools. I wrote my thesis in musicology on one of his LPs because it seemed to me that his leaving the counter-culture market to produce an LP with ABBA in Sweden represented a shift in ideology quite remarkable even by Norwegian standards. This move suddenly increased his sales potential from approximately 6,000 to 100,000 per LP and made him a very popular musician. The question of whether his music changed was not my main reason for writing about him; I wanted to catch the atmosphere of a typical Norwegian pop product, to see how it activated the dreams and associations of the audience.

Jahn Teigen is perhaps the most popular singer in Norway today. He even became briefly familiar outside Norway too, as the first artist ever to score nil points in the Eurovision song contest. This actually made him a local hero back home and ever since he has been immensely popular. Jahn's musical career began in the late sixties when he was the singer in a Norwegian progressive rock group for several years without any success. He now performs in collaboration with two friends and what has given them their unique position in recent years is their simple, bizarre sense of humour, based on excessive parodies of international hit songs. Their song, 'Det er Norge som er bra', is a parody of the folk-line music from the eastern part of the country, on the Swedish border, where this kind of dance music is very popular. Jahn puts a new text to the song trying to display the opinions behind the music, the kind of nationalist ideology of which this music is a vital part. The text is heavily ironic: 'Norway is good, the Norwegians are best, they can drink quite a lot and they vomit at every party, so I think there should be only Norwegians living in this nice country.' In the refrain there is a short call of 'Hei' which is traditionally performed as a loud shout. This is transformed in Teigen's version and takes on an aesthetic quality all its own. The song reached number two in the Norwegian charts of 1980.

'I get frightened of my voice': on *avant-garde* rock in Hungary

The early 1980s saw the emergence of a highly innovative and influential set of musical styles and practices in Hungary that was variably referred to as new wave, (with adjectives such as amateur, underground or *avant-garde*), rockandroll and independent music making. These labels define various aspects of this phenomenon, approaching it as a subcultural style, as an artistic–musical attitude or as a particular position in the structure of the whole youth music field.[2]

Iain Chambers (1985) observes in the introduction to his book on English pop history:

Pop music is a field of continual novelties. In some cases, these merely involve the latest twist in marketing strategy, the quick business eye for a possible trend. More frequently, fresh proposals represent a real intrusion upon an earlier organization of the music and its surrounding culture. Whenever a sound powerful enough to threaten existing arrangements emerges, previous interpretations, choices and tastes are put in question. (pp. xi–xii)

In the Hungarian pop music field such an intricate relationship between fresh musical proposals and imaginative business strategies is unprecedented. Most typically, the record industry fails or refuses to notice the emergent innovative trends, partly because of the lack of incentives on the part of its employees, partly because of the political control it is supposed to exercise over its products (Szemere, 1985). If audience demand becomes a real social pressure, the usual response is an intrusion into the material to be published or a strategy of substitution – the aim is to redirect audiences to *ersatz* products, to recording artists of the industry's choice (Hadas, 1983). More often than not, the demanded music with its original performers does get issued but with such delay that the recordings can, at best, only function as archive pieces reminiscent of some of the great moments of Hungarian pop history.[3] As for the new wave *avant-garde*, no quick businessman recognised that the live shows of the most popular bands in the period between 1980 and 1984 were attracting up to a thousand people to venues designed for just a few hundred. Instead, barely known, musically immature bands were promoted and marketed as 'new wave'.[4] Out of the seven or eight most significant *avant-garde* new wave bands, only two have had the opportunity to issue albums, even though each of them had the repertoire for at least two LPs.

The cultural significance of the movement, despite its apparent decline since the mid-1980s, is difficult to overestimate, in view of its novel attitudes, lyrical themes, sounds, and performance practices, i.e. what Chambers referred to as 'a new organization of the music and its surrounding culture'. (For a detailed account of the musical innovations of new wave, see Hajnóczy, 1986.) Unlike the previous *avant* styles in Hungary (such as the surrealistic 'musical circus' of the group Kex at the turn of the 1960s – see Hajnóczy, 1984 – or the jazz-rock of the early 1970s associated with the Syrius), 'new wave' did manage to sustain a fairly autonomous and self-contained subculture, and took the initial steps towards creating an infrastructure for minority music making.

In the following pages I will attempt to give a description of the short-lived new wave movement with special regard to its 'fresh proposals' which, even if they did not threaten, did challenge the 'existing arrangements'.

The pop music landscape at the turn of the 1970s

'Music is for everyone.'
    (Zoltan Kodaly, 1882–1967)

'Crowded place, it's just one step to bump into something. Music is for everyone.'
    (Control Group)

At the end of the sleepy and vacuous 1970s, youth music with all its institutional and subcultural conflicts became a carrier and, to a lesser degree, absorber of manifold social tensions. It was a particular moment in an ongoing economic recession when a sense of insecurity was spreading over and across diverse sectors of society. Typically, it was the young who were affected most painfully by a loss of faith in future prospects and who responded in the most desperate forms. The apparent breakdown in communication between its various groups and the establishment was increasingly a concern of the media.

While a craze for a rock'n'roll revival raised the super-professional group Hungária to the top of the charts with sounds and images catering for escapism, sociographic accounts in print as well as on film threw light on the self-destructive life-style of the most militant core of the hard rocker subculture, many members of which abandoned their families if they ever had any (Köbányai, 1979). Obviously, for these youngsters music was the only medium of articulating social criticism, often in a completely nihilistic form. Hostility between them and disco kids, another working-class youth subculture, often assumed violent forms (Maróthy, 1982). The rockers repeatedly had to turn against their 'sincere and hard-as-stone' bands too, as these bands (formed of established musicians fifteen to twenty years their elders) transferred their allegiance to media manipulators.

Those musicians who did seriously undertake to be a mouthpiece for these youth groups inevitably clashed with the gate-keepers of the pop business. In fact, one wing of the early punk movement (represented by the group Beatrice) gained their nation-wide fame not so much by the other-than-inspired music they played (a blend of heavy metal and British punk) than by their resistance to the attempts of the media to domesticate them. There is a striking parallel here to the career of the Sex Pistols. Just as the Pistols use of swear words to TV reporter Bill Grundy and the ensuing public outrage became constituent of their image as a punk band (Vermorel, 1978), so did Beatrice member Feró's conflict with the Record Company's label manager Péter Erdös shape the public perception of this group with all its repercussions.

The Beatrice can be viewed as the 'critical social(ist) realist' wing of the punk movement (Chris Bohn's phrase, 1981), voicing social dissent in a crude and direct fashion. Yet they were instinctive rather than self-conscious punks: the label 'punk', which the authorities tended to regard as a right-wing, even fascistic movement, was used by the Beatrice's adversaries, the official guards of 'law and order', as a trigger-word for the campaign which gradually led to their silencing.

In the meantime, there was a notable revival of the amateur movement whose growing impact reached various age-groups and social strata. A self-conscious subculture with all the sartorial and hair-style extravaganza of punk was nurtured in centres such as the Young Artists' Club, art galleries and college venues. Its beginnings date back to 1978 when Gergely Molnár and his band (The Spions) held three extremely brutal and provocative punk concerts for a selected elite. The sophisticated multi-media action may well justify the term 'art-punk' or *avant-garde* rock. The Spions' leader, faithful to the tradition of Hungarian *avant-gardists*, defected to the West. As Feró of the Beatrice became the hero of the 'ragged' punk rockers, Gergely Molnár's myth was fed by underground publications and he himself celebrated as the initiator of the *avant-garde* punk/ new wave.

The avant-garde new wave as a subculture

No need for powder
No need for cackle
No need for funky, no need for punk
What you need is the underground[5]
    (Committee)

The new wave music scene began to appeal to a broader public in 1980–81, when numerous bands emerged with harshly provocative or outlandish names such as Petting, Orgasm and Riding Coroners; others produced a shock effect by adopting the name of existing institutions like the (Albert Einstein) Committee (alluding to the Central Committee of the Hungarian Socialist Labour Party), Europe Publishing House and URH (an abbreviation for either 'Ultra Short Wave', a reference to police patrol, or 'Ultra Rock Agency'). It is tempting to interpret this 'redoubling' technique of naming as a slightly anarchistic assertion of an alternative social realm – if without such defiant irony, the same idea is apparent in the name 'Control Group'. Other bands operated with self-irony – 'Neurotic', 'Trabant' (the brand-name of the cheapest and lowest quality car in the socialist market).

Dave Laing (1985) has argued that the stage names of British punks marked a mildly radical variation on hippy/underground precedents, but because in Hungarian rock history there had been no 'Grateful Deads' or 'Electric Prunes', no underground/psychedelic tradition, names such as the above did prove particularly effective in both recruiting followers and bewildering and outraging the public at large. Shock tactics, however, rapidly lose their effectiveness, whether attained by an appropriate stage name or by particular performance practices. Punk, with its obsession with shock, soon gave way to 'new wave', which allowed for more differentiated and individuated forms of artistic expression. What defined *avant-garde* new wave as a subcultural style can be related, first, to a shared set of sociological parameters; second, to a shared attitude arising from a particular moment of social/historical awareness (postmodernism); and third, to the textual incorporation of other art forms.

Musicians and their audience

To start with a sociological description, most of the new wave performers came from the bohemia and other non-established professional groups and were aged between twenty and thirty. Amateurs in music, quite a few were simultaneously or had been previously involved in other artistic activities such as visual arts, filming or drama. A few of them had a musical past in jazz-rock or folk.

Initially, new wave seemed to revive the early informality of the beat club scene of the 1960s; musicians and audiences were of the same age-group and from a similar social background. In contrast to the beat era, though, when fans' loyalty was pledged to one band only, in the new wave subculture the prominent groups attracted the same audiences to a live venue. There was no rivalry between the bands, which came to be reflected in the occasional spontaneous exchanges of musicians, in the fluidity of line-ups as well as in a preference for joint concerts. Nor was public unity threatened by the gradual changes in the composition of the audience, as the originally predominant bohemian/intellectual elite were absorbed in a younger, more ordinary rock audience public which included mostly college and high school students as well as a smaller group of working-class hard core punks.[6]

The technical, economic and organisational aspects of musical communication

As has been mentioned in my introduction, new wave rockandroll has not become integrated into the Hungarian pop music industry.

The few sympathetic broadcasters, journalists and label managers were unable to achieve official recognition for this style. Altogether three albums and a few singles came out to represent a large and varied set of styles, which had an impact not only on the followers in the same subculture but on mainstream rock as well. Even these records appeared rather late. The first LP by the Committee (*Up to Adventure!*, 1983) was made up of material that had been played for at least three years at concerts; the publication of the group's second album (*Icecreamballet*, 1985) coincided with the collapse of the group. Europe Publishing House had also long been over the peak of their popularity when the Company assessed their competence worthy of record (*Popmusic*, 1987).

The existence of *avant-garde* new wave depended entirely upon 'enthusiasts' (as Wallis and Malm, 1984 used this term); most of all, it depended on organisers at college venues. These were usually students, who besides doing publicity work, ensured the preservation of the music by recording the live events for the musical 'archives' of the college. Although the primary aim of this was documentation, it actually made possible an extensive circulation of duplicated tapes among the fans. This was a non-commercial practice: for example, a recording of a 1981 URH concert, instead of being sold, could typically be exchanged for a home-taped Joy Division album. As a result of the enthusiasts' activities, sound recordings occasionally reached foreign musicians and businessmen working for independent labels (Rittn-Tittn, Recommended Records, etc.). In this fashion almost every group had the opportunity to appear a couple of times in *avant-garde* rock venues or participate in Festivals in Western Europe.

Mention should also be made of a couple of film studios which through their responsiveness to (and partly because of their involvement in) the subculture, preceded and surpassed all other media not only in reproducing and distributing tapes but also in encouraging new wave musical creativity. (The Committee and the Riding Coroners appeared in Gabor Bódy's film *The Dog's Night Song*; János Xantus' *Eskimo Woman Is Cold* featured the Trabant.)

But despite these other channels, live shows remained the chief mode of communication between performers and the public. As amateurs, the bands worked under very poor technological conditions with careless technical crews hired by the venue. Concerts were often cancelled at the last moment, either by local authorities or for technical reasons. Meanwhile, the shows were fairly lucrative because of the sheer size of the audiences, and so a highly exploitative practice prevailed: the bands, because of their status as amateurs, received extremely low or no fees at all.

Musical communication: attitudes, themes, sounds and images

The common theme of *avant-garde* new wave texts[7] is an all-pervasive anxiety and frustration produced by a particular form of social/historical awareness. This awareness can be defined predominantly in negative terms, i.e. by a lost or blurred sense of the temporal and spatial axes of existence. The disturbing Hamletian statement 'The time is out of joint' could be the leitmotiv or this otherwise stylistically diverse music.[8] The particular state of mind conveyed is more directly rooted in what Grossberg (1984a) described as the post-modern condition:

We have been thrown into a maelstrom of constant change, apparently under no-one's control and without direction. Both the past and the future have collapsed into the present, and our lives are organized without any appeal to the place of the present within an historical continuum. We have neither a sense of indebtedness to the past nor of our obligation to the future. (p. 107)

Let me quote some of its Hungarian song lyrical articulations: 'You arrive as a traveller who lost its way/History is a rusty city'; 'Dirty times, I ought to love them/The future is here and will never end'; 'I'm somewhere else/Yet I'll be here' (EPH); 'Existence is a background' (Trabant); 'No-one called you and you will live here . . . But you'll disappear from here too since you're fed up'/(Control Group); 'No time!/No space!/A triple salto high up!'/(Riding Coroners).

According to Csengey (1983), post-war Hungarian youth generations grew into adulthood with the decisive experience of their own non-existence (p. 9). Whereas the youth of the 1940s could sing about 'shaking the world by tomorrow' and even the sixties beat generation had at one time the illusion of becoming active and creative members of a then-renewing society ('I don't wanna stand when the earth moves' proclaimed the group Illés), the children of the seventies and eighties had seen only shrinking prospects, in the broadest sense of the word, and witnessed a rapid devaluation of some of the basic constitutive principles and ideological premises of the hegemony. Passive or active, they became outsiders: 'We are no-one's children/Just happened to be born here/And still are alive' (Europe). The site of self-assertion became displaced: 'Overgrown souls are hiding in cellars' (Europe); the expropriation of social space, the separation from the straight world, might assume anarchistic flavours: 'I am you and you are me/We are in the same army' (Control Group); a crisis of identity and values, also pervading media discourses, took the form of either satire or self-satire: 'Value, value, without value, without value-free value/One can hardly react/One cannot raise his voice/ One can hardly resist' (Committee).

It would be wrong, however, to overemphasise the unity of attitudes displayed by new wave, or even to suggest that the movement was entirely set in a pessimistic key. Over the years some of the groups realigned and reshaped their outlook or developed their original concept into new directions.

Let me proceed to a brief discussion of the groups.

We're made of rabbit and will end up as bunnies.

The group Committee was founded by visual artists, which explains their debt to contemporary multimedia performance styles. In fact, their shows were initially held on their own varnishing days. Stage setting, costumes, movements and gestures were harsh and caricature-like, frequently obscene. However, a carefully balanced dramatic effect was produced by foregrounding three contrasting complementary personalities (a female and two male singers). Talks, jokes and comments between and over musical items were inseparable components of the production, therefore this 'music' had no studio version: the album *Up to Adventure!* was edited from fragments of recorded live events. (*Icecreamballet* contained music composed for their self-produced film.) The Committee labelled their product 'catastrophe music'. It drew elements from numerous pop styles (reggae, jazzy impros, trivial *schlager*) and frequently a V-Effekt is produced by their mere juxtaposition and re-contextualisation. For example, banal lyrics are sung over a swaying atonal melody or given an instrumental counterpoint. Inversely, 'word salads containing obscenities and every imaginable waste product of language' (W. Benjamin quoted by Laing, *ibid.*) are set to worn-out musical patterns.

On this Dadaist circus stage all our established notions, conventions and clichés get ridiculed. As the chosen motto above suggests, self-satire, humour and irony became the Committee's way of coping with the frustrating sense of being cornered.

It's the grave of the unknown soldier where you're sitting
It's so familiar still depressing how it's stinking. (URH/Control)

The Control Group, like the Committee, also based its concept on the dramatic potentials inherent in the confrontation and collaboration of a female and two male singers. Stage work, sophisticated multimedia effects, as well as the occasional involvement of the audience in the performance were tools for creating a 'total theatre'.

Whereas the Committee celebrates the perceived disorder and chaos with a cacophony of harsh colours (visually as well as through the use of metonymy), the Control Group's music is wrapped up in black. (The female singer, posturing as a *chanteuse*, is also clad in a black dress.) This is a 'rock macabre'[9] abounding in visions of individual and collective death and self-destruction. There is a fascinating oscillation between the metaphoric/allegorical and the realistic/experiential level in the articulation of an all-pervasive sense of fear and paranoia. The context of this is also multi-layered: Orwellian images of totalitarianism translated into the 'everyday' are blended with apocalyptic visions of a destroyed civilisation. This is the heart of the Control's anarchistic politics: the antagonism of peace and war is cynically resolved, they are treated as posing equal threats to the individual: 'Today it's war, tomorrow it's peace/ But when will it be over?/ Today it's peace and tomorrow it's war/ Yet you don't despair'. Tragic pathos is counterbalanced with an elusiveness of the lyrical/dramatic subjects; singers are foregrounded ambiguously either as representing a collective identity or as confronting actors of the mini-dramas unfolded within the musical items. Grossberg's (1984b) description of post-punk as 'oddly detached yet furiously energetic and affective' (p. 249) perhaps fits this group more than any other Hungarian bands in this style. The Control achieves it by a contrast between a passionate, declamatory singing technique and the wry repetitive minimalism of the instrumental accompaniment constructed of modal, atonal or chromatic fragments and bare harmonic structures.

My watch says it's been tomorrow for long.

The Europe Publishing House (also translates as Europe to Rent) with its all-male line-up and exclusive concern with the musical aspect of production falls closest to mainstream rockandroll, yet their attitude and musical language ensured that their place amongst the more off-beat bands was never questioned by members of the subculture. Further mainstream features are, firstly, the arrangement of the group around a 'front man', the singer-songwriter-guitarist Jeno Menyhart, and, secondly, his apparent identity with the protagonist of his lyrics (for an extensive discussion of the subtle relationship between lyrical subjects and performers in various pop styles, see Laing, *ibid.*). One aspect of the popularity of Europe, might be precisely the group's powerful and intense way of articulating and displaying a 'personal history', and Menyhart's affective investment in overt subjectivity. Paradoxically, a masochistic sense of self-inquiry and a desperate attempt to mark a purely individual difference produced, unintentionally, songs that became the 'collective property' of the audience, their sing-along 'anthems'. There is a strong intertextuality between the Control and the Europe, which goes back to previous collaboration between some members in the URH. Shared thematic/lyrical motifs are however, used to different effects. For example, the 'war-equals-peace' theme was set by the Control to a music reminiscent of Brecht–Weill songs, conveying a sense of detachment. The Europe's version ('We'll be killed, sweetheart/war and peace are of equal danger to us') articulates fear in a creepily direct way by murmuring the words over the sheer creaking noise of some unidentifiable electric machine, interspersed with the subdued sounds of siren, bells and machine-guns. The different stances of the two groups can be observed in their treatments of another common theme, the search for ecstasy in what can be called a collective 'death-dance'. Again, the Control uses trivial musical material to create distance ('This'll be then the last tango'), whereas Europe's 'one more dance!' is set to a furious rock'n'roll. Most remarkable is the fashion in which the Europe has elaborated the punk ideology of 'No future'. This notion has ambiguous, even contradictory connotations in the texts: not only threat or boredom ('Future has become present') but also challenge and fascination. This derives from a sci-fi-influenced concept of the FUTURE with capital letters. It is the tension between the fantasies constructed around it and the depressingly anachronistic realities ('What is today has for long been past') that provides the keynote of the songs (for more on this see Szemere, 1985).

Despite the apparent debt to Bowie, Lou Reed and the Talking Heads, the Europe has a recognisable style of its own: this is an acerbic sound composed of a rich harmonic vocabulary, favouring the Frygian and Lydian modes, and subtle polyrhythmic structures. Mention must also be made of Menyhart's use of a variety of vocal techniques in exploring the potentials of human voice.

In terms of popularity, the Committee, the Control Group and the Europe Publishing House can be regarded as the most significant new wave acts, but a lot of other musicians also helped open up new possibilities for rock and roll in the early 1980s.

'I am a picture projected onto myself' could be the motto of both the Trabant and the Balaton, originally separate groups retaining their names, despite their eventual musical symbiosis. Owing to the scarcity of public appearances, their home-made amateur recordings served as their main means of communication. The Trabant/Balaton's music concept shows resembled the Velvet Underground's: not only in their relative disregard for public appeal, but also in their mixed media technique and their blurring of the boundaries between artistic/music activities and everyday life. The contours of these individual music pieces are vague, so as to create a flow of loosely related accounts of the minutiae of the everyday, refracted through psychedelia. The Trabant/Balaton celebrate the precarious boundary between the 'real' and the 'unreal', a floating sensation, by immersing themselves in a completely self-enclosed space of their own. Musical and lyrical trivia taken from 1960s pop styles are re-worked by exaggerated simplicity and also disrupted by micro-dissonances and the insertion of entirely alien textual elements.

All is artificial
but we won't be artificial.

Osaba Hajnóczy (1984) has described the Riding Coroners as a 'pre- and post-punk delirious hard-core group' (p. 5). In fact, the group was formed as early as the mid-1970s, but until the new wave tide they were virtually unnoticed. Their prominence is associated with the connections between shamanistic folk music and punk. Attila Grandpierre (1984), leader of the group has made quite serious theoretical attempts to define and legitimate punk as the revival of shamanistic practices. It is tempting to attribute his ideas to the punks' general obsession with (or craving for) a charismatic figure, a superstar, a hero and a leader. No doubt, a great deal of nostalgia is attached to reviving this prehistoric version.

The Riding Coroners' live shows are literally cultic rituals, aimed at releasing the psychosomatic energies of the subconscious. Many of the fans, skinhead-looking 'hard' punks and young bohemians, are ready to participate actively in the event with agitated body movements, shouts and screams as suggested by the dynamics of the musical process. Occasionally, there is also a visual emphasis on simulated tribal rituals with costumes, make-up and hair styles which can include raw meat and bunches of grass attached to T-shirts or birds' feathers covering the skin all over.

The music creates a completely self-contained and closed acoustic space, the illusion of a trip in time and space, into an environment where nothing reminds the listener of everyday realities and concerns. An apparently chaotic but carefully construed soundscape is produced by the vocals, guitars and an array of drums, timpani and other, non-conventional percussion. Excessive amplification, fuzz and echo are heavily relied on to produce a thick noise. The typical concert is made up of just a few longer musical units bearing no title and following one another without pause. The whole process of the performance stimulates as well as acts out ecstasy.

Conclusion

The year 1983 marked the end of the most intense phase of new wave *avant-gardism*. Most of the groups were shattered by internal controversies or seemed unable to produce new programmes. Members of the Control separated to form three other bands. The Committee and the Trabant/Balaton gradually collapsed. The Europe gave up public appearances for a year and even after their return, concerts became few and far between. Only the Riding Coroners have been able to sustain continuity with growing impact upon the audiences.

The stylistic innovations proposed by these bands started to infiltrate into mainstream rock but served more directly as a set of models for the younger generation at the *avant-garde* fringes. The scene as a whole however lost its subcultural unity and identity. New, self-conscious subtrends emerged like the 'industrial' and 'instinct' musicians, the latter influenced by the Riding Coroners' shaman ideology. Yet with very few exceptions, these musics, to borrow Grossberg's term, no longer empowered their fans, or, to view it dialectically, fans could no longer empower the music. The decreased attendance at live venues epitomised the change most dramatically..

As a legacy of the movement, a more differentiated infrastructure of minority music making has evolved. Over the past few years, foreign alternative rock bands have become a regular feature on the Hungarian stage, and local bands have had the opportunity to tour abroad. Certain venues have specialised in supporting *avant-garde* music and a slightly increased media attention could be observed recently for off-beat trends. Yet the significance of these developments should not be overstated in view of the serious financial, organisational and technological problems (inaccessibility of studios, lack of management, etc.) which most groups still have to face.

In searching for the multiple reasons for the decay of the new wave, one particular point needs to be noted. The expression of pessimism and frustration have become virtually ubiquitous in 'mainstream' discourses on present-day Hungarian social issues. As part of a policy of outspokenness, the rhetoric of crisis has found its way even into the traditionally optimistic editorials of the Party's daily paper. The dramatically worsening economic situation, to put it very simply, is being paralleled by a policy of liberalisation. It is increasingly difficult to be subversive or even different by articulating frustration and despair.

In 1984 an *avant-garde* publication came out entitled *Jó vilás* (Good world) in which artists, post-punk musicians and culture critics suggested the rise of a 'new mentality' opposing the 'depressed' and 'decadent' official culture (see Grandpierre, 1984). As the editor László Beke stated, artists working in the spirit of a new optimism 'are producing a "good world" day by day, at times with hard efforts . . . constantly reiterating values such as beauty, goodness, friendship, love, dynamic yet intimate human community

. . .' (p. 136). Even though aware of the ambiguities surrounding these notions, contributors to *Good world* claimed to take them at their face value. However, the breakthrough of this new trend, what happens when it grows beyond making mere elitist gestures, provoking public puzzlement or misunderstanding, remains to be seen.

Notes

1 This is a substantially expanded and revised version of the paper 'On *avant-garde* rock in Hungary' delivered at the Second Internatinal Conference on Popular Music Studies, Reggio Emilia, Italy, 1983. (Published in *Popular Music Perspectives 2*, IASPM, Goteborg, Exeter, Ottawa, Reggio Emilia, 1985, pp. 183–7) The quotation in the title is taken from a song by the group Europe Publishing House.

2 Most remarkable is the adoption of the term 'rockandroll' with a new meaning: whereas in mainstream discourses on popular music in Hungary this has signified the 1950s dance music style (i.e. 'rock'n' roll'), these musicians and their fans took over the broader, affectively charged understanding of rockandroll with its connotations of authenticity and relevance. It also marked a new approach to rock as a cultural tradition, important aspects of which had been repressed in its 'East Side' version. More emphatically and explicitly than ever before in its Hungarian history new wavers reminded us that this genre has been more than just a musical idiom: visual images and stage movement might play equally important parts in conveying ideas and feelings. Ultimately, rockandroll was proposed as an alternative culture with ideologies of its own, 'taking fun seriously', (Grossberg, 1987) to a degree where it appeared to be the organiser of a particular life-style. This was also the first time that the association of rockandroll with sex and dress got articulated through music, lyrics and performance style, or more precisely, became an artistic statement, shaped by the politics of punk.

3 Grotesquely enough, some bands get contracted by western companies sooner than by Hungaroton. The hard-folk group Kolinda produced three albums in France; the jazz rock group Syrius' recording was made in Australia and issued under license a couple of years later in Hungary.

4 In an attempt at more credibility, 'old wave' musicians were encouraged by label managers to imitate the stylistic *clichés* of foreign new wave. These rock bands gathered around the Hungaroton label 'Start' and received the degrading qualification 'official' new wave by audiences as well as journalists.

5 The word 'underground' in the original version is an untranslatable pun: besides the grotesque phonetic pronunciation of the word, the phoneme 'e' is replaced with 'o' ('undorgrund') thus the first part of the compound assumed the meaning of 'disgust'.

6   The 'hard-core' punks represented another populist, working-class subtrend. It drew on the British 'oi' and some of the bands were legally persecuted for racist (anti-Gypsy) propaganda or slander.

7   This is also to say that the punk and post-punk *bricolage* drew (even if instinctively) upon a considerably broader cultural tradition for expressing alienation than merely twentieth century 'isms'. The investigation of punk's reliance upon, e.g. nineteenth- and twentieth-century negativist and existentialist schools of thought, deserves more attention and points beyond the scope of this paper.

8   The term 'post-punk' would be a more adequate description for this style than the vague term 'new wave'. My reluctance to use it can be explained by the fact that this label remains virtually unknown in Hungary.

9   The phrase was suggested by Janos Maróthy in one of our extensive discussions on new wave rock.

References

Bonn, Chris (1981), Hungarian Rhapsody and other Magyar melodies, *New Musical Express*, XVII, pp. 16–18.

Chambers, Iain (1985), *Urban rhythms: Pop Music and Popular Culture*, Macmillan, London.

Csengey, Dénes (1983), '... És Mi Most Itt Vagyunk', Maguetö, Budapest.

Grandpierre, Attila (1984), 'A punk-rock összefüggései a samán zenével mint népzenével', *Jo Vilag*, ed. Beke and Szöke, Böicsész Index, Budapest, Elte Btk pp. 91–97. In English: 'Punk as a rebirth of shamanist folk music', unpublished typescript.

Grossberg, Lawrence (1984a),' "I'd rather feel bad than not feel anything at all": rock and roll, pleasure and power', *Enclitic*, VIII, pp. 95–112.

—— (1984b), 'Another boring day in paradise: rock and roll and the empowerment of everyday life' *Popular Music 4*, ed. Middleton and Horn, Cambridge University Press, Cambridge, pp. 225–58.

—— (1987), 'Rock and roll in search of an audience, or taking fun (too?) seriously', *Popular Music and Communication*, ed. Lull, Sage Publications, Newbury Park.

Hadas, Miklos (1983), 'Ugy dalolok, ahogy én akarok: a popzenei ipar müködésének vázlata', *Valosag*, XXVI, pp. 71–8.

Hajnóczy, Csaba (1984), *Voice of Hungary*, Vol. 1, International Network Rittn Tittn, Vienna, Budapest, New York, Memo.

—— (1986), '100 popdal', *Magyar Zene*, XXVII, pp. 284–94.

Köbányai, János(1979), 'Biztosiótü és börnadrás', *Mozgo Vilas*, V, 2, pp. 64–77.

Laing, Dave (1985), *One Chord Wonders: Power and Meaning in Punk Rock*, Open University Press, Milton Keynes.

Maróthy, János (1982), *Zenei Tömegmüfajok Magyarországon 1956–81*, unpublished typescript.

Szemere, Anna (1985), 'Pop music in Hungary' *Communication Research*, Sage Publications, XII, 3, pp. 401–11.

—— (1985), 'A jövö itt van és sose lesz vége: tér és idöképzetek az Európa Kiadó együttes zene és szövesvilágában', *Magyar Zene*, XXVI, pp. 70–75.

Vermorel, Fred and Judy (1978), *Sex Pistols: The Inside Story*, W.H. Allen and Co., London.

Wallis, Roger and Malm, Krister (1984), *Big Sounds from Small Peoples: The Music Industry in Small Countries*, Constable, London.

Pop and government policy in the Netherlands

For some years now a debate has been going on in Holland about rock music and the responsibilities of the central government.[1] The government itself was dragged into that debate and 'forced' to take a position by political pressure: it was provoked by the Stichting Popmuziek Nederland (The Netherlands Pop Music Foundation). SPN was established in 1975 by a group of people as an alternative to what they called 'commercialised pop'. They were concerned that dependence on the music industry would force commercial standards upon rock and that the wealth of musical forms would therefore become emaciated. At the same time they put forward the claim that rock is much more than commercialised mass culture – it is creative self-expression and a free attitude to life as well. Inspired by the credo that 'there is a relationship between the problems of artistic freedom, musical innovation, live music on small stages, and the educational impact of rock music', they campaigned for a rock centre to be set up in Amsterdam, which 'might be able to activate rock music socially and artistically – a service institution helping a nationwide organisation of musical specialists, a trade group of non-commercial rock music'. The SPN-founding fathers aimed at an open meeting place with a regular staff of fifteen musicians who would be engaged for a certain period on a part-time or full-time basis. The centre was supposed to gather and distribute information; to organise workshops, jam sessions and experiments in music; to set up a house band and help other groups to get organised; to offer low-priced rock performances to people who would otherwise not hear such music; to design, manufacture, and lease good and inexpensive equipment; to make contact with educational institutions by providing a rock curriculum and course tutors, and, finally, to work with other artists, for instance by writing music for theatre productions, pantomime and so on.[2]

SPN did eventually get ƒ50,000 from the Ministry of Culture, Recreation and Social Work, and looking back at its subsequent history it is clear that SPN's activities have been focused on (1) artistic innovation; (2) rock music and education; (3) the social and economic position of rock musicians; and (4) the organisation of pop-collectives and performance facilities. In my opinion the organisation and support of local and regional pop-collectives, the SPN's efforts to establish a *network* of rock venues, practice rooms, and information centres has been its most important task. SPN is a spear-head of a form of self-help and self-organisation typical of the Dutch welfare state. According to SPN's figures there are now some eighty-two pop collectives throughout the country, receiving financial help in total amounting to ƒ757,325.

In the early eighties SPN submitted a plan for supplementary grants for their venues which would enable them to hire the kind of bands they would otherwise not be able to book by guaranteeing them a reasonable rate of pay. For three periods of twelve weeks (with the concerts at the weekends) central government was asked to guarantee the net-salary of the bands (at a minimum rate of ƒ1,500) while the venues were to take care of the taxes and premiums. At the time there was no money available, but in 1984 SPN received ƒ200,000 to spend on this scheme, and the money was allotted to twenty-seven venues. In 1985 SPN was given ƒ350,000 and put an advertisement in a well-known music magazine, *OOR*, asking venues who wanted to be considered for funds to write in. To be eligible they had to meet the following conditions: a capacity of more than 200 visitors, regular shows featuring Dutch rock groups, and a professional organisation and administrative system.[3]

There is no doubting SPN's success, then, in winning state support for rock performance. What is less clear is the reason for the government's support and its impact on Dutch music. Is the SPN funded as a matter of cultural or social welfare policy? Can state supported musicians credibly retain any sense of rock as an oppositional culture? One way to get at some answers to these questions is to look, briefly, at two of the main issues that have been tackled by SPN: rock education and rock employment.

Rock and education

Many young children and adolescents, who play the guitar a little,
or like fiddling with drums at home, really want to learn to play rock
music well, if necessary at a music school. Even in 'classical' schools
instruction in rock is in much demand. The problem is that there are
hardly any teachers trained in the idiom. The conservatories which
train music teachers are traditionally oriented, while professional
rock musicians do not have a pedagogical qualification and cannot,
therefore, be engaged as paid experts in youth centres. In 1975 the
Ministry of Culture started investigating whether and in what form
a popular music training programme for teachers at music schools
could be set up (this was after a committee, representing various
music educational institutions, had raised the problem in 1972).

SPN took up the issue, arguing that it was only performing rock
musicians who understood the techniques involved – rock's special
way of playing, arranging and improvising music, its particular
types of equipment. SNP thus advocated removing the legal and
financial obstructions to 'unqualified' musicians working as teachers
in music schools and community centres. In 1982 SPN conducted
an inquiry among 163 music schools throughout the country:
ninety-eight of them believed that rock music should be incorporated
in the curriculum; at the same time they noted a lack of suitable
accommodation, equipment and funds, as well as the absence of
capable teachers. With the help of various people from the
conservatories, music schools and social work institutions, SPN
then designed a suitable instruction programme. Subsidised by the
Ministry of Culture, in the spring of 1984 a number of courses to
instruct future rock music teachers were organised in the regions of
Drenthe and Noord-Holland.[4] Whatever the eventual outcome of
this programme, it is clear that it will make rock an aspect of
'official' welfare state culture, and put rock musicians themselves in
an odd position – within the 'establishment' as teachers, outside it as
performers.

Rock employment

From its beginnings SPN drew attention to the difficult socio-
economic position of the rock musician, declaring that 'because of
the norms of commercialism the rock musician is not a free artist,
but a labour force not in control of the means of production' and

noting too that because of the high rates of unemployment, many rock musicians were dependent on social welfare. The sharp attack on 'capitalism' has by now disappeared from the SPN's vocabulary, but the focus on trade union-like promotion of musicians' interests has remained. In 1974 ANOUK (the Dutch artists' association) had already carried out a small exploratory research project on unemployment among rock musicians. At that time 132 performers were officially registered totally (63 per cent) or partially (37 per cent) unemployed – more people than the complete Concertgebouw Orchestra, as SPN commented later on.[5]

Asked about their income position 15 per cent of the bands I surveyed claimed to earn enough from their performances alone, 33 per cent enjoyed another source of income, and 27 per cent got some kind of social benefit. On the average these bands received a fee of ƒ982 a performance, but 57 per cent of them got an amount not higher than ƒ500, while 22 per cent earned between ƒ500 and ƒ1,000. Another illustrative figure: 62 per cent of these bands (made up of five to six people) enjoyed an annual performing income of no more than ƒ10,000. Apart from the investment in expensive equipment, matters like transport, lighting and sounds entail a great deal of expense: they devoured 67 per cent of earnings.

I think it will be enough to conclude here that rock is an expensive hobby. The above figures mainly cover amateur bands and a small number of semi-professionals, but according to a survey in 1977 only 9 per cent of the 'really' professional rock musicians had an income from making music only, 23 per cent lived on social security benefits, and 64 per cent got an income from making music and an additional welfare payment. These benefits came from the City Social Welfare Agency (GSD) (65 per cent) or from some trade association (27 per cent). (It is quite unclear, by the way, whether or not a rock musician belongs to the hotel and catering industry or to some other trade.) A lot of artists and groups were thus shown to be officially registered as 'looking for a job'.

At that time, in the late seventies, many amateur rock musicians (93 per cent of whom were under twenty-five) had never been in touch with the labour exchange at all. Seemingly, even then these bands constituted an alternative world of their own, with hardly any contact with official institutions (but now SPN shows them the right way!). And to the (overwhelming) majority of rock groups the social and financial outlook was not that bright at all: the image of the rock star living a life of luxury is not in the least bit realistic.

The response of the central government to this situation is rather ambiguous. On the one hand it sees in rock a great number of possibilities for work, just because it is a form of production which attracts many consumers – the government is, therefore, not unwilling to inject a lot of money into this 'economically important' field.[6] On the other hand the problems of musical unemployment are great, and the theme of social assistance payments thus plays an

Table 11.1 Official unemployment registration of rock musicians (in percentages)

	Amateurs	Semi-professional	Professional	TOTAL
Never been registered	65	42	9	42
Has been registered for some time, in the past	16	29	18	21
Still registered	16	19	73	32
No information[a]	3	10	-	5
Total	100	100	100	100

[a] No answer was given to this item in the questionnaire

Source: Pop als werk, a Music Magazine – OOR publication April 1978, p. 41.

important role in the government's thinking too. Policies on culture become policies on employment, and lead to much discussion of rock musicians' careers and what kind of job they should be allowed to do or to keep on doing without losing their right to unemployment benefits. What should the government do to support professional rock musicians? Should it guarantee their fees? Subsidise the purchase of equipment or musical compositions? SPN suggests a BKR-settlement for rock artists; this is a kind of social welfare arrangement for the plastic arts through which the government commits itself to buy works regularly from the artists in return for which they receive life support benefits. A BKR deal for rock has not had much support, though, since the government wants to reduce its BKR obligations generally.

Then there are the complex laws on work and work conditions and the intricate system of taxes with which musicians are confronted. The Netherlands have developed a refined system of social insurance, and especially here the bureaucratic complexity of a modern welfare state manifests itself. An extensive exposé on this would take us too far, so I will only make some general observations.

In his or her job the rock musician meets three bureaucratic parties: the superintendent, the trade association and the Inland Revenue. Quite frequently he or she is playing a role somewhere in between being a self-employed entrepreneur and being a person in the service of someone else. It is not always easy to discriminate between amateurism (hobby) and professionalism (additional job) and it is not always quite clear whether the individual artist or the group is the central unit. The problem is to decide whether in legal terms, a rock musician is an artist to whom special regulations, for instance on wage tax, are applicable. And it is difficult too to calculate the unemployment benefits: they depend on the classical working pattern of an eight-hour working day – so in what cases might a musician be labelled 'unemployed'? The same goes for sick-pay – can a musician get ill during rehearsal? And the state's usual labour placement service hardly functions in the case of the rock musician, since in their field commercial mediation through publicity, etc., is what leads to work.

The introduction of VAT taxes, to raise another problem, on services rendered by the artist, or on youth centres which had previously been VAT exempt, seriously complicates the relationship between employer and employee, and tax and revenue affairs do seem to pose the most complex economic problems which musicians face. In co-operation with SPN a working-group 'Rock and Revenue' was thus set up and, in 1982, an information book on the legal–fiscal affairs of a rock group produced.[7] More recently SPN has helped set up a professional organisation for rock musicians: BV POP – a kind of voluntary association (rather than a labour union) intended to advance the social and financial interests of this 'oppressed' group, vis à vis the government. BV POP is also meant to be a clearing house for all kinds of experience and knowledge concerning rock as entertainment – one of the first things BV POP did was to apply for a position within the management of the national copyright organisation.

Conclusion

The question is what government intervention in the Dutch rock field has actually brought about. To begin with, it is obvious that the many government documents on rock music do not show a consistent or worked out position – financial allotments and rhetorical slogans do not make a policy. Generally speaking the central government's position has moved from the view that 'the commercial circuit is the natural environment of rock music' to the thesis that 'rock is an art form like any other'. This implies that policies on the arts come into play in the rock world as well (and there certainly has been a change of atmosphere), but so far this seems to be a matter of a verbal message of support rather than a well-thought-out basis for administrative proposals.

The central government's policies on art might be qualified as neo-liberalist: they are very restricted and almost exclusively directed to creating conditions for the advance of the arts. To the government the starting point is that the arts must develop autonomously and it will try to give all the initiatives of citizens a fair chance. The social diffusion of art, and therefore education and character-shaping, plays an important role in government thinking. It is not quite clear what this means for rock music. The government admits to giving uneven attention to the various musical genres: serious classical music and jazz are much better subsidised. As a 'weak sector in music', rock might then be considered for more financial aid, but then again, in a more or less democratic system, endowments for rock as art would mean the same criteria of excellence as are applied in the case of any other form of art. And the problems with rock are that the relationship between the professional and amateur performer is quite different from that of the established music world, and that there are no easy ways to test rock's aesthetic qualities.

My impression is that because of this the government handles rock music essentially as an amateur art. This adds to the tension, or at least to an unclear relationship in this area between the government's art and social welfare policies. To put it somewhat crudely: because of the decentralisation of activities in social work (provincial and local authorities get a budget and decide themselves how to distribute the money), whatever national policies of rock-as-art are adopted, they are soon tied up with local practices of rock-as-social welfare. This means that the musicians do not only have to compete for money with other traditional art forms like classical music and even jazz, but with affairs of social work as well – to mention a few: the local football club, the jogging track, the meeting place of young Mediterranean immigrants, and the old ladies' bookclub.

Notes

1 This is extracted from a longer paper entitled 'Sex and drugs and rock'n'roll *vs* tulips, cheese and rock'n'roll'. Thanks to Mrs Tingloo for help with the translation.
2 The committee that founded SPN consisted of people from the ANOUK artists' associaton, the artists' labour-union organisation (Kunstenaarsbond FNV), the Association of Music Teachers, the jazz scene (BIM-Huis) and ex rock musicians. SPN-ideas were published for the first time in a brochure *Het Popplan (je kan er altijd nog op dansen)*, Amsterdam, 1975.
3 *OOR*, xii, 15 June 1985.
4 *Meester? Doet U Ook Pop?*, SPN publication, Amsterdam, January 1985.
5 *Het Popplan*, p. 13.
6 *Kunsten en Werkgelegenheid*, by Drs P. van Klink, publication of the Ministry of Culture (WVC), Rijswijk, 1981.
7 *Pop & Paperassen*, Publication-Serviceburo's and Kunstenbond, Amsterdam, 1982.

Rock for Ethiopia

Editor's note

The two papers that follow read rather differently from the rest of the contributions to this book. I've made no attempt to edit them for publication but left them as they were presented – in the present tense, addressed to a large and vociferous audience which had been arguing about the meaning of the Live Aid since this particular IASPM conference had begun. What was at issue was our ability as popular music scholars to make sense of immediate popular music issues, and by the summer of 1985 it was clear that the most significant, most political musical event of the year – the 'text' that we should be able to read – was the charity rock phenomenon. And what concerns me here is less the content of these papers, both taken from the Live Aid session – Stan Rijven's illustrated guide to the 'band-aid-wagon'; Will Straw's attempt to place Live Aid in political pop history – than their form, and the methodological questions they raise: what does popular music scholarship add to popular music meaning and experience? Does our superior knowledge, our sense of sounds' wider social or historical or economic circumstances really further understanding of how pop works in people's lives?

By leaving these papers as they were first heard I hope therefore to capture what was most important about them: their tone – cool, slightly cynical, deliberately contrasted to the media euphoria then surrounding Live Aid outside. As IASPM members we were rightly detached from the hype but it is arguable that we missed the point – 1985's charity rock moves affected people in ways that a detached analysis didn't always acknowledge. But then popular music scholars are pop fans too, their theories determined by their tastes, by their own sense of market identity, their sense of distinction from (or identity with) the crowd. Not all arguments can be made in retrospect and it's as important to consider scholarship on the wing, as it were, as well as neatly tied up, when all is clear.

Stan Rijven
Introduction

On Sunday 25 November 1984 the preparations for this very conference ended in Exeter, England. At the same moment thirty-seven English pop stars popped into a studio in London. In one night 'Do they know it's Christmas?' was born. Probably for the first time Bob Geldof, leader of the Boomtown Rats and founder of this first Band-Aid project, liked Mondays.

On 13 July 1985, when the third IASPM conference comes to an end, Live Aid will be on television worldwide. The biggest live-show in pop history, broadcast directly from Sydney, Australia; Wembley, London and the JFK stadium in Philadelphia. Among the performers: Adam Ant, Boomtown Rats, David Bowie, Brian Ferry, Elton John, The Pretenders, Queen, Sade, Sting, U2, Wham, The Who and Paul McCartney in London; Eric Clapton, Duran Duran, Bob Dylan, Waylon Jennings, Billy Joel, Judas Priest, Mick Jagger, Santana, Simple Minds, Stevie Wonder and Tears (are not enough) for Fears in Philadelphia. To make the spectacle attractive Phil Collins will attend both shows, a fast Concorde enabling him to be the *Deus-ex-machina*. Seven tele-communication satellites will beam this Aid-event live to an estimated one billion viewers in about 150 countries, including the Soviet Union and China, a real Woodstock '85 on video at home.

In less than nine months the Band-Aid phenomenon has grown from an incidental seed to a baby fostered by hundreds of pop-parents; in no time Band-Aid became a word in the international *pop-vocabulaire*. As a new tropical disease, or to put it more precisely, a new philanthropical disease, Band-Aids spread all over the pop world. The famine fashion turned into a safe political issue for the pop aristocracy that all of a sudden heard a new melody: swing low, sweet charity.

But what does this opportunistic wave of positivism tell us? What moves these celebrities? Is it a guilt syndrome? Is it the longing for the authenticity that artists lose when becoming megastars? Are we reading a new chapter in a book about pop and politics or is it just a 1985 version of pop and marketing politics? And why this boomtown-effect? Everybody jumped on the Band-Aid-wagon, afraid of missing a train that leads to the country of free publicity. As if the surgeon general had determined that *not* smoking this cigarette is dangerous to your career. Bob Geldof puts it this way in the British *Sunday Express* of 14 April 1985: 'I've said to a couple of people, if they won't contribute, who'll tell the press, them or me? It's not the nicest kind of emotional pressure. It's the most blatant kind of moral blackmail.' But, before answering these questions, I'd like to make clearer what Band-Aid is, how it has been presented to the pop audience.

(1) Band-Aid – 'Do they know it's Christmas?'

This was the first Band-Aid song and the prototype for all that would follow. In Britain, Christmas singles, even if they are sung by Barry Manilow and Julio Iglesias in duet, sell like Christmas trees. In marketing terms, perfect timing. The single sold about ten million copies and raised about eight million pounds. It could have been more if Mrs Thatcher hadn't been so willing to take the sales tax. The cover stresses, in its Victorian *kitsch*, the contrast between well-to-do high class kids and the reality Ethiopian children live in. A visualisation of the lyrics that contain the same self-satisfied attitude of we–them thinking. At the back the whole British pop-aristocracy stand in brotherhood together, in total opposition to what pop fans are used to, because the pop media always stress the differences in order to model the necessary individual images. A Band-Aid logo shows a creative moment of irony (*the world as a plate, knife and fork in place*). This formula – an eye-catching cover, a feeling of togetherness and an individual Band-Aid logo – returns on many other sleeves. For instance on the most famous and best selling of all, 'We are the world'.

(2) USA for Africa – 'We are the world'

It's time to lend a hand to life
so let's start giving.

Again that nineteenth-century charity idea.

And the truth, you know, Love is all we need.

Paraphrasing the Beatles' love and peace anthem.

The single sold half a million copies in the first forty-eight hours, becoming CBS's fastest seller ever. Together with an album, videos and the merchandising of posters and T-shirts, United Support of Artists gross fifty million dollars, aimed not only for immediate and long-term relief in Africa, but 10 per cent also went to the hungry and homeless in the USA itself. USA for America, funny and sour at the same time; I will come back to this later. It is remarkable that for the first time black artists took the initiative and headed the organisation of a big musical event. Harry Belafonte became the American Bob Geldof, Quincy Jones did the record session, Michael Jackson and Lionel Richie wrote the song. Further, the selection of artists is interesting: a broad cross-section of soul, rock, country and singer-songwriters. Meanwhile the Band-Aid virus had many victims.

(3) 'Starvation', a second British version, was performed by musicians from bands like UB40 and the former Specials, who have shown engagement in the past on issues like Rock Against Racism.

Starvation is spreading through the nation
there must be someone to help the situation
whether you are white, black, red or an indian
we all share the same blood.

This *ad hoc* collective stressed multi-racial issues; it did not want to play with false images on the cover but associated with the Two Tone idea of integrating white and black musicians.

(4) The flip side of this twelve-inch was 'Tam tam pour L'Éthiopie', the first Band-Aid of a whole continent. Fifty African artists – among them Youssou N'Dour from Senegal, Hugh Masekela from Botswana, Manu Dibango from Cameroun and King Sunny Ade from Nigeria – were involved. It was the only Band-Aid record with music that really mattered. Because of my bad Wolof, Swahili and Lingala I'm not able to offer the right translation.

(5) Band für Ethiopia – 'Nackt im wind'

Naked in the wind that roars and destructs
that kills without plan
because he knows people forget quickly.

Through metaphors the lyrics show a feeling of guilt towards famine. The German pop-elite from Nena and Alphaville to Udo Lindenberg and Spliff, jumped on two bandwagons. Besides international Band-Aid, they picked up on the German campaign for African famine relief at the beginning of this year. The cover therefore shows the same picture as had been used for posters and television in Germany.

(6) For French speaking people some trance from France: **Chanteurs sans frontières** sing 'Éthiopie', with

Let's give them a future
in exchange for nothing
let's give them life
just life alone.

The same gratuitous 'swing low sweet charity' attitude. The music itself makes 'Do They Know It's Christmas?' sound like a flashy pop song. Thirty-six voices, from actors like Gérard Dépardieu and Mitterand's running-mate Coluche, to musicians such as Julian Clerc, Véronique Sanson and France's premier rock band, Téléphone. The cover was characterised by the French semiotic approach – Beaujolais bottle with SOS letters in the sands, and the back featured a tableau of the troupe and in the corner, a 'Singing in the Rain' logo – a French cloud dropping musical notes on Ethiopia.

(7) Hilton Fyle and African Cruise – 'Ethiopia'

(8) Tribu – 'Kyrie Ethiopia'

With no cover, Hilton Fyle's music mixes sound archives with Boney M-aidentity. Together with Tribu's 'Kyrie Ethiopia', an example of the broader use of music, marketing and morality.

Other Band-Aid projects

But before becoming a Band-Aid scratcher myself I'd better mention other projects. Canadians must know by heart 'Tears are not enough' from Northern Lights, including Joni Mitchell, Gordon Lightfoot and Bryan Adams. South Africa had its Kruger Rand-Aid with the song 'Operation Hunger'. Flanders in Belgium had the song 'Leven zonder honger' ('Life without hunger'); Dutch artists tuliped together for 'Samen' which means 'together', the song will be released next week. Austria, Italy and Jamaica have also showed their donationalism. On a continental scale Australia came from down under with 'EAT' (an abbreviation of East Africa Tragedy). The velvet crooner Julio Iglesias formed a Latin American *conjunto*, in which José Feliciano and Placido Domingo also took part, for 'Cantaré, cantarás' ('I sing, you sing').

Since we ran out of countries the latest trend in famine fashion is musicians grouped around a certain style. Heavy metal performers like Judas Priest and Quiet Riot have recorded 'Hear an aid', their way of jumping on the headbandwagon. Gospellers, country-artists and even doowop singers have become *aidicted*. Also individual artists like Tribu plugged in. You may ask yourself: what is next? Well, the British band The Blood have released an anti-Band-Aid song!

Conclusions

All these projects share:

(1) an air of patriotism, concentrated as they are on nationalities, so-called 'donationalism'. This is linked up with

(2) an accent on community, togetherness. But they are offering a community feeling that does not really exist in the audience. There is not the identification youth anthems like 'My Generation', 'God Save The Queen' or 'Fixing to Die Rag' gave. Those songs were part of your own experience, your own emotions. Band-Aid turns politics into commodities. Identification? Aidentification!!

(3) except for 'Tam Tam Pour L'Éthiopie', the same muzak characteristics, transparent frameworks built on the conventions of pop song-writing that only sell because of the Band-Aid connotation;

(4) a high media sensibility that feeds on itself – charity opens all doors. The video gets extra attention, every public move made by Geldof, Belafonte or other prominent members is registered by the press. Every newspaper receives Band-Aid information as a news

item on telex. Of course the development of video and satellites offers possibilities that, for instance, The Concert for Bangaladesh could not dream of;

(5) a naive political attitude combined with a superior morality.
'If we can come together we can change the world forever' is the central line in the Canadian Band-Aid.
'Let us realise that a change can only come when we stand together as one' sing the Americans.
'Do they know it's Christmas?'

Will Straw

What I want to do here is make a series of remarks and observations centred primarily on the 'We Are The World' single, but pertinent in most cases to the other charity records. In the latter part of the paper, I would ideally like to open up some debate on the forms of involvement of rock musicians in political causes.

(1) I would stress, first of all, that the participation of artists in the various Ethiopia records is in many ways less significant than the involvement of the music industries, and that this is usually overlooked. The waiving of record label, distributor and retailer profits is much more unprecedented and spectacular than the gathering of artists for charity purposes. The demand that these artists then go on to make records for the miners, or for Nicaragua, while well-intentioned, misses the extent to which industry involvement, the greatest source of the money raised, depends upon the construction of a humanist, apparently non-partisan consensus. One can defend this consensus as strategically necessary, or condemn it as a source of depoliticisation, but one cannot deny its being essential to the success of the project.

I stress this because it is relevant to a point which follows: that the credibility, understanding and sincerity of the artists involved in the Ethiopia records has little pertinence to a debate over the political appropriateness of charity as a solution to famine. In the flurry of debate over the tasteless and self-serving artist involvement in these projects, it should be pointed out that, even if Paul Weller or Billy Bragg sang and played all the instruments, the bulk of the money would come from the deferred income of multinational record companies.

(2) The most striking textual quality of the 'We Are The World' single is its absolute coherence. That coherence grows out of the momentum it carries and through which, in a peculiar way, it can be read as the celebration of a new pop mainstream and its recent successes. The narratives of how each of the Ethiopia singles came to be are essential to the meanings of those records, but none expresses this sense of momentum better than that for the 'We Are The World' single, with its passage from success at the American Music Awards to the coming together for the production of the record. The ambiguity of the new mainstream is that, while it is built around the single, perfectionist production values, and relatively formulaic rhythms, it is much more characterised than is the more recent British pop by a collection of distinctive and recognisable voices: Michael Jackson, Bruce Springsteen, Cyndi Lauper, Lionel Richie, and so on. The aesthetic success of the song, I would argue, is that while these voices are expressive, that expressiveness is exploited for its narrative value, rather than as a succession of individual moments of testimony. The recognisability of these voices is such that the song's normal harmonic tensions are doubled by the tensions attendant upon the identification of the successive voices. The song does, for me, build in an effective way, but part of that effectiveness is the centrality of its voices to the coherence of American pop music in 1985. Part of the 'cringe factor' in the Canadian single comes from its lacking this coherence: it is a record of dispersal, pulling together artists from different countries, genres and linguistic groups.

In this respect, I agree with the argument that the lyrics of 'We Are The World' resonate with imperial sentiment, but I think that this aspect of the song's meanings comes as much from its consecration of success and coherence as from specific lyrical content and from the subordination of individual voices to a structure of building to a climax.

(3) What struck me the first time I heard the Ethiopia records was that, ten or fifteen years ago, these projects would have taken the form of double or triple album sets, probably consisting of extended live jams. The operative assumption was that unfettered personal expression stood as guarantee of the sincerity and credibility of the whole enterprise. The punk critique of this, of course, said that the disengagement from pop and other apparently commodified forms

in the 1970s had, among other things, resulted in an emphasis on musical virtuosity which was self-indulgent and exclusionary.

What has happened in the intervening years is something like the weakening of the modernist project in rock culture – the notion that it is important, above and beyond all else, for artistic liberation to embody the utopian impulse and act as a model for social liberation. The master-narrative of this kind of politics is one of embodiment: that the rock community or the rock experience embody certain political impulses, and that these are homologous to larger desired social-political projects. Most all-star benefit concerts fifteen years ago ended with all the artists on stage, singing a traditional song like 'Will The Circle Be Unbroken?' It was always essential to the desired transcendence of these moments that this closing song not be written by any of those present, that it express a sense of tradition and community essential to rock culture's mythologies, even if this was largely irrelevant to the lives of the vast majority of audience members.

The problem of this sort of rock politics is that embodiment and homology are no guarantee of political intervention. Recent re-thinkings of rock politics have been precisely in the direction of strategy, intervention and the calculation of effects within particular contexts but these have had a difficult time. The messiness of a pragmatic rock politics is that it inevitably trades on the crasser aspects of the pop music machinery, when what the master-narrative of rock utopianism has always demanded is that these be transcended.

I see these remarks as pertinent to the Ethiopia songs inasmuch as debate has paid much less attention to the questions of desired political effects and achieving these, than to the degree to which the enterprise signifies and embodies community and integrity. I want to talk now about the ways in which the discourses of rock culture define and evaluate political intervention. In part, this involves playing devil's advocate in order to make what I consider important political distinctions, but I wish to argue more substantively that the political usefulness of rock music needs to be reconsidered.

I take it for granted that most of us here find the various charity projects tasteless, self-serving for those involved, symptomatic of existing geo-political relations and politically inappropriate, and that we never much liked Bob Geldof anyway. What I want to argue is that debates over the whole enterprise conflate a number of distinct issues, and that questions of a geo-political nature usually become subordinate to the ongoing assigning of credibility to musicians within rock culture.

There are two sets of questions involved here. The first is that of the appropriateness of charity as a response to famine in Ethiopia. The positions in this debate should by now be familiar, ranging from pro-charity stands for humanitarian reasons or through left fraternalism, through to anti-charity positions rooted either in a Marxist analysis of imperialism or an anti-Soviet refusal of aid to an apparent client state. All of these positions are represented regularly in articles or letters in the rock and general press. The second set of debates has to do with the perceived scandal of well-off rock stars proclaiming a concern for the famine victims in Ethiopia. Polemics revolve around the degree of sincerity and understanding of those involved, and the extent to which participation in these charities produces such returns as ego-reinforcement or heightened media visibility.

I would argue that this second set of issues has taken precedence over, and been conflated with, the first. To a large extent, the question of whether or not charity is an appropriate response becomes an argument over who has the right to offer this charity. A distinction needs to be made. If the raising of charity money is a legitimate response to the African famine, then it remains so, regardless of the sincerity or credibility of those involved in granting it. If charity is not the appropriate response, this likewise remains the case whether those offering it are American Grammy winners or British reggae stars or African musicians. Nothing could be less relevant to the situation in Ethiopia than the accumulated credibility which those involved carry within rock culture, or the likelihood of their having any idea whatsoever of the experienced reality or historical basis of the Ethiopian famine.

Part of rock's disengagement from older show business traditions was its devalorising of those forms of political involvement which most blatantly trade on the resources and attention-getting attributes of the star: fund-raising and political endorsements, which have long histories within, for example, the film industry. The positive impulse here, of course, was the conviction that professional creative output and political partisanship should be integrated and serve each other. The popularity of this impulse coincided with the rise of the artist-songwriter within rock music.

The negative effect of this has been the enshrining of a specific kind of political activity above all others, even when it cannot be demonstrated to have discernible political effects. This political activity is what Michael Neumann calls the activity of bearing witness to injustice and social condition. The artist sees, understands, and testifies, and all three are extremely important to the construction of the credible rock persona. There are a number of points I wish to make about this.

(1) Firstly, it is notably within rock culture that one finds the fullest examples today of the *intellectuel engagé*. As Lyotard has suggested, the impulse of the *intellectuel engagé* is almost always towards the embodiment of a collective subject of humanity rather than of particular interest groups. In rock culture, ideologies of purity and expression have, among other things, encouraged the transcendent refusal to do anything so mundane as lend one's name to a political party, project or candidate. There are notable exceptions to this, but the tendency persists to valorise a politics of the exemplary life rather than of the strategic result.

(2) The effect of this has been that rock's discourse on politics is primarily concerned with nudging people rather than instances of political intervention. Writing about rock artists is preoccupied with the imminent arrival of the moment of co-optation and the dilution of purity, and its discourse might be described as one of vigilance and attentiveness to shifts in the degree of earned credibility. This is all part of the rigour and irreverence which typifies magazines like *New Musical Express*, but it also means that, for example, the right to speak politically is considered as much more crucial than the political effects of speaking. The arguments over Wham's involvement in a miners' benefit are symptomatic of this, with their expressed anxiety that the sincerity of that group might not be sufficient to warrant them the credibility capital which participation might bring.

(3) The preoccupation with the right to bear witness is part of a disdain for messy politics. What is interesting in the arguments over Cyndi Lauper or 1960s girl groups is that, while one might admit that these produced welcome shifts within rock's discourse about rock, sexuality and pleasure, there is usually the stated fear that

these effects might be accidental and unintended. One demands of the exemplary rock life that it involve the transparency of results to intentions, and intentions to convictions, even when all this may prove to have no political impact whatsoever. I don't think we can base support for these exemplary lives in a lazy sociology of role models and disown that same sociology when confronted with the moral panics over, for example, Heavy Metal.

(4) The most under-rated contribution rock musicians can make to politics is their money, or ways in which that money might be raised. The difficulty rock culture has with the giving of money stems from the fact that it is much less obviously heroic than bearing witness to the problems which that money might resolve. The issue of charity as a response to the Ethiopian situation is in a sense separate, but it has nothing to do with whether Bob Geldof's discovery of famine was accidental or his understanding of it superficial. These are important to characterisations of Bob Geldof, and thus to rock culture, but not to the legitimacy of the enterprise. Again, I would argue that a calculation of political objectives and strategies needs to be separated from an aesthetic distaste for the gaudy trappings of low-brow show business.

(5) Part of the interest of the Ethiopian projects is the manner in which the tensions within them may have politicised an issue in a way which the exclusive participation of more credible rock personalities would not. The rudimentary elements of the debate over wealth, charity and rock music have filtered far beyond the rock press and rock bohemia and this is ultimately far more politically useful than the self-congratulation we would have felt had the only Ethiopian record been that by British reggae artists. What is over-estimated is the extent to which the various Ethiopian records are accompanied by an unambiguous ideological closure for those who do not think in an informed and rigorous fashion about the issues. What the culture of rock music and politics should encourage and accomplish is the extension and focusing of these debates.

Charles Hamm

Afterword

As this volume attests, the decade of the 1980s saw the emergence of popular music research as a legitimate, coherent and distinctive field of study, largely as a result of the establishment and growth of the International Association for the Study of Popular Music (IASPM), which quickly became a focus and rallying point for scholars in various parts of the world.

The handful of books on popular music published in the decade before IASPM's founding were scattered efforts, written in isolation by people with no common academic discipline or journal, no organisation or network to facilitate communication and debate.[1]

But the 1980s brought institutionalisation, beginning with IASPM itself, which in its brief lifespan has pieced together a network of scholars, organised national and international conferences, and generated various publications: the two volumes of *Popular Music Perspectives;* the newsletter *RPM;* numerous monographs and newsletters by national branches. The decade also brought the journal *Popular Music,* put out by Cambridge University Press, mostly the work of IASPM members, and the gradual acceptance by colleges and universities of popular music study into the canon of the academically acceptable, despite lingering resistance. Undergraduate and postgraduate lecture courses and seminars in popular music have proliferated. Centres for the study of popular music have been established at Humboldt University in East Berlin, the University of Nevada at Las Vegas, Liverpool University, Middle Tennessee State University, Strathclyde University in Glasgow, the University of Natal in Durban, and elsewhere. Faculty appointments, promotions and tenure decisions have begun to be made on the basis of scholarship in popular music; theses and dissertations have been written and accepted; university presses now vie with commercial publishers for book-length studies of popular music.

In the process of becoming institutionalised, popular music research has developed a profile all its own, as Simon Frith points out in the introduction to this volume. This profile, characterised by a propensity for multi-disciplinary and international perspectives and an enthusiasm for confronting the 'politics of pop', came into focus in the course of IASPM's first international conferences and its early publications.

Participants in these conferences came from many academic disciplines and professions, including sociology, journalism, anthropology, ethnomusicology, library science, history, political theory, performance, historical musicology, folklore, labour history, and music education. Some initial problems of communication, resulting from disciplinary jargon, were soon overcome by a communal willingness to grapple with the methodologies and terminologies of different disciplines. Also, it quickly became evident that many members of the new organisation shared ideological concerns cutting across disciplinary boundaries; the oppositional and democratic potential of rock music; a fascination with the popular sociological themes of post-war youth and leisure time; popular music as an agent of class struggle; the impact of cultural imperialism and hegemony on the modern world; the dialectic between the genres of popular music produced and promoted by the most powerful record companies, increasingly allied with large transnational corporations, and the more varied and democratic genres promoted by the 'enthusiastics' in various countries.[2] These themes run through most of the papers in the present volume.

Other aspects of popular music have been of less concern, perhaps because the specific nature of IASPM's engagements with 'the political issues of pop power and taste' has been shaped by the demographics of its membership. There have been few attempts at musical – rather than social and political – analysis of popular genres. Mainstream popular music, as opposed to subcultural and other oppositional genres, has been relatively ignored. Most popular music research has been adamantly ahistorical, or restricted its view of history to the post-1950s era. Certain popular genres, jazz for instance, scarcely figured in IASPM's international conferences and publications.[3] IASPM discourse has been persistently theoretical, critical and political, and even though a number of journalists have been active in the organisation, there have been only rare instances of writing in which issues are illuminated through the brilliance of the literary style itself, as in some of Simon Frith's work and Stan Rijven's introduction to 'Rock for Ethiopia' in the present volume.

Natural alliances have emerged, with contemporary trends in literary criticism, with British counterculture theory, with gender studies, with semiotics, with various schools of neo-Marxist thought. Adorno, though often criticised, and Walter Benjamin are important spiritual ancestors. A deep concern for class struggle underlies much of what has been written; ethnicity as a cultural determinant has been less often explored. At the risk of over-generalisation, I'd say that the character of popular music research of the 1980s has been in general much closer to the social sciences than to the humanities, more European than American, more theoretical than empirical, more synchronic than historical, more political than descriptive.

And to date, more Western than non-Western. Even though IASPM, as a matter of conviction and policy, has constantly and with some success sought to expand its membership to countries in all parts of the globe, there have been economic and political restraints, and the majority of its members are from NATO countries, as Philip Tagg has often remarked.

As a result, entire repertories of popular music have been virtually ignored. Martin Hatch's 'Popular music in Indonesia' is a rare look at the mushrooming popular musical life of Eastern Asia, which in the 1970s and 80s has witnessed the emergence of regional popular genres consumed by countless millions of people in Japan, Hong Kong, Taiwan, Indonesia, Korea, Vietnam, and now the People's Republic of China. Bernard Broere's 'El Chambú – a study of popular musics in Nariño, South Colombia' is a valuable ethno-musicological analysis of one local repertory in Latin America, and other IASPM members have studied oppositional political song in Chile and elsewhere in Latin America. But as Coriún Aharonián reminded the IASPM membership on one occasion, performers and styles popular with millions of Latin Americans continue to remain little more than a rumour in the Anglo-American world, and to popular music research. Likewise Motti Regev's 'The field of popular music in Israel' is a rare look, and an indirect one at that, at the music of the Arab world.

Popular music research in the 1980s has only occasionally broken the pattern still dogging such disciplines as anthropology, ethnology and ethnomusicology, whereby knowledge of the cultures of Third World countries still comes chiefly from scholarship by Europeans and North Americans. All essays in the present volume concerned with Europe (Slovenia, Italy, Norway, Hungary, and the Netherlands) are written by natives of these countries, as are the studies of popular music in Israel and Canada. By contrast, the articles dealing with Indonesia, Colombia and Cuba are by Europeans or North Americans, and the one study of African music is a joint effort by a West African and a European.

This is not to criticise Euro-Americans who choose to write about cultures other than their own. The articles by Hatch, Broere and Manuel in the present volumes are valuable contributions; without them, we would know little or nothing about the cultures they have chosen to study. They also serve to underline differences between the type of work often done by scholars not born into a given culture, as opposed to those native to it: the former tends to focus on description, definition, taxonomy; the latter often confronts the life blood of the subject, as witness the articles by Barber-Kersovan, Regev and Szemere.

To pursue this point a bit further, the second half of the 1980s has brought unprecedented international interest in African popular music, both in performance and in scholarship. But most Europeans and North Americans know this music mostly from performances in the West, or from recordings produced for export; and anyone who has heard African pop music in Africa itself understands that mediation usually takes place when this music is performed abroad, through the intervention of entrepreneurs and managers and the intrusion of musicians from other parts of Africa or even the West. Likewise, much of the writing about this music is based on the shape it takes abroad, not at home. Take, for instance, one of the numerous recent book-length studies of African pop, *African All-Stars: The Pop Music of a Continent* by Chris Stapleton and Chris May,[4] in which a disproportionate amount of space is devoted to African musicians who have managed to find their way to Europe. The section on South Africa is devoted largely to profiles of the Manhattan Brothers, Miriam Makeba, Hugh Masekela, Malombo Jazz, Sipho Mabuse, Malopoets, Ray Phiri, Savuka, and Ladysmith Black Mambazo – a list that would strike a black South African as decidely curious, both for its inclusions (Makeba is twice identified as 'The Queen of African Song,' even though she left South Africa in 1959 and her repertory until recently has consisted of a mixture of American pop and jazz standards, and arranged and mediated versions of 'folk' songs from various countries) and for the fact that it omits most of the musicians most popular *within* the country in the past decade – Steve Kekana, the Soul Brothers, Brenda Fasi, Moses Mchunu, Babsy Mlangeni, Harari.

Will Straw's remark at Montreal in 1985 that 'I take it for granted that most of us here find the various charity projects tasteless, self-serving for those involved, symptomatic of existing geo-political relations and politically inappropriate, and that we never much liked Bob Geldof anyway' situated the ideological climate of that conference with admirable and chilling precision. The only problem, for me, lies in the phrase 'most of us here'. Shortly after that conference, I heard 'We Are the World' coming from radios and cassette players in villages in Botswana, in various towns in Zimbabwe, and in the South African 'National States' of Venda, Ciskei and Bophutatswana. From simple observation, and from discussions with a range of people in these countries, including officials of the Zimbabwe Broadcasting Corporation, I cannot believe that the song had the same meaning in southern Africa as it did for the Euro-American academics assembled in Montreal.

My intent is not to criticise the reading of that song offered in Montreal, but merely to suggest that other readings are not only possible but essential if popular music research is to become a truly global discipline. To achieve the latter goal, we must not only deal with music from all parts of the world as subject matter, but also confront issues of the perception and reception of popular music in cultures other than our own.

There are encouraging signs that IASPM is continuing to reach out to the entire world. The international conference of 1987, held in Ghana, established closer ties with African scholars and musicians and exposed Western participants to African ways of making music, and thinking about it. There is a thriving new national branch in Japan, another in Bulgaria, and the strong possibility of yet others in the People's Republic of China and Czechoslovakia.

Popular music research has established itself as a discipline to be reckoned with in the academic world. The present volume stands as a testament to work in progress, impressive but unfinished.

Notes

1   Dave Laing, *The sound of our times*, Sheed & Ward, London, 1969;
    Charlie Gillett, *The sound of the city: the rise of rock and roll*,
    Outerbridge & Dientsfrey, New York, 1970; Richard Middleton, *Pop
    music and the blues*, Gollancz, London, 1972; Steve Chapple and Reebee
    Garofalo, *Rock'n'roll is here to pay: the history and politics of the music
    industry*, Nelson-Hall, Chicago, 1977; John Shepherd *et al.*, *Whose
    Music? a sociology of musical languages*, Latimer New Dimensions,
    London, 1977; Greil Marcus, *Mystery train*, E.P. Dutton, New York,
    1977; Simon Frith, *The sociology of rock*, Constable Ltd., London,
    1978; Philip Tagg, *Kojak, 50 seconds of television music: toward the
    analysis of affect in popular music*, Musikvetenskapliga Institutionen,
    Göteborg, 1979; Charles Hamm, *Yesterdays: popular song in America*,
    W. W. Norton, New York, 1979; Dave Harker, *One for the money:
    politics and popular song*, Hutchinson, London, 1980.
2   Cf. Roger Wallis and Krister Malm, *Big sounds from small peoples; the
    music industry in small countries*, Pendragon, New York, 1984.
3   Only IASPM/USA, the branch established in the United States, has
    consistently dealt with jazz in its national conferences.
4   London & New York: Quartet Books, 1987.